Idit Alphandary
**Forgiveness and Resentment in the Aftermath of Mass Atrocity**

# Perspectives on Jewish Texts and Contexts

**Edited by**
Vivian Liska

Editorial Board
Robert Alter, Steven E. Aschheim, Leora Batnitzky, Richard I. Cohen,
Mark H. Gelber, Moshe Halbertal, Christine Hayes, Moshe Idel,
Menachem Lorberbaum, Samuel Moyn, Ilana Pardes, Alvin Rosenfeld,
David Ruderman

# Volume 24

Idit Alphandary

# Forgiveness and Resentment in the Aftermath of Mass Atrocity

—

Jewish Voices in Literature and Film

DE GRUYTER

ISBN 978-3-11-221535-7
e-ISBN (PDF) 978-3-11-131769-4
e-ISBN (EPUB) 978-3-11-131781-6
ISSN 2199-6962

**Library of Congress Control Number: 2023941439**

**Bibliographic information published by the Deutsche Nationalbibliothek**
The Deutsche Nationalbibliothek lists this publication in the Deutsche Nationalbibliografie;
detailed bibliographic data are available on the internet at http://dnb.dnb.de.

© 2025 Walter de Gruyter GmbH, Berlin/Boston
This volume is text- and page-identical with the hardback published in 2024.
Cover image: Rembrandt Harmensz. van Rijn. Return of the Prodigal Son. ГЭ-742 (a detail).
Photograph © The State Hermitage Museum/photo by Alexander Koksharov.
Typesetting: Integra Software Services Pvt. Ltd.
Printing and binding: CPI books GmbH, Leck

www.degruyter.com

# Acknowledgements

I would like to thank Ewa Ziarek, Henry Sussman, Carol Jacobs, Thomas Brudholm, Vivian Liska, and Leszek Koczanowicz for providing opportunities to contextualize the general scope of this work. The "Languages of Emotion" cluster at the Free University in Berlin, the Fortunoff Video Archive for Holocaust Testimonies at Yale University, Steven Connor of the CRASSH Institute at Cambridge University, Briony Jones of Swisspeace at the University of Basel, and Lyudmila Sholokhova of the Dorot Jewish Division at the New York Public Library all provided material resources and opportunities to present this work. Shimon Kornitzer provided much needed encouragement at critical moments during the completion of the manuscript. I thank Routledge, Katarzyna Lukas at *Schulz Forum*, and Peg Birmingham at *Philosophy Today* for permission to reuse some of my previously published work.

# Contents

**Acknowledgements —— V**

**List of figures —— XI**

**Introduction**
**Theorizing forgiveness and resentment in the presence of radical evil —— 1**
    Arendt's forgiveness, Améry's resentment —— 4
    The interdependence of forgiveness and resentment —— 9
    Exploring forgiveness and resentment through literature and film —— 12

**Chapter 1**
**Forgiveness, resentment and reconciliation – on W. G. Sebald —— 18**

**Interchapter 1**
**Aesthetic falsehood and emotion – on Bruno Schulz's *The Sanatorium Under the Hourglass* and Wojciech Has's *The Hourglass Sanatorium* —— 39**
    Foreword: Aesthetic falsehoods in 1937 usher in decent politics in 1973 —— 39
    1    "Somewhere on a distant shore" (Schulz 2018, 189) —— 46
    2    Forgiveness and resentment: Reterritorializing the life and work of Bruno Schulz —— 51
    3    Can something new ever happen? —— 58

**Chapter 2**
**Love and worldliness – on Hannah Arendt —— 61**
    Private and public love —— 62
    Lovers of the world —— 64
    The politics of love —— 72
    Love in plurality —— 78
    Radical evil as the absence of responsibility —— 80
    Love, forgiveness, and promises —— 83
    The loophole of existence —— 87
    Conclusion —— 92

**Interchapter 2**
**The necessary fragility of paradox – on Christian Petzold's *Phoenix* —— 93**
    On the dead and the possibility of a future —— 93
    Petzold's Levinas: "Show me your face now" —— 98

Petzold's Sebald: "We have a plague of flies" —— **101**
Petzold's Paul Celan, I —— **101**
Petzold's Alain Resnais: The railroad and the past —— **103**
Petzold's Paul Celan, II: "I feel more drawn to our dead than to our living" —— **104**

## Chapter 3
## The sincerity of forgiveness – on Heinrich Böll and Jean Améry —— **106**
Forgiveness, resentment, and madness —— **111**
Jewish biography and German contemporaneity —— **115**
*The Clown* —— **120**
Resentment and innocence —— **124**
Criticizing Catholicism in the open —— **126**
Forgiveness as rupture —— **126**
Afterword —— **130**

## Interchapter 3
## Negative possessions – on Wladislaw Pasikowski's *Aftermath* (*Poklosie*) —— **133**
The everyday life of disavowal —— **133**
The irreducible difference of two traumas: Victim and perpetrator —— **135**
Tracking shots: A recent archeology of the land —— **137**
Difference: The old; the madwoman; the nomad; the crucified; the Jew —— **142**
Inspect the old cottage; don't speak to the people —— **146**

## Chapter 4
## From emotion to national renewal – on J.M. Coetzee —— **150**
Normalizing emotions? —— **150**
Emotions do not have an essence: Conflating love and desire —— **154**
A historical precedent: The truth and reconciliation committee —— **157**
Emotional and social transformation —— **164**
The translation of emotions —— **166**
Love and shame in the public sphere —— **173**
Global themes: Love, forgiveness, nonviolent resistance —— **176**
Judith Butler: Nonviolent resistance and moral substitutability of "I" and "You" —— **178**
Memory as restitution in the wake of difference, translation of identity —— **181**
Conclusion —— **183**

**Interchapter 4**
**Memory and nonviolence – on Raoul Peck's *I Am Not Your Negro* —— 184**
    Detour: On globalism and nonviolent resistance —— **185**
    Is memory's language wrong? —— **191**
    Memory and difference —— **196**

**Coda**
**Forgiveness, justice, and historical responsibility —— 200**

**Bibliography —— 207**

**Index —— 215**

# List of figures

| | |
|---|---|
| **Figure 1** | "Max Ferber," the room that Ferber dream-walks into —— **34** |
| **Figures 2, 3** | *The Hourglass Sanatorium*, the cemetery shots that open and close the film, DVD screen shots —— **56** |
| **Figures 4, 5** | *Night and Fog*, DVD screen shots —— **104** |
| **Figure 6** | *Aftermath*, the burning field, DVD screen shot —— **145** |
| **Figure 7** | *Aftermath*, digging into the ground, DVD screen shot —— **146** |
| **Figure 8** | *Aftermath*, the madwoman screamed to let the Jews go, DVD screen shot —— **147** |
| **Figure 9** | *Aftermath*, Jozef is crucified, DVD screen shot —— **148** |
| **Figure 10** | *I Am Not Your Negro*, a Black girl is choosing to go to a desegregated school, DVD screen shot —— **192** |
| **Figure 11** | *I An Not Your Negro*, James Baldwin, DVD screen shot —— **196** |
| **Figure 12** | *I Am Not Your Negro*, Malcolm X, Martin Luther King, Jr., Medgar Evers, DVD screen shot —— **197** |

# Introduction
# Theorizing forgiveness and resentment in the presence of radical evil

This book examines a series of narratives of forgiveness and resentment, with the aim of showing that these two emotions are relational and interdependent in the context of coping with trauma. Forgiveness and resentment are not, as they might first appear, mutually exclusive. It is through the interaction between them that victims of mass atrocity become agents of personal and cultural change. These pages argue that the sentiment "to forgive is to forget" is incorrect, counterproductive, perhaps even dangerous.

But what are forgiveness and resentment? How are they related to memory? How to deal with the paradoxes that emerge when forgiveness and resentment coexist? Michael Rothberg asserts that memory is the past made present (Rothberg 2009, 3), while Gilles Deleuze amends this notion, suggesting instead that, if the present is the repeater of the past, then the future may, in the presence of the active force of difference, disintegrate such repetition: "The present is the repeater, the past is repetition itself, but the future is that which is repeated." Deleuze suggests that the future fights against habit and memory in a way that allows difference to pervade repetition: "but making it [the future] the thought and the production of the 'absolutely different'; making it so that repetition is, for itself, difference in itself" (Deleuze 1994, 94).

When forgiveness and resentment merge, I maintain, they become saboteurs of repetition. Together, forgiveness and resentment interrupt the present, reframe the past, and shape the future. In the context of national trauma resulting from mass atrocity, memory and trust are not, cannot be, automatically tied together. The presence of both forgiveness and resentment, however, can reduce the chasm between memory and trust, by fashioning new connections of identity and alterity that can open paths to truly ethical coexistence between victims, offenders, and their descendants.

Forgiveness follows the recognition that change is possible, both for the individual and for society as a whole, both for victim and perpetrator. In *No Future Without Forgiveness*, Archbishop Desmond Tutu argues that, because forgiveness is a personal process, perpetrators must be allowed to participate in the kind of dialogue that shows that they are not monsters, that they are as human as their victims: "In the spirit of *ubuntu,* the central concern is the healing of breaches, the redressing of imbalances, the restoration of broken relationships, a seeking to rehabilitate both the victim and the perpetrator, who should be given the opportunity to be reintegrated into the community he has injured by his offense" (Tutu 1999, 46). Coexistence between victims and offenders depends upon trust and a particular orientation to memory, one in which forgiveness and resentment are both actively present. In the Western literary epistemology, emotions cohere either by affirming love and hatred, or by promoting shame and regret. But there are other epistemologies, of which Tutu's is but one example, those that translate the Western epistemology and advance new values – which I will call *negative possessions* – to combat the trauma wrought by atrocity and genocide.

The central idea in this book grew out of my reading of a subchapter – "Irreversibility and the Power to Forgive" – in Hannah Arendt's *The Human Condition*.[1] Arendt's analysis of forgiveness is strongly tied to her understanding of love. I was overwhelmed by how difficult it is for her to decide whether forgiveness and love are only interpersonal affects, or whether they can effect change in the social and political spheres. Arendt seeks to protect forgiveness and love from being corrupted by the public sphere. In order to accomplish this she limits them to the life of the couple, of the family. She argues that forgiveness is personal because, like love, it focuses on the *who* – who commits the evil deed – and not on the *what* – the deed itself. The ability to focus on the humanity of the offender, not to fall into an economy of vengeance or reprisal, gives rise to forgiveness.

Resentment is the insistence on attaching moral responsibility to perpetrators, be they individual persons or entire societies. The resentful witness communicates with the perpetrator, and in doing so demands justice. The resentful witness demands that evil be documented, that memory persist, yet does not commit to one necessary future. The resentful witness articulates new possibilities of difference.

Forgiveness is difficult. So is resentment. In regards to the difficulty of resentment, victims must expose their own traumatic suffering in order to compel the Other's moral and cultural respect. This book suggests that a forgiving victim envisions a world in which she/he must descend into a moral abyss *before* she/he can envision psychological healing, social trust, or the restoration of a moral existence. Going beyond personal pain and moral disappointment leaves room for the – partially fictional – hope that, somewhere in the future, there will come recognition and collaboration between victim and offender. Forgiveness is an emotion that operates within a reciprocal relationship with the Other.

On the surface it seems as if forgiveness and resentment are mutually exclusive. It seems that the one who forgives must relinquish resentment, and the one who resents does not contemplate forgiveness. But emotions seldom fall into neat

---

[1] See the interview with Lyudmila Sholokhova, May 5, 2022. See https://www.nypl.org/blog/2022/05/05/researcher-spotlight-idit-alphandary accessed on August 1, 2022.

categories. I have found that it is only possible to understand forgiveness when one realizes that resentment is a form of memory, of loyalty, a remembering that can legitimize forgiveness. Resentment can be a springboard to the restoration of mutual recognition between witnesses, be they victims or offenders. For the witness, forgiveness is a leap of faith, a wager on the good, not a negation of morality. Resentment is a desire and a knowledge that compels the victim to address the nation in an attempt to cause deterritorialization, and to create a line of flight that s/he can use to shape a future, a new life.

This book explores works and thinkers that highlight the intimate link between forgiveness and resentment in a variety of contexts: post-Holocaust Europe, post-Apartheid South Africa, the battle to end colonialism in India, the struggle for Black Civil Rights in the United States. I argue that, in each of these cases, forgiveness and resentment are emotions that shape memory, and have the potential to transform the value of the present and the possibilities of the future. The number and diversity of my examples are meant to promote a discussion of forgiveness and resentment that is global in scope. I seek to examine these emotions in their transnational, translinguistic, and transcultural characters. Yet the reader will notice that, throughout the following chapters, I return repeatedly to the writings of Hannah Arendt and Jean Améry, two thinkers who wrestled with the paradox of forgiveness and resentment in a very specific context: the aftermath of the Nazi regime and the Holocaust of European Jewry. The reason, as I show below, is that every contemporary thinker who negotiates these emotions in the context of crimes against humanity is in conversation with Arendt on the subject of forgiveness, and with Améry on the subject of resentment. Following in the footsteps of Arendt, I associate forgiveness with emotions like love for, and trust in, the humanity of the other person – be they victim or offender. Following Améry, I relate resentment to remembering, and to the inability to rationalize, to give meaning to the dehumanization that people and nations inflict on those they consider undesirable or expendable.

Forgiveness is difficult, because the offender commits an overwhelming wrong against the victim, and yet the victim is supposed to react with love, with innocence, with trust in the Other. But resentment is just as difficult, because a rancorous victim is morally committed to enlighten the culture which perpetrated evil, to compel that culture to undergo transformation, to activate deterritorialization, to open up future potential for new assemblages to which individuals and communities can belong. Forgiveness and resentment prove that memory is not monolithic, that it is subject to changes that correlate with the passage of time, the changing of values, and the fluctuation of personal and social circumstance. Forgiveness and resentment build new worlds in their encounter with pain.

My template, my paradigm for the discussion on forgiveness and resentment is the Holocaust, most specifically, the works of European Jewish intellectuals in the aftermath of that incomprehensible catastrophe. This reflects my personal interests, but also the seminal importance that the Holocaust has had in debates about crimes against humanity. In many ways the aftermath of the Holocaust established the current language on radical violence and on collective trauma (LaCapra 2001). It remains a frame of reference in the quest for healing and for change for religious, ethnic, and national groups around the world.

Because the Holocaust has been particularly entangled in questions of transitional justice, it informs my analytical approach to texts concerning events in other, very different places and contexts. My ultimate goal is to show that forgiveness and resentment are not mutually exclusive, that they are necessary to each other, for their purpose should be to translate a Western ethical epistemology into new forms of knowledge relevant to non-European languages and communities.[2]

## Arendt's forgiveness, Améry's resentment

The act of storytelling often memorializes violence. In doing so, one would think, it encourages resentment, and discourages forgiveness, towards the victimizers. But resentment is a necessary retort to the phenomenological experience of atrocity. Resentment offers a new vocabulary with which to rebuild morality in the aftermath of overwhelming evil. For Améry, resentment should be embraced and understood as historical remembering and responsibility (Brudholm 2008). Forgiveness begins with resentment. Améry is unapologetic about the festering resentment he feels towards his abusers, yet he reaches out to them, to listen, to be informed, and perhaps even to rearrange his own conception of politics in light of the harm he suffered. In other words, *positive* narratives of forgiveness entail a kernel of bitter resentment, while *negative* narratives of resentment carry a gesture of healing and correction.

The enigma of love surfaces because, as Arendt points out, love is "worldless," it belongs to the lovers only interested in *who* the other is, in her/his singularity. And yet she explains that, in order to know *who* a person is, one has to know

---

[2] This introduction is influenced by Michael Rothberg's *Multidirectional Memory Remembering the Holocaust in the Age of Decolonization.* Rothberg's analysis of the memory of the Holocaust offers tools to examine remembrance of mass atrocity across crosscultural, crosstemporal, and crossreligeous contexts: "The greatest hope for a new comparatism lies in opening up the separate containers of memory and identity that buttress competitive thinking and becoming aware of the mutual constitution and ongoing transformation of the objects of comparison" (Rothberg 2009, 18).

*what* causes this person to engage in speech and action in plurality. Storytelling is crucial to Arendt's ability to explain *who* human beings are, because their speech and actions in plurality reveal their humanity. Arendt is aware that people speak and act in a "web of relations," so that everything they say and do finds its place in the existing structure of relations. And yet, without the new beginnings that speakers and actors in plurality initiate these relations would not have existed.

In their social and political lives with others, human beings reveal their ability to act, judge, trust, and suffer. For those who seek to build the world, *amor mundi* is the guiding ethos, they are lovers of the world, armed with a love not corrupted by politics. People who act from *amor mundi* are courageous. They address public affairs driven by thought and passion, not just by a desire to satisfy their own interests. Those who favor forgiveness, and those who stress resentment, are courageous lovers of the world, as Arendt notes: "courage and even boldness are already present in leaving one's private hiding place and showing who one is, in disclosing and exposing one's self" (Arendt 1958, 186).

Arendt is aware of how language shapes and transforms culture. She speaks as a victim, not just as a Jewish survivor who fled Germany in 1933, but as a philosopher whose native German language was destroyed by Hitler's totalitarian regime. In the aftermath of the Third Reich, Arendt encourages her readers to transform the totalitarian hues of the German language through acts of resistance. She explains how the language of forgiveness and love can save a society from political and moral stagnation. I aim to show that Arendt's criticism of totalitarianism and racism is grounded in fluctuations of language. These shifts occur before ideologies can gain the force needed to mobilize the population towards racism, anti-Semitism, and genocide.

Writing to Jaspers in 1946, Arendt comments about the United States: "the society organizes and orients itself along 'racial lines.' [This racial issue] is greatly aggravated by the Negro question; that is America has a real 'race' problem and not just a racial ideology" (Arendt and Jaspers 1992, 31). Arendt locates American racism in the language that attaches itself to democracy, through her analysis of the ways "democratic language" truly frames Black people and their Blackness. She feels an instinctive kinship with those who are brutalized by their nation's language, those who are pushed to "the fringes of society" (Arendt and Jaspers 1992, 29).

For Arendt, it is crucial that forgiveness remain not pure. If pure forgiveness is related only to emotions like resentment or love, then not pure forgiveness is tied together with a penal logic and with political healing. Because the law either punishes or forgives, "men are unable to forgive what they cannot punish and [. . .] cannot punish what has turned out to be unforgiveable" (Arendt 1958, 241). How does one punish a German perpetrator for the destruction of European Jewry? How does one forgive this annihilation? Arendt argues that forgiveness is personal, but not necessarily individual. Forgiveness is the shape that love takes in the public sphere.

In her examination of the role that love has in Arendt's *Denktagebuch*, her diary of thinking, Tatjana Noemi Tömmel focuses on the concept of "Volo ut sis: *Love as Unconditional Affirmation*" (Tömmel 2017, 116). *Volo ut sis*, "I love you, I want you to be," is a phrase that belongs to those whose love is unworldly because they only need each other. The same phrase belongs to those who are motivated by *amor mundi* to speak and act with the goal of building a better world. Améry is the singular example of a survivor who judges. He indicts Nazi Germany for its crimes, but also the international community, for being too quick to seek forgiveness and reconciliation. His speech and actions add up to an affirmation of negative possession, to restoring a moral meaning to history. Améry speaks and acts out of love, despite his fear that few among his contemporaries are interested in the story of his resentments.

A speaker and actor in the public sphere does not turn love into politics, but its presence shows that the political realm cannot function without the memory and knowledge of private love. Love means that people are in need of affirmation, because they come into a web of relations that exists before they arrive and continues after they leave the world. Arendt puts it thus: "[w]e have not made ourselves, we stand in need of confirmation. We are strangers, we stand in need of being welcome. *I want you to be*" (cited in Tömmel 2017, 118). The loss of a human perspective on *bare life* causes Améry to speak in favor of restoring justice and solidarity, love and care in and for the world.

Améry, born in Austria to an assimilated Jewish family, emigrated to Belgium in the 1940s, and there lived with his wife while a member of the anti-Nazi resistance under an assumed name. He was captured and tortured by the Gestapo, interned at Auschwitz, and eventually freed from Bergen-Belsen at the end of the war. Afterward he wrote many volumes of essays and two novels, before committing suicide in 1978. While the older generation wanted to forget the Nazi past, young citizens from the Left condemned fascism and warned the world against countries that emulated fascist policies. To an "eyewitness" like Améry, their attitude towards fascism's dangers appears "utterly stupid" (Améry 1980, viii). Améry wants to reveal "emotions? For all I care, yes" (Améry 1980, xi). What matters to him is to acknowledge "the state of someone who was *overcome*" (Améry 1980, xiv, italics added). He seeks to create a bridge over the moral chasm between the victim, in the state of being overcome, and his German readers: "But it must not be done by hollow, thoughtless, utterly false conciliatoriness. On the contrary: since it is a moral chasm, let it for now remain wide open" (Améry 1980, ix). Today, we would call this overcome state post-traumatic stress disorder. But, for Améry, to be overcome is "to fulfill the law of enlightenment and at the same time transcend it [and] reach intellectual realms in which *ratio* does not lead to shallow rationalism" (Améry 1980, xi).

The language of the Enlightenment, and the silence that it leaves behind, are central to Améry. He aims to translate Western epistemology and institute the relevance of moral judgment to genocide by turning to emotions, those affects that ethics has traditionally dismissed as obstacles to finding truth. Forgiveness and resentment do not rationally explain the abyss of evil. These emotions call on the victim to survive evil by being overcome with both conscious and unconscious suffering.

Améry is the most sophisticated proponent of resentment. He demands that both victim and perpetrator be united in their overcome state. The perpetrator has to return to the realm of trauma – to *the real* – in order to understand the abyss of his wickedness, without seeking shallow justifications. Forgiveness, only becomes tangible when it is grounded in the same psychological and moral abyss as resentment, the space in which one is overcome by an inability to articulate remedies for suffering. Améry believes that the moral abyss between the victim and the perpetrator will be bridged: "someday *time* will close it, that is certain" (Améry 1980, ix). To allow young generations to mend the tear between victim and perpetrator is to use, rather than abuse, history. Yet victims and perpetrators can trust each other only if they descend into the abyss of evil and remain in the state of *being overcome* by passion.

Passion signifies suffering and endurance, love and resignation. Victim and perpetrator can acknowledge both guilt and pain when they are overcome by passion. The twelve years of National Socialism in Germany, and the suffering they produced, are why "all of us [victims and perpetrators] are still faced with a dark riddle" (Améry 1980, viii). Améry names this dark riddle a "realized negation of the world," or a "negative possession" (Améry 1980, 78). In this sense negative possessions guide forgiveness and resentment – values that restore a moral dimension to our historical understanding of evil. Negative possessions force us to write history refracted through emotion. Writing history through the lens of forgiveness and resentment is what keeps history from becoming useless as a concept.

Améry is considering forgiveness and resentment as both a moral and historical frame (Améry 1980, 68). He demands that Germans acknowledge guilt, that they disclose the truth about the atrocities they committed. This can be done in political speech, in courts of law, in the education system, in literature, theater, film, in the visual arts. Germany must promote history, so that remembering becomes a cultural commitment to memorialize the Jewish culture it worked so hard to eradicate. Memory cannot deteriorate into sentimental nostalgia. It must enable a working through of the ungraspable crimes. At the same time, the negative possessions that Améry envisions do not currently exist in historical research, education, or the arts. Negative possessions aim to subvert and humble history and ethics, to allow these disciplines to grapple with how far off the mark of evil they are when demanding that facts and judgment restore morality.³

Dialogue, the relinquishing of the phantasy of sovereignty, and the acceptance of the value of passivity and powerlessness, are worldly states that meet the moral exigencies of forgiveness and resentment. Améry remains the example of how emotions cannot be substituted by simply bringing the culprit to justice, even though he seeks indictment to every Nazi criminal. When Améry is in dialogue with his reader, he demands recognition for negative possessions, recognition beyond jurisdiction, and articulates German guilt and repentance. But he cannot be satisfied that guilt is explained, that repentance brings closure to the historical narrative, so that evil is neutralized and history is balanced.

Améry expects his reader to be overcome by atrocity, filled with passion for the victims' suffering, the perpetrators' guilt. Holocaust testimonies render the memory of atrocities meaningful and relevant to the present because the present lends a context in which incomprehensible evil must be valued using emotions. Primo Levi's testimony clarifies why he thinks that, despite Améry's resentment, Améry cannot avoid keeping open the possibility that survivors and perpetrators will be equals in the future, responsible for Germany's negative possessions. Survivors and perpetrators cannot share life in the world if they try to gloss over atrocity, either by forgetfulness or by being so resentful that they sever all human connection. In *The Drowned and the Saved*, Levi confesses that "Améry called me 'the forgiver'" (Levi 1988, 137). Levi denies that he can forgive the Nazis, but admits that forgiveness is at stake. Life in Auschwitz, he recalls, was rife with human interactions like friendship and enmities. They were "food that certainly contributed to keeping a part of me alive and that subsequently supplied me with the material for thinking and making books" (Levi 1988, 141). These examples of the open scope of forgiveness show that, during and after the Holocaust, the victim denies that Nazism is potent enough to negate the human capacity to restore fellow feelings. Only a democratic dialogue imbued with emotion can bridge the chasm that prevents the victim and perpetrator to forge memory and trust which can match the violence that circulates in all cultures.

---

**3** In this sense I diverge from Amir Engel's position. According to Engle, Améry's resentments promote a "nonconsiequeatial mode" of memory. He stresses that Améry's resentments are not pervaded by a kernel of forgiveness but, on the contrary, that "Memory, which is not contrived of clichés and platitudes, is action's most powerful antidote" (Engel 2020, 18). I argue that Améry wants to implicate enlightenment in phenomenology and thereby translate Western epistemology, move away from the discussion of epistemological truths to the discussion of emotions and the passion of bare life.

Forgiveness is a moral threshold, a reciprocal and intersubjective emotion to which the victim is obligated in the face of the utter loss of human values. Améry demands that Germany "no longer repress or hush up the twelve years that for us others really were a thousand, but claim them as its realized negation of the world and it self, as its own negative possession" (Améry 1980, 78). Resentment is not expressed only in returning the blow to the perpetrator. Negative possessions are a translation of Western epistemology. They signify new literary and artistic practices that can help us navigate mass atrocity, precisely by presenting readers with the paradox of forgiveness intertwined with resentment.

## The interdependence of forgiveness and resentment

Sigmund Freud's understanding of mourning and melancholia presents an internal paradox that mirrors that which unites forgiveness with resentment: the attempt to simultaneously survive and remain faithful to the dead. Freud argues that the work of mourning causes the ego to distance itself from reality, in order to remain attached to the dead loved one. In mourning grief is slowly consumed, so that the ego can welcome new attachments. On the other hand, the melancholic ego is impoverished because it suffers two losses: the loss of the object and the loss of the ego. Freud explains that the melancholic is ambivalent and can neither love nor hate the dead person. In order to break free from ambivalence, the melancholic remains loyal to the dead by feeling guilty:

> The shadow of the object fell upon the ego, and the latter could henceforth be judged by a special agency, as though it were an object, the forsaken object. In this way an object-loss was transformed into an ego-loss and the conflict between the ego and the loved person into a cleavage between the critical activity of the ego and the ego as altered by identification (Freud Vol. 14 1957 [1917], 249).

There is a clear line between Freud's notion of mourning and Paul Celan's "Conversation in the Mountains," where the Jew is obligated to memory even while he cathects new objects in the world:

> But they, those cousins, have no eyes, alas. Or, more exactly: they have, even they have eyes, but with a veil hanging in front of them, no, not in front, behind them, a movable veil. No sooner does an image enter than it gets caught in the web, and a thread starts spinning, spinning itself around the image, a veil-thread; spins itself around the image and begets a child, half image, half veil (Celan 1986, 18).

The metonymy of the veil suggests that observations in the world are implicated in memories of the dead. This prosopopoeia, or personification of abstract birth and death, is used to show that a Jewish child is born from melancholic remembering in search of a new self. Despite melancholy, the protagonist's return to memory enables him to remain close to his own experience of death: "me, maybe accompanied – now – by the love of those I didn't love, me on the way to myself, up here" (Celan 1986, 22). The world into which the poet is born does not precede the existence of the poem. Prosopopoeia also means that the poem creates images of veiling and being born, giving a face to that which does not have a face.

Like Arendt, Celan and Améry indict the German mother tongue. Discrimination and anti-Semitism have always been inscribed in the language. With this in mind, how does a German intellectual use language to establish guilt and repentance? How does a Jewish German use that very same language to articulate suffering, resentment, forgiveness? If both German offenders and victims admit that German is the language of the murderers, then what moral authority could the German speaking intellectual yield? *The Question of German Guilt* by Karl Jaspers is an early text that confronts these questions of moral linguistics. I suggest that Jaspers strongly influenced Améry's writings on resentment. Jaspers, like Améry, lays the burden of guilt on the lap of Germans:

> the ones who knew, or could know and yet walked in ways which self-analysis reveals to them as culpable error – whether conveniently closing their eyes to events, or permitting themselves to be intoxicated, seduced or bought with personal advantages, or obeying from fear (Jaspers 2000, 57–58).

He argues that these conforming Germans are "guilty of being alive." "We did not go into the streets when our Jewish friends were led away," he asserts, "We did not scream until we too were destroyed. We preferred to stay alive, on the feeble, if logical, ground that our death could not have helped anyone. We are guilty of being alive" (Jaspers 2000, 65–66). The repentant German intellectual is conscious of political, moral, and metaphysical guilt. Each German must accept individual "solitude" from which a future German soul might be born (Jaspers 2000, 68). Metaphysical guilt may force Germans to recognize that "historically we remain bound to the closer, narrower communities, and we should lose the ground under our feet without them" (Jaspers 2000, 69). Jaspers acknowledges that the loss of solidarity with the Other brought about disaster. Améry follows suit when he states that, if he is to be released from his solitude, Germans must feel morally abandoned. Jaspers seeks to acknowledge his negative possessions when he states that his task as a German is urgent for "guilt brings a people face to face with nothingness" (Jaspers 2005, 75).

In his seminal analysis of forgiveness, Vladimir Jankélévitch shows that, when writing about forgiveness and resentment, the rhetorical use of *chiasmus* has the most profound effect on a reader. Forgiveness, he argues, is an *event* that restores innocence to the world. The chiasmus of forgiveness entangled in resentment means that neither forgiveness nor resentment can explain their appearance. In relation to radical evil, Jankélévitch insists that "the debate between forgiveness and the unforgiveable will never have an end" (Jankélévitch 2005, 162). Forgiveness exists because it is haunted by resentment. Resentment exists because it is haunted by forgiveness. Forgiveness cannot understand. It is a performative emotion and is therefore able to cleanse the world from meanings that affirm wickedness: "this extreme and almost heartrending tension is that of the mad forgiveness that is accorded to the wicked person" (Jankélévitch 2005, 164).

Jacques Derrida agrees with Jankélévitch, but only to a point. Jankélévitch asserts that forgiveness is only necessary in the face of crimes against humanity. He wrestles with how it is possible to forgive the wickedness of those who deny the humanity of the Other. Forgiveness and resentment are necessarily interconnected – unless the forgiving victim remains resentful, then the victim is not forgiving. Rather, that victim is attempting to forget the trauma, or denying that the wicked is human enough to accept moral responsibility, not even in a changed world. Derrida deals with the same difficulty, yet he is intolerant of the paradox of forgiveness and resentment, and leaves only pure forgiveness as an option.

Derrida believes that, because forgiveness is pure, it is mad and therefore impossible. He denies that pure forgiveness overcomes resentment, because pure forgiveness does not advance the politics of reconciliation. Instead he stresses that forgiveness begins in resentment. I suggest that, for Derrida, "the only thing that calls for forgiveness" (Derrida 2001, 32) is the unforgiveable, because he has two historical figures in mind. Améry is the first. The second is the widow of a murdered Black South African victim, who, during a meeting of the Truth and Reconciliation Committee, refuses to forgive her husband's murderers. This stance informs Derrida's philosophical negotiation of forgiveness and resentment. Both Améry and the widow send the perpetrator to ask forgiveness from the dead, for only the dead victim can forgive (Derrida 2001, 43–44). The survivors attach forgiveness to the past, and to the fact that the survivor's identity is forever linked to past horrors, to a past in which they were powerless. Derrida's vision of forgiveness generates no reward, not even psychological healing, for when a reward is contemplated then forgiveness is not pure.

Derrida argues that forgiveness inspires reciprocal emotions. He is closest to associating both forgiveness and resentment with the state of being overwhelmed, with language's loss of its ability to explain forgiveness and resentment. Forgiveness must remain a madness of the impossible – impossible to understand forgiveness and impossible not to understand this emotion when it applies to crimes against humanity.

For Derrida, "the only thing that calls for forgiveness" is the unforgiveable (Derrida 2001, 32). The unforgiveable is the unforgettable crime that must forever be etched in memory. Yet Derrida has put himself in a philosophical bind. He acknowledges the necessity of repetition at the same time that he roots for the exigencies of difference. When we remember we repeat, and yet forgiveness introduces difference. When we forget we lure difference. And yet, the return of the repressed, "forgotten" traumatic past is the most common form of repetition without difference, without forgiveness. In the face of the unforgivable, resentment safeguards subjective memories and interpretations of the past of both culture and identity. I believe the attachment to practical ethics is implicated in phantasies of autonomy, sovereignty, and power. Derrida associates forgiveness with a sovereign decision that takes shape in a powerless victim. The victim is the one whose sovereignty is destroyed by a perpetrator who phantasizes to be sovereign.

The victim has no power before the sovereign perpetrator, who has excessive, destructive power. In many cultures the aftermath of catastrophe teaches that, even when the perpetrator makes certain human beings superfluous, the emerging society, and politics still depend on the Other, develop symptoms that show that neither the victim nor the perpetrator are sovereign, neither the victim nor the perpetrator are completely powerful or powerless. This brings Améry to mind, in that it trusts in both resignation and abandonment and their opposite, vigorous resentment. Derrida institutes a victim and a perpetrator who undergo transformation, inaugurating an *ethics beyond ethics*. They abide by the emotions that equalize them: the perpetrator and the victim acknowledge guilt and shame, they acknowledge mutual respect, and they are guided by emotions that accept the value of love and forgiveness. Ultimately, Derrida is asking how nonsovereignty and powerlessness propel acts of forgiveness without closure? I will refer to the power inherent in forgiveness, in the hands of the powerless, as "Power(lessness)."

Derrida observes that if forgiveness is only conscious but not transparent – conducted by the sovereign and outside the public realm – then forgiveness is not pure. Pure forgiveness is compound. It "must plunge, but lucidly, into the night of the unintelligible" (Derrida 2001, 49). For Derrida, unconscious forgiveness is always hyperbolical, *lucid but unintelligible*, and therefore pure. Pure forgiveness is directly related to the traumatic past – the unintelligible – but accesses moral difference in the present – the lucid.

## Exploring forgiveness and resentment through literature and film

Literature manipulates language: it generates repetition, difference, neologisms, unknown segmentation of phonemes all in order to encompass the lucid and the unintelligible. Literature elaborates metaphors, and reveals new themes. It questions the reliability of narrators in order to break free from, and destroy the terms of possibility of, a sovereign language. In the chapters of this book I explore how the poetic function of literature can restore lucidity while remaining aware of unintelligible suffering. The narratives and images I discuss plunge the reader into *chiasmus*, revealing how prosopopoeia can become a means through which a lucid victim can remain loyal to the dead and still advance difference, be alive.

Prosopopoeia is a rhetorical device, a form of personification, a form of repetition, and the site of an emerging difference. The writer who employs prosopopoeia borrows the voice of another, usually a dead master, but with a different rhythm or accent, so that the synthesis of repetition and difference brings this other writer into being. Personification can bring an adversary back into language. It can animate the dead and deliver their thoughts. It can allow them to be interlocutors who address us from beyond the grave. The enunciations of the dead, those who have no face, no voice, cannot be logically analyzed, but they can nevertheless bring the dead back into the present, carry their memory into the future, interrupt the passage of time without forcing closure. These rhetorical possibilities make prosopopoeia suitable for parody, but they also make personification suitable for autobiography and testimony – for in these genres the speaker tries to articulate aspects of her/his life that are dead to her/him.

Prosopopoeia allows the writer and the reader to understand tragic events that surpass the imagination, that are incomprehensible. Prosopopoeia brings together skepticism – the writer's/reader's bewilderment, can this be true? – and sincerity – the writer's/reader's acknowledgement that truth can be made lucid only if repetition and difference are veiled by fiction and metaphor. Prosopopoeia stresses death, but the dead appear as an interruption that introduces potentials in life, not as a finality, it gives voice to and makes the dead accessible and visible.

In a famous article on the role of making a face and suffering defacement in the autobiographical genre, Paul de Man reads Romantic poetry and arrives at the following definition of prosopopoeia: "Voice assumes mouth, eye, and finally face, a chain that is manifest in the etymology of the trope's name, *prosopon poien*, to confer a mask or a face (prosopon). Prosopopoeia is the trope of autobiography, by which one's name [. . .] is made as intelligible and memorable as a face" (de Man 1984, 76). Language does not explain. It brands on the reader the affective paradoxes that are available to it. A proficient author uses both structural and contextual paradoxes to expose the shortcomings of language to handle and produce affect and judgment. Prosopopoeia leaves intact the unintelligibility, of the dead but it grants lucidity to the memory of the dead. It introduces difference to repetition.

My work means to show how literature resides in the in-between: in-between language and the ineffable, in between dream and action, in between forgiveness and resentment. Language lends conscious meanings to the unconsciousness of a writing/reading experience. The writer's and the reader's judgment of the world undergoes unexpected alteration, wherein unconscious affects suspend habitual meanings in language.

Literature mandates the performative force of negative possessions. Negative possessions are embodied in metaphors, rhetorical tropes, and repetitions. These transformations are the remedies that philosophers such as Arendt, Jaspers, Améry, and Levi prescribe to the German native tongue, in order to alter everyday speech, making it receptive to reciprocal emotions. Literature renders forgiveness and resentment tangible when they are submerged in the powerlessness of literary discourse. Literature exerts moral force because it is not a sovereign origin of reasoning and naming, but a set of tropes that coalesce around mobilizing affective and linguistic potentials. The diachronic axis, or the history of a language, diverts reasoned and affective potentials when it comes in touch with the synchronic axis or the present of the language so that literature always thwarts fixed language positions of meaning and power.

Forgiveness and resentment are malleable in literature because subject positions are interdependent in the text, so that both guilt and repentance, shame and regret activate our ability to experience paradox. In the following chapters I underline instances in which literature makes the language of the powerless present, at the same time as it makes the language of the powerful foreign, and so creates the palimpsest of different languages, and brings them into layered confrontation. I underline how literature translates whole epistemologies and vacates the authority of known power positions, and how the position of the Other can exert an equal force, which propels new epistemologies into action.

Derrida contends that language opens the possibility of non-knowledge. Literature, in his view, refers only to its own textuality. It remains tangible even when it plunges knowledge and meaning into an abyss:

> But is it not necessary for all literature to exceed literature? [. . .] What would be a literature that would be only what it is, literature? It would no longer be itself if it were itself [. . .] Surely one could speak of "literariness" as a *belonging to* literature, as of the inclusion of a phenomenon or an object, even a work, within a field, a domain, a region whose frontiers would be pure and whose titles indivisible [. . .] The work, the opus, does not belong to the field [of language], it is the transformer of the field (Derrida 1992, 215).

The performative language that issues from literature transforms language itself, and enables both writer and reader to move between subject positions. The authors I discuss in this book embody the power of literature to access emotions because their works translate these emotions: they are designed to give voice to difference and heterogeneity, to move away from the attempt to master knowledge.

The first chapter examines forgiveness and resentment in the story "Max Ferber" by W. G. Sebald. As a child, Ferber was smuggled out of Germany before the Holocaust. In the story's present, he tells the narrator, who is a fictional stand-in for Sebald, the story of how he grew from a refugee into a renowned and successful painter. Ferber is resigned, *overcome* by fatigue and abject loss, but his powerlessness does not escape the chiasmus of forgiveness and resentment. I show that the overlap between Sebald's resentment toward Germany and Ferber's forgiveness and resentment of the narrator/Sebald, and by extension of Germany, establish a new reality. It is a reality in which radical evil is not implicated in the political language of power, but belongs instead to the language of love, dialogue, and respect.

When people are in relationships that allow them to be swayed by emotions, they are immersed in the nonsovereing structure of reciprocal love, and are more vulnerable to forgiveness and resentment. They are not primarily practicing autonomy and sovereignty. Yet these emotions are never pure. They are shaped by memory, as Sebald shows in "Max Ferber": "As I now thought back, it seemed unforgivable that I should have omitted, or failed, in those Manchester times, to ask Ferber the questions he must surely have expected from me" (Sebald 1996, 178). The narrator/Sebald and Ferber meet sporadically for twenty years. This is how long it takes to establish a real relationship, and begin a conversation about repentance, forgiveness, and resentment. Negative possessions replace silence.

The second chapter is devoted to an extensive examination of Arendt's work. Arendt understands that radical evil relies on turning human beings to superfluity, and reducing their humanity to the phenomenology of *bare life*. Her discussion of how totalitarianism strips persons of their humanity informs my analysis of the anti-colonial struggle in India, the quest for truth and reconciliation in South Africa, and the fight for civil rights in the United States.

In the third chapter, I juxtapose the writings of Jaspers, Améry, and Heinrich Böll. In Böll's *The Clown*, the protagonist Hans Schnier expresses his resentment through the routines of pantomime: his face is painted white, he is always silent. He repairs the German language using the strategy of *the look from beyond the grave (regard de l'outre-tombe)*. Böll, I argue, sabotages duplicitous verbiage by ensnaring his characters in prosopopoeia and chiasmus. Hans' white mask alludes to death, to the dead, and he borrows the voices of the dead to explore his own resentment. A silent, masked clown leads the way to the phenomenology of emotions.

Like Améry, Böll embraces the powerlessness of philosophy and literature in order to unearth the truth. Memory and trust can return to German politics and culture only if Germany carefully collects its negative possessions, turns its most frightful memories into tangible narratives. The work of articulating negative possessions is a form of repetition that allows difference in meanings and actions to emerge. Böll offers Germany an opportunity to be part of a conversation about the guilt, shame, and regret that have been obscured by the theater of monetary compensation and diplomatic reconciliation. The state of being overcome leads to a dialogue that fashions memory and can foster trust between Germans and those they consider Other.

At the core of the fourth chapter are the meetings of the Truth and Reconciliation Committee in South Africa in the aftermath of Apartheid, and the translation of Western epistemology's treatment of the emotions to a new literary language grounded in the notion of *Ubuntu*. Ubuntu stresses that human beings are tied to one another inherently and inextricably, in action and in emotion, so that when the one inflicts pain on the other both are dehumanized. By the same token, when the offender sincerely regrets and repents then the humanities of both offender and victim are restored.

I approach the notion of Ubuntu through an extended analysis of J. M. Coetzee's novel *Disgrace*. The novel shows that, in post-Apartheid South Africa, emotions that appear personal have immense cultural and social impact. David Lurie, the protagonist, is a university Professor accused of raping a student, and he knows himself to be "a *thing*, that is, a monster," (Coetzee 1999, 34). Lurie must therefore face the authority of a disciplinary committee. This body, in turn, serves as a metaphor for the Truth and Reconciliation Committee, and serves Coetzee to examine questions of public confession, encounters between perpetrators and victims, amnesty, punishment, and more. I show that Coetzee creates characters that transcend the bounds of Western – legalistic, philosophically abstract – notions of truth or justice, and instead embrace love, hatred, guilt, shame, becoming animal, becoming woman, and disgrace to create clusters of meaning that point the way towards true forgiveness and reconciliation. I argue that this is the position from which witnesses truly forgive or truly resent forgiveness in *Disgrace*'s South Africa. As the philosopher Sami Pihlström from Finland argues, forgiveness is "an extreme possibility that is itself necessary for them [moral systems] to be possible" (Pihlström 2017, 529). Only where all ethical systems are collapsed do we find forgiveness which brings the need to acknowledge unforgivable atrocities to the fore. "Not only forgiveness forgives the inexcusable; it can, paradoxically, at least seek to forgive the unforgiveable" (Pihlström 2017, 531). In *Disgrace*, Lurie does not undergo moral evolution but his desire undergoes a process that Deleuze and Guattari name involution. Lurie becomes involved in South Africa, its diversity: the differences that he and his daughter face on a cultural, social, economic, and personal levels.

In between the chapters I have added four "interchapters," in which I explore forgiveness and resentment through a focus on films that have significance to me personally: *The Hourglass Sanatorium* by Wojciech Has (1973), *Phoenix* by Christian Petzold (2014), *Aftermath* by Wladyalaw Pasikowski, (2012), and *I Am Not Your Negro* by Raoul Peck (2016). I am a cinephile, sensitive to the fact that films make sense of and change the structure of reflection and desire in my everyday life. Films reflect on and structure my experience. They allow me to distance myself from known images of *who* and *what* I am. When I leave the movie theater, the film forces me to find the right words to describe a world of associations and connotations that are instigated by it. I am forced to relocate *my* view and my *words* in an attempt to relate the filmic experience to other people.

The film-philosophy of forgiveness and resentment discloses the Power(lessness) of the *real* (Lacan 1971; Kristeva 2002) that my chapters articulate. With the exception of the second, each interchapter is connected to a book and to the philosophical ideas that I examine in the chapters. The films allow me to examine the relational and affective Power(lessness) that emerge from forgiveness and resentment in the lives of singular characters and communities, which exist in the shadow of the mass atrocity that they suffered.

Philosophers try to illuminate forgiveness and resentment when they separate these emotions from each other, avoid a paradox in the realms of meaning, ethics, and action. Avishai Margalit comes very close to admitting that forgiveness and resentment are locked together if each one of these emotion is to have any meaning or the power to propel the world into action. In *The Ethics of Memory*, Margalit states that democracy must acknowledge emotions that look to the past. He examines religious and everyday forgiveness but wants to establish a philosophical explanation of everyday forgiveness, not divine forgiveness. Although he alludes to resentment he does not name this emotion. Margalit wants to show that forgiveness is only sincere if it does not equal to forgetting, he calls forgiveness true when it covers up the evil that was done at the same time that it leaves the one who forgives and the one who asks for forgiveness conscious of the harms that they suffered and dealt respectively:

> Blotting out is analogous to deleting; covering up is like crossing out. I shall argue that the image of covering up is conceptually, psychologically, and morally preferable to the picture of blotting out—that it is better to cross out than to delete the memories of an offense. In short, I argue that forgiveness is based on disregarding the sin rather than forgetting it (Margalit 2002, 197).

# Chapter 1
# Forgiveness, resentment and reconciliation – on W. G. Sebald

According to Julia Kristeva, forgiveness is an act of love extended to the other (Kristeva and Rice 2002).[1] Forgiveness, from this perspective, is dialogical, in that it enables the victim to regain power and become a forceful voice (Grunebaum 2002, 308; Kluger 2002, 313; Benjamin 1997, 286). Forgiveness, however, reveals a paradox when it manifests as a response to crimes against humanity: how can the unforgivable be forgiven? This is the paradox Arendt, Derrida, Jankélevitch, and so many others wrestle with. The solution, I will argue throughout this book, is found in the work of Jean Améry, particularly in his insight that, in the face of the unforgiveable, forgiveness becomes sincere when it carries resentment within it.

Améry teaches that resentment is also dialogical, in that it delivers the victim from abandonment. Abandonment, in Améry's view, begins with exclusion and culminates in unforgiveable crimes. But resentment allows the victim to return to society as a powerful actor, a survivor, a witness. Resentment allows for trust in the emotions. It allows for the restoration of a culture's ability to accept guilt, to repent, to grant victims equality and respect, to change for the better.

W.G. Sebald's story "Max Ferber" connects the emotions of forgiveness and resentment to love. It shows the role forgiveness and resentment play in opening up new spaces for thinking and feeling. Sebald, like Améry, encourages German culture to accept the Holocaust as its negative possession. With Améry in mind, Sebald affirms that "the issue, then, is not to resolve but to reveal the conflict" (Sebald 2003, 157–58). The objective, notably, is not to reach closure, but to continue the conversation, which will start anew from a different vantage point, and will instill hope that language can change, and in doing so cause the culture of its speakers to change as well.

In order to achieve this rhetorical feat, "Max Ferber" initiates an intertextual exchange with Bruno Schulz. Sebald accesses Schulz's world of alien hallucinations and poetics, only to find that he is lost in the labyrinth of Schulz's mythology: his Jewish community, the subversive literature and art produced by him. The intertextual exchange between the narrator/Sebald, the protagonist Ferber,

---

[1] Some scholars contend that forgiveness is a prosocial propensity or that it is mistakenly understood as a speech-act. Govier (2002), like Kristeva, insists that forgiveness is not a speech act but occurs within the bounds of a continuous dialogue with the guilty party. See also McCullough 2001.

and the murdered Schulz give literary shape to the relevance of negative possessions to the emotions of love, forgiveness, resentment repentance, and suffering.

"Max Ferber" amplifies the moral paradox of forgiveness and resentment. The story vividly describes the fatigue of Ferber, the forgiving victim who lives in isolation. At the same time, Ferber is presented as a powerful protagonist who enjoys a fulfilling personal and cultural life. He is a well-known painter living in Manchester, who exhibits his work at first-rate venues such as the Tate Gallery in London. Yet Ferber remains loyal to the dead, both in his daily, isolated life, and in his work. Sebald, on his part, takes advantage of Ferber's loyalty to a world of memories and ghostly presences.

The text takes Ferber to task for his tendency to break in the face of the cruelty of reality, to *give way*, and live in a hallucinated *real* furnished by deceased masters. Ferber and his deceased relatives are fictional, but the story is populated by many historical personages, including Schulz, Vladimir Nabokov, Ludwig Wittgenstein, and Queen Victoria. Ferber is not real, Wittgenstein is real, and yet they were both émigrés who left Germany to live in England, as was Sebald, whose life-story permeates the text. I read Sebald's method of conflating the fictional and the real as a way of signaling that, in the aftermath of mass atrocity, in relation to emotions, many of the facts to which people remain attached are not needed to explain the world, but to allow them to avoid the state of *being overcome* by suffering and loss. Sebald's ability to create a world which is grounded in discontinuity, caesura, and prosopopoeia leads the reader to the realm of trauma, where the emotions are tied to the search for truth and justice for the victims.

Ferber came to Manchester from Germany when he was fifteen. By the age of eighteen he "lodged at 104 Palatine Road – the selfsame house where Ludwig Wittgenstein, then a twenty-year-old engineering student, had lived in 1908" (Sebald 1996, 166). Ferber is twenty years the narrator's senior. They meet in 1966, when the Sebald comes from Zurich to live in Manchester, as "a student who planned [. . .] to pursue research, bringing with him a variety of letters and papers of identification and recommendation" (Sebald 1996, 150). The German Sebald and the German-Jewish Ferber remain close friends for the next quarter of a century, despite the fact that there is a lapse of almost twenty years between their first and second meetings. For the narrator, Manchester is "a necropolis or mausoleum" (Sebald 1996, 151). Ferber stays in Manchester because he feels at home in the city's center, "where all seemed one solid mass of utter blackness [. . .]. I [Ferber] believed I had found my destiny" (Sebald 168–69).

It turns out the destinies of the narrator/Sebald and the protagonist/Ferber were joined together before they came to know each other. Sebald was a student in Basel, while the only trip Ferber ever took abroad was to Geneva Lake. This information is important because Ferber went to see the Isenheim paintings of Grünewald in Lake Geneva. Not only are the real Sebald and the fictional Ferber geographically circling each other, but they circle around the emotions of love, forgiveness, resentment, and suffering as they learn to articulate traumatic memories using friendship, literature, and art:

> I [Ferber] gradually understood that, beyond a certain point, pain blots out one thing that is essential to its being experienced – consciousness – and so perhaps extinguishes itself; we know very little about this. What is certain, though, is that mental suffering is effectively without end. One may think one has reached the very limit, but there are always more torments to come (Sebald 1996, 170).

The suffering that Ferber experiences is related to Sebald's suffering, because both are wrestling with forgiveness, resentment, repentance, with negative possessions, in the aftermath of the Holocaust.

Ferber contemplates suffering at Lake Geneva because of a memory. He remembers his father, who was an art dealer as Hitler was rising to power, and who used to organize special exhibitions in Montreux during the summer months. He once took his twelve-year-old son with him. By then, Ferber was already a committed painter. Hitler's rise to power truncated the Ferbers' lives. The boy was smuggled out of Germany to England. His parents were murdered. Sebald was likewise strongly affected by Hitler's rule, which led him to decide to write his doctoral thesis in Switzerland, and to eventually leave the German speaking countries altogether to work in England.

Sebald the author fashions a textual grid in which the similarities between the narrator/Sebald and Ferber are greater than the differences. Sebald stages his responsibility to Ferber's story to the point that it allows the narrator/Sebald to be overcome, to seek forgiveness, to feel both repentance and resentment, the only emotions that can redeem them both from abandonment. The real Sebald was born in Bavaria, just like the fictional Ferber. Sebald lived and worked as an academic at the University of Manchester in the 1960s, when the fictional Ferber had his studio in that city. Later, Sebald remained in exile in England as an academic and translator at the University of East Anglia, until his death in 2001. Meanwhile Ferber, his protagonist, lives and dies in exile. When the narrator reads in the newspaper that Ferber's new exhibition is opening at the Tate in 1989, he learns that Ferber came to England as a fifteen-year-old, and that his parents were exterminated in Riga. This prompts Sebald's remorse. He acknowledges that "it seemed unforgivable" that he did not ask Ferber about his biography during those years in Manchester (Sebald 1996, 178).

As part of his repentance, the narrator returns to Manchester when he is about fifty years old, and finds the seventy-year-old Ferber still painting. The friends catch up on each other's biography, including their "exile in England, the immigrant city of Manchester and its irreversible decline" (Sebald 1996, 181). Sebald's repentance, that is, his acceptance of the diaries that Ferber's mother left her son but which Ferber cannot bear to read, prompts the protagonist/Ferber's first steps towards forgiving atrocity.

Ferber leaves the documents in the narrator's care in the hope that he may be saved from abandonment, by a change of hands of the avatars of suffering. It is in them, through them, that Sebald engages in prosopopoeia: the words of the dead in the diary inform the acts of the living. Prosopopoeia gives a face to the dead, a material moral existence.

The return of the dead is crucial to both Sebald and Ferber, even though the former was not a perpetrator (he was born at the end of the War) and the latter was not a victim (having been smuggled out of Germany before the horrors of Nazism began to materialize). Ferber cherishes the sporadic memories he retains from his childhood, but he forgets two main things: his parents' faces and his native tongue, "which I [Ferber] have not once spoken since I parted from my parents at Oberweisenfeld airport in Munich in 1939, and which survives in me as no more than an echo, a muted and incomprehensible murmur" (Sebald 1996, 182). This is typical of one who has suffered traumatic loss, an excessive pain that muffles the ability to either feel or explain sorrow. This emotional experience, immersion in negative possessions, becomes a moral obligation, to give a face to lost loved ones, and to force the German language to learn to articulate guilt and repentance. German as well articulates exclusion and enactments of murder.

Sebald's German remained very much alive in his work, numerous fictional biographies, poetry, and volumes of nonfiction. He insisted on personally vetting and supervising his English translators. The sufferings of the German and the German Jew are asymmetrical, yet can become a negative possession if the narrator and Ferber, existing at the opposite poles of the moral divide, engage in dialogue, and from it produce new kinds of literature and art. When they acknowledge the humanity of the Other, the arts can reveal the truth of suffering, and bring forth repentance, resentment, and forgiveness in its place. Sebald's novel use of prosopopoeia reveals the fragile balance between silence, erasure, and the birth of narrative voice, as it creates innovative language structures with which to represent the suffering that exists in the aftermath of genocide.

Derrida's daydream, which I discussed in the introduction, suggests that the forgiving victim is both forceful and powerless when she/he forgives. If the force and powerlessness dyad constitute a viable philosophical option, as I believe it does, then it might compel a recognition of the ethical limitations of politics. In the democratic state politics are preoccupied with treaties, with reconciliation and restitution, with national healing. Yet all of these entail sovereignty as the protection of interests. Derrida argues that pure forgiveness cannot cater to individual or collective interests in this way. Yet Derrida suggests that the singular victim exceeds the goodwill of the state in her/his forgiveness. Whatever agreements are reached, the forgiveness and resentment of the singular victim are antithetical to political reasoning and profit.

Forgiveness and resentment challenge every political arrangement, by forcing societies to acknowledge suffering and engage in an honest discussion about evil. Works of literature, such as "Max Ferber," which bring them to the fore, leave an indelible mark on history, as documents that disseminate the intelligibility and acuteness of suffering. This literary/artistic discourse/image of powerlessness institutes a sense of forceful action. The forgiving and the resentful victims are always singular. In "Max Ferber," forgiveness and resentment are inherently personal, moral and powerless. They constitute acts undertaken without promise of reward.[2]

When forgiveness is not in the service of diplomatic or political goals, it issues from powerless force. Force without power entails that the victim is not merely trying to gain advantage over the perpetrator, but is engaging in dialogue with the evildoer. The victim has a moral obligation to rebuild the world after the catastrophe. Yet the victim does not view her/his act as morally superior to the perpetrator. S/he does not think that the act of forgiveness should depend on practical considerations. Rather, the victim wants to restore trust and be delivered from her/his abandonment.

This remains true when resentment enters the picture. Resentment purports that the perpetrator accept guilt, feel remorse, and show dignity to the victim, in an imagined new world that they may create and share as equals. Améry shows how the perpetrator's repentance takes the form of a negative possession. Germany should not absolve itself through compensation for the victims. It should shoulder its guilt through disclosing the truth. By producing texts that archive and narrate its guilt and repentance, Germany can transform its language from one of racism, anti-Semitism, and propaganda to one of repentance and responsibility.

---

[2] In her study of Derrida's *On Forgiveness*, Kim Worthington (2002) suggests that pure forgiveness is what makes the politics of reconciliation moral. I disagree that forgiveness is pure. Sincere forgiveness shelters a kernel of resentment. "Max Ferber" creates a world in which politics is foreign to the force of both victim and perpetrator. This literary world achieves greater moral and psychological clarity than the real one, while leaving the victim and the perpetrator in their passivity and powerlessness. "Max Ferber" also brings a sense of psychological and social healing.

Améry's rehabilitation of resentment is directed at Nietzsche's aversion to both resentment and forgiveness. Améry cites Nietzsche in order to launch a discussion of resentment's virtues:

> There seems to be a general agreement that the final say on resentment is that of Friedrich Nietzsche, in whose *Genealogy of Morals* we read: ". . . resentment defines such creatures who are denied genuine reaction, that of the deed, and who compensate for it through an imaginary revenge . . . The resentful person is neither sincere nor naïve, nor honest and forthright with himself. His soul squints; his mind loves hiding places and back doors; everything concealed gives him the feeling that it is his world, his security, his balm . . ." Thus spake the man who dreamed of the synthesis of the brute with the superman. He must be answered by those who witnessed the union of the brute with the subhuman; they were present as victims when a certain humankind joyously celebrated a festival of cruelty, as Nietzsche himself has expressed it—in anticipation of a few modern anthropological theories (Améry 1980, 68).

Some scholars argue that Nietzsche views resentment only as a debilitating emotion. Psychologists follow this interpretation when they denounce the man of resentment. Nietzsche, according to Améry, suggests that the man of resentment is pathologically passive, hiding from the truth of real power. Rather than better his situation by acting on reality, the man of resentment imagines a successful future revenge that will destroy the power he imagines to be the author of his suffering. Améry suggests that Nietzsche understood resentment to be a bargaining chip between power inequities. The man of resentment was imprisoned by slave mentality. He was not sovereign, and therefore did not try to regain power. As I suggested earlier, resentment can work together with – and might be necessary to – the master's mentality as well as the slave's. Améry substitutes political interests with guilt and truth:

> I do not want to become the accomplice of my torturers; rather, I demand that the latter negate themselves and in the negation coordinate with me. The pile of corpses that lie between them and me cannot be removed in the process of internalization, so it seems to me, but, on the contrary, through actualization, or more strongly stated, by actively settling the unresolved conflict in the field of historical practice (Améry 1980, 69).

The disclosure of truth is an action that demands the perpetrator negate himself. This negation constitutes action for both the victim and the perpetrator, wherein they both accept responsibility for negative possession. Negative possessions are the cultural containers that transmit German responsibility for National Socialism. German intellectuals institute negative possession when they try to articulate the ineffable moral abyss that Germany must consciously acknowledge in order to be a moral, and therefore a nation of justice and equality.

In "Resentments," Améry insists that when Holocaust survivors refuse to forgive their murderers and choose instead to retain their resentment, they investigate the nature of suffering: "I lack the desire, the talent, and the conviction for something like that [to internalize our bare suffering and bear it in emotional asceticism]" (Améry 1980, 69). Améry condemns "the Jews who in this hour were already trembling with forgiveness and reconciliation" (Améry 1980, 65). He thus implies that diplomatic relations between Germany and Israel, and particularly the Reparations Agreement signed on September 10, 1952 between the German Chancellor Konrad Adenauer and the Israeli Prime Minister David Ben-Gurion,[3] emerge from a willingness to forgive Germany and make resentment unnecessary or regressive:

> The German people bear no grudge against the Jewish people, he [a German businessman] said. As proof he cited his government's magnanimous policy of reparations, which was, incidentally, well appreciated by the young state of Israel. In the presence of this man, whose mind was so at ease, I felt miserable: Shylock demanding his pound of flesh. [. . .] The Germans no longer had any hard feelings toward the resistance fighters and Jews. How could these still demand atonement? (Améry 1980, 67).

For Améry, resentment is manifested in the demand for legal indictments against the German perpetrators. At the same time, resentment awakens an expectation for moral understanding and the articulation of suffering.

Like forgiveness, resentment opens up a space for repentance. A critical aspect of resentment is its position to the political realm. Like forgiveness, resentment is also outside of, and anathema to, politics. "What matters to me," says Améry, "is the description of the subjective state of the victim" (Améry 1980, 64). But resentment need not preclude the possibility of acknowledging forgiveness as that which lies outside and is Other to politics.[4] Améry calls for dialogue, demanding openness in order to expose historical truth. The German perpetrator must become acquainted with the stories and the history of European Jewry in order to accept his or her own guilt. In the aftermath of the Holocaust, Améry seeks to institute conditions that would enable the people of Germany to acknowledge their role in enabling Hitler and the Nazi party, while laying claim to this guilt as

---

[3] For more details about the personal relations between the leaders Adenauer and Ben-Gurion, see Witzthum (2019).

[4] Studies of testimonies from the Truth and Reconciliation Committee in South Africa make it clear that witnesses who do not want to forgive the perpetrators appeal to their right to resentment. The same reaction is found in testimonies from the *gacaca* court in Rwanda. Brudholm and Rosoux examine the works of Esther Mujawayo, a survivor of genocide in Rwanda. At the same time, testimonies in the film *Long Night's Journey Into Day* show that, even within the same family, certain members forgive the perpetrator after he confesses his crimes, while others refuse to forgive him, while others first refuse forgiveness but grant it after confession. See Brudholm and Rosoux 2009, 41–48, and Deborah Hoffmann and Frances Reid 2000.

the "negation of the world and itself, as its own negative possession" (Améry 1980, 78). He insists that the country accept and fully acknowledge the indictments against Germany and the German people, and that it engage in dialogue about these texts, which constitute the country's negative cultural possessions. In his 1958 Brehmen Speech, the German-Jewish poet Paul Celan takes a similar stance when he says:

> Only one thing remained reachable, close and secure amid all losses: language. Yes, language. In spite of everything, it remained secure against loss. But it had to go through its own lack of answers, through terrifying silence, through the thousand darknesses of murderous speech. It went through. It gave me no words for what was happening, but went through it. Went through and could resurface, 'enriched' by it all (Celan 1986, 34).

The German language, in other words, can be enriched if it engages in an intra- and inter-subjective dialogue about the Holocaust.

"Max Ferber" seeks to portray the tension that living victims experience, those who wrestle with memories in which contradictory feelings of forgiveness and resentment are played out. I will show that, although Sebald's narrator can speak only in the name of repentance, he seeks to learn the language of forgiveness and resentment from his protagonists, both the dead and the surviving victims of the Holocaust. This search for traces of memory leads Sebald to probe images and specters, mystery and folklore, religion and history. In his narrative, sovereignty is without power. Language and images emerge from dead and fatigued victims who overcome suffering by introducing the value of ephemeral hope. Sebald must construct more riddles before he can offer his readers a "'final' . . . thing of shreds and patches, utterly botched," a narrative that protects the emotions from reaching closure, and renders forgiveness, resentment, and thinking morally equivalent to each other, as they all contribute to opening a conversation about the Holocaust (Sebald 1996, 231).[5]

The value of forgiveness and resentment lies precisely in the urge towards critical thinking, listening, and dialogue. In its dismissal of the relation of forgiveness to the politics of reconciliation, resentment bears a striking resemblance to divine forgiveness, and, more specifically, to "the divine manifestation of sovereign power," which "dissolves law for the sake of life itself" (Friedlander 2012,

---

5 Giorgio Agamben insists that forgiveness and resentment are relevant to each other, because resentment makes historically contingent the crime that forgiveness forgives. Agamben states that resentment prevents us from forgetting the unforgettable crimes that institutions want us to forget (Agamben 2005, 39, 138, 142). Magdalena Zolkos (2007) proposes that after resentment is consumed, the victim can fathom forgiveness.

132). Resentment and forgiveness emerge from force without power. They absolve the perpetrator not of guilt, but of law.[6]

For Arendt and Derrida, forgiveness arrives like a revolution – radically altering the known, automatic course of events (Arendt 1858, 237). As Derrida explains, the law can be changed only when it is faced with the "'hyperbolic' ethical vision of forgiveness" (Derrida 2001, 51). This revolution doesn't have to happen in words. Gestures can also usher in revolutionary ideas and behavior toward the Other. Arendt finds revolutionary examples of the good as Otherness in the gestures of Dostoyevsky's Christ and in those gestures that belong to Melville's Billy Budd (Arendt 1965, 86).[7] When it comes to goodness as Otherness, the Other can be the Jew, the historical Christ, or a victim who suffers for the sake of a greater good.

Walter Benjamin precedes Derrida by connecting forgiveness to postponement. According to Benjamin, forgiveness receives its meaning from its opposite, which is retribution. The final act of retribution arrives at the Last Judgment, which is endlessly postponed. Thus, writes Benjamin, "this significance is revealed not in the world of law, where retribution rules, but only in the moral universe, where forgiveness comes out to meet it. In order to struggle against retribution, forgiveness finds its powerful ally in time" (Benjamin 1996, 286). Meanwhile, Derrida claims that "a finalized forgiveness is not forgiveness; it is only a political strategy or a psycho-therapeutic economy" (Derrida 2001, 50). Derrida is aware that politics is run by institutions that are not interested in the suffering of the singular victim, but in national healing and the proper management of institutional failures. Benjamin underscores that legal institutions establish a coherent line of action, not a moral reply to subjective suffering. Yet both Derrida and Benjamin show that forgiveness, that is, the victim's treatment of evil, revolutionizes the very *raison d'être* of retributive justice, and that this revolution is never ending because the need to revolutionize politics is constant.

In "Max Ferber," the narrator/Sebald is repentant, but he behaves as if asking for forgiveness might be wrong, since it involves a pragmatic request. The narrator's remorse becomes clear as he reflects on the past: "as I now thought back, it seemed unforgivable that I should have omitted, or failed, in those Manchester times, to ask Ferber the questions he must surely have expected from me" (Sebald 1996, 178). [Unverzeihbar erschien es mir nun im Nachdenken, daß ich es damals in Manchester entweder verabsäumt oder nicht fertiggebracht hatte, Ferber jene Fragen zu stellen, die er erwartet haben mußte von mir . . .] (Sebald 2013 [1992],

---

[6] Avishai Margalit (2002) argues that divine forgiveness blots out guilt while human forgiveness only leaves traces of guilt that remain etched in human memory.
[7] *The Master and Margarita* is a contemporary example of this forgiveness: a force without power that Christ extends in his gestures. See Bulgakov 1995, 193–94.

262, ellipses added). These questions concern Ferber's experience as a German Jew, who fled from Germany as a child and grew up in England as an orphan. Sebald is remorseful because he is German, his memories conjured by reflection.

Ruth Kluger notes that the German who has a stake in his nation's past must "take the good with the bad and own up to the crimes that were committed by your parents and grandparents" (Kluger 2002, 311). How does Sebald repent? The fictional Ferber haunts Sebald for many years. More importantly, Ferber's lost German ancestors haunt Sebald. The more the narrator seeks to metaphorically recover the dead and salvage their heritage, the more powerless he becomes.

Sebald populates his story with the ghosts of deceased Jews who are "legendary" – only their names are known (Sebald 1996, 157). On his canvases, Ferber depicts the missing bodies of the extinct German-Jewish world:

> The following morning, the moment the model had sat down and he [Ferber] had taken a look at him or her, he would erase the portrait yet again, and once more set about excavating the features of his model, who by now was distinctly wearied by this manner of working, from a surface already badly damaged by the continual destruction. The facial features and eyes, said Ferber, remained ultimately unknowable for him (Sebald 1996, 162).

Ferber's art consists of applying paint to canvas and then scratching it off. His work depicts loss through the absence of color and image. The images that he erases are portraits. In this way Ferber resembles the narrator (and author): both employ negation. Sebald follows in the footsteps of Ferber when he uses prosopopoeia. He creates a fictional world and populates it with ghostly presences. He creates, in short, negative possessions. Yet who initiates the pursuit of ghosts? Is it Sebald who follows in the footsteps of Ferber, or is it Ferber who accepts the law of the narrative, following Sebald's dictates? Sebald wrote hundreds of pages in order to give an account of Ferber's life, but fell short, because "by far the greatest part [of the writing] had been crossed out, discarded, or obliterated by additions" (Sebald 1996, 230). Sebald acknowledges that, in fiction, negative possessions share a great deal with the ineffable.

I mentioned that the narrator initially meets Ferber in 1966, but their decisive meeting occurs over twenty years later, in 1989. Ferber's story is prophetic in relation to Sebald's narrative because the objective paintings that Ferber constructs affect Sebald as a subject. They open in him "a sort of gaol or oubliette" (Sebald 1996, 178). Sebald's unconscious is influenced by the paintings, and his older self responds in the way of desire. His desire is woken by Ferber's mother's diaries and old family pictures. These portraits depict Ferber's deceased family members, whose portraits he can no longer paint, the faces he no longer remembers.

"Max Ferber" is highlighted with numerous black-and-white images, which are supposed to make the places and the people look real. Instead, the images make the world to which the people belonged seem ghostly.[8] Derrida argues that the language of forgiveness is fundamentally the domain of the dead, because only the dead can legitimately forgive. Forgiveness, like memory, is continuously accosted by the dead. The dead are debtors, at the same time as they are a source of inspiration. They compel the survivors to continue living, continue forgiving, continue resenting, and continue practicing force despite having no political power.

Derrida states that "pure and unconditional forgiveness, in order to have its own meaning, must have no 'meaning,' no finality, even no intelligibility. It is a madness of the impossible" (Derrida 2001, 44–45). This leads Thomas Brudholm and Valéry Rosoux to conclude that pure forgiveness is impossible (Brudholm and Rosoux 2009, 49). However, they fail to address the plausibility of pure philosophy, pure thinking, and pure resentment.[9] In my view, Sebald's turning to the dead stems from powerlessness or extreme fatigue. The gesture is enmeshed with the ghosts of those who died in the Holocaust, as well as with the mythological ghosts that guide and guard art, such as Orpheus, Persephone, and the Wandering Jew.

It is in reading the diaries of Luisa Lanzberg, Ferber's mother, that Sebald comes across the concept of forgiveness and of the sacrificial victim. These are diaries that Ferber kept for many years but read only twice. Lanzberg writes:

> Autumn arrives, and the autumn holidays are approaching. First comes Rosh Hashanah, bringing in the New Year. [. . .] A week and a half later is Yom Kippur. Father, in his death robes, moves about the house like a ghost. A mood of rue and penitence prevails. None of us will eat until the stars rise. Then we wish each other *ein gutes Anbeißen*. And four days later it is already the Feast of Tabernacles. [. . .] On the two main and four half feast days we shall take our meals in the sukkah (Sebald 1996, 201).

This description is written in the present tense, as if to suggest that Jewish life and practice continued to flourish in Steinach. The passage incorporates proper Hebrew names of the holidays of Rosh Hashanah, Yom Kippur, and Sukkot, sug-

---

[8] The picture at the end of the story is particularly haunting. Sebald documents the material history of this picture's discovery in a pawned piece of luggage in Vienna. The image is of three women working in the Litzmannstadt ghetto in Lodz, which in the 1940s is known as "*Polski Manchester.*" Genewein is the German photographer who took snapshots of industry and commerce in the ghetto. Sebald does not include these visual records in the story. Instead, he describes a picture the reader cannot see, in which women laborers look directly into the eyes of the viewer. Carol Jacobs finds another one of Genewein's pictures in a museum and reproduces it. See Sebald 1996, 235–36 and Jacobs 2004, 223.

[9] It is important to recall that continental philosophy and psychoanalysis greatly trust *le regard de l'outre-tombe* – the *look from beyond the grave* – when it is related to literature, to mystery and irresponsibility, to melancholia, to eagerness and extreme horror, and to film that can change the future through an impossible glimpse of the remembered past. See Blanchot 1955, 226; Lévinas 1979, 55–64; Freud 1957, 266; Bataille 1998, 71 and Deleuze 1986, 116–125.

gesting that these holidays are mainstays of local life. One wonders, can it be that there was a time when Jewish culture and identity were so much part and parcel of German life?

In a particularly moving passage from Lanzberg's diaries, she recalls how "we [the school-children] also have a guessing game. For instance, we have to guess the three things that give and take in infinite plenty. Of course no one knows the answer, which Herr Beim then tells us in tones of great significance: the earth, the sea, and the Reich. Perhaps the best thing about that day is that, before we go home, we are allowed to jump over the Hanukkah candles, which have been fixed to the threshold with drops of wax" (Sebald 1996, 204). The bounty of the Reich and the light of the Hanukkah candles are joined seamlessly in these notes written between 1939 and 1941. Pure, mad forgiveness inheres in these lines. Lanzberg lovingly recalls the Reich of her childhood memories, despite the fact that, by the time of her writing, the Reich has become the Third Reich. Without political power to change her situation, she asks for forgiveness as she refers to the Jewish Day of Atonement. She forgives her persecutors, in order to restore innocence to the world and thereby protect her son from radical evil. She wants to give her son, Max, childhood memories that might pacify him, when he reads them in England as a free man.

Metaphorically, the narrator stages a funeral for the Jewish ghosts that haunt the depths of German history.[10] He visits Steinach, where he contemplates the graves in the Jewish cemetery. This gives him an opportunity to recite the names of absent Jews, names like the ones that in Manchester had "a legendary ring" (Sebald 1996, 157). In the Jewish cemetery, these names become indigenous to the German land and language: "but the names I could still read – Hamburger, Kissinger, Werthaimer, Friedländer, Arnsberg, Auerbach, Grunwald, Leuthhold, Seeligmann, Frank, Hertz, Goldstaub, Baumblatt and Blumenthal – made me think that perhaps there was nothing that the Germans begrudged the Jews so much as their beautiful names, so intimately bound up with the country they lived in and with its language" (Sebald 1996, 224). The sounds of the Jewish names echo meaningfully in the text. Sebald understands how the Jewish German is a threat to the

---

**10** In the 1960s, Gershom Scholem wrote that a dialogue never existed between Jews and Germans. Scholem dismisses the value of both forgiveness and resentment, trusting only in reasonable, good will: "Bridges are needed to pass over abysses; they are constructed; they are the product of conscious thinking and willing. Moral bridges, I repeat, are the product of goodwill. If they are to endure, they must be firmly anchored in both sides" (Scholem 1976, 63). I return to this assertion in the third chapter, to show that Scholem continues to speak about love between Germans and Jews, a concept that belongs to the realm of forgiveness and resentment more so than to social and cultural reasoning.

German culture of the 1960s. Mourning recalls the vacillation of consciousness between resentment and unconditional repentance. Yet Sebald enacts resentment alongside his repentance, salvaging these Jewish names from being lost in oblivion. He is claiming negative possessions.

Sebald's references to deceased authors, philosophers, and legendary figures such as the Wandering Jew create a constellation of references. It includes Jews in literary modernism, Jews at work, and Jews from Drohobycz. The signifiers in this constellation form a system of metonymies so potent that Sebald is drawn into this world of Jewish work and creativity until he blends with the artist Bruno Schulz, whose work saturates "Max Ferber." Schulz's poetics have the quality of a dream, and the structure of the labyrinth. Forgiveness and resentment are caught up in the labyrinth because what must be forgiven is Schulz's murder, but since this is impossible, then reinstalling Schulz's work is an action that belongs to the ineffable, and yet it expresses guilt and repentance, turning Schulz's murder into a negative possession.

Schultz's "Cinnamon Shops" leads the reader to believe that whatever happens to the protagonist does not simply belong to reality. On the contrary, the *imaginary* and the *real* (to use Lacan's language) are responsible for the progression of narrative and the surfacing of the first person narrator's consciousness: "when the city reached out deeper and deeper into the *labyrinth* of winter nights, and was shaken reluctantly into consciousness by the short dawn, my father was already lost, sold and surrendered to the other sphere" (Schulz 1963, 14, italics added). Because the father is lost in his own theater, "murmuring and whispering indistinctly in tune with the interior monologue that wholly preoccupied him," the boy surrenders to the pleasure involved in perceiving reality trough fantasy and the imagination (Schulz 1963, 54).

Like Sebald's, Schulz's writings are semiautobiographical. In "Cinnamon Shops," the boy – Schulz as a youth – leaves the theater and walks into the night to fetch his father's wallet. Rather than go straight home and back, however, the boy gets lost in his own dreams: "On that night the sky laid bare its internal construction in many sections, which, like quasi-anatomical exhibits, showed the spirals and whorls of light, the pale green solids of darkness, the plasma of space, the tissue of *dreams*" (Schulz 1963, 55 italics added). Sebald borrows this structure from Schulz. Dreams impose singularity on reality and make reality correspond to subjectivity. When it emerges from the labyrinth of subjective meanings, reality acquires seductive qualities that reshape it, making it equally foreign and intimate.

Schultz makes an appearance in Ferber's dream about an art gallery in Queen Victoria's Crystal Palace. The Crystal Palace, perhaps the epitome of the illusory grandeur of empire, an enormous structure made of glass, cast iron, wood, and concrete, was erected in Hyde Park in 1851. From May to October of that year, it hosted the Great Exhibition, the first World's Fair. Prince Albert, husband to Queen Victoria, was the leading proponent of this mega event. The Great Exhibition, which attracted over five million visitors, was meant to "promote British manufactures to an international audience, and to improve the 'taste' of domestic consumers" (Gardner 2018, 187). The Palace's measurements were awe inspiring: 564 meters in length, 92,000 square meters of floor space. Albert intended the Crystal Palace to be the inaugural monument of modernism. In 1852 it was moved to Sydenham Hill, in south London, and there hosted the "Festival of Empire" in 1911. The Second Crystal Palace was destroyed in a fire in 1936. In 2013, London Mayor Boris Johnson proposed that it be rebuilt, for which he was roundly rebuffed. "The Crystal Palace," said one critic, "functions perfectly well in its absence (perhaps even more so than if it were here)" (cited in Gardner 2018, 196).

The illusion that the Crystal Palace calls forth is expressed in the admiration of exotic objects, of distant continents, of foreign customs, while glossing over the death and atrocity caused by imperialism. But the might of Empire and its fall leave traces in memory and unconscious dreaming. It is in this context that Ferber's dream must be understood. Rather than be seduced by the magnificent objects on display, Ferber involuntarily arrives to a secret room filled with paintings that prompt him to go back in time and commune with the dead.

Ferber relates his dream to the narrator:

> Somewhat to the side, a stranger was sitting on the ottoman. In his lap he was holding a model of the temple of Solomon, made of pinewood, papier-mâché and gold paint. Frohmann, from Drohobycz, he said, bowing slightly, going on to explain that it had taken him seven years to build the temple, from the biblical description, and that he was now traveling from ghetto to ghetto exhibiting the model.[11] Just look said Frohmann: you can see every crenellation on the towers, every curtain, every threshold, every sacred vessel. And I, said Ferber, bent down over the diminutive temple and realized, for the first time in my life, what a true work of art looks like[12] (Sebald 1996, 176).

Frohmann is an allusion to the protagonist of Joseph Roth's reportage "Solomon's Temple in Berlin."[13] In Roth's report, the miniature Temple is part of an allegory

---

[11] The German *Frohmann* relates happiness and divine grace to wandering. This coincidence with the name of the character Frohmann is not incidental. The trope of the wandering Jew lends a moral tint to happiness, as if these two traits must appear together in the ethical world, where forgiveness arrives like a revolution for the sake of life itself. Gorgio Agamben would call this an outlook on life from a "Messianic vocation" or a "Messianic modality" (Agamben 2005, 23–39).

[12] The most fitting description of this dream and the desire it arouses appears in Freud's famous footnote no. 2: "There is at least one spot in every dream at which it is unplumbable – a naval, as it were, that is its point of contact with the unknown" (Freud 1995, 135).

[13] I thank Carol Jacobs for drawing my attention to this text. See Roth, 2003.

about contemporary Jews in Berlin. Yet, in "Max Ferber," Frohmann/Schwarzbach commemorates the destruction of the Jewish Temple by creating a miniature replica. Frohmann/Schwarzbach signifies pure forgiveness, repentance, and resentment, rebuilding that which is destroyed while his labor comes to the world as a gift – the gift of commemorating a people for the sake of life itself. These acts of commemoration and forgiveness are, as Derrida describes, mad. They do not belong to either an economy or a therapeutic ecology.

The world that Frohmann/Schwarzbach belongs to is neither interested in purity nor in forgiveness. In it "the people are godless and republican [. . .] [They] chew over the day's news and the exchange rates" (Roth 2003, 43–44). These Jews are assimilated, and they delude themselves: "what an untenable idea anti-Semitism is" (Roth 2003, 41). This moment of "traveling from ghetto to ghetto exhibiting the model" serves as a metaphor for the value of pure forgiveness (Sebald 1996, 176). Forgiveness never reaches closure, yet it allows us to imagine the existence of a world that is subject to something other than reward, and vengeance. Building the replica of the Temple is an act of forgiving a history of destruction and loss for the sake of restoration.

It is hard to speak about Drohobycz without calling forth Schulz's ghost. Schulz was born in Drohobycz, and murdered in the ghetto by the Gestapo officer Karl Günther. Sebald's resentment toward his native German culture is expressed in the imaginary avenging of this murder, which enhances the narrator's repentance when he structures Ferber's vision around Schulz's poetics.

As I discussed earlier, the narrator of "Cinnamon Shops" goes to the theater with his parents. When they are seated in the hall the father realizes that he forgot his wallet at home. The young boy is asked to run and fetch it before the beginning of the play. The youth takes a shortcut, the beautiful night activates his imagination, and he loses his way. The streets that open up in front of his eyes are "reflected streets, streets which are doubles, make believe streets" (Schulz 1963, 55). These streets are, in fact, the linings of the real streets on Market Square. They are refracted through the boy's emotions, memories, and aspirations. The youth calls the shops on these streets "cinnamon shops because of the dark paneling of their walls" (Schulz 1963, 56). Sebald borrows from Schulz the dream-like quality and transplants it to Ferber's dream, a dream that has Ferber lost in the halls of the Crystal Palace.

The room that Ferber wanders into is the lining of other rooms. It is a make-believe room that can be reached only if one walks through a *tromp-l'oeil* door. Although the other rooms are bright, this room is dark. Sebald offers a picture of the room that Ferber dream-walks into. In this picture, the walls have dark paneling, just like those of the cinnamon shops (Sebald 1996, 175, [see Figure 1]).

Schulz's cinnamon shops smell of exotic foreignness and showcase exotic items from distant countries:

> Dimly lit, their dark and solemn interiors were redolent of the smell of paint, varnish, and incense; of the aroma of distant countries and rare commodities. You could find in them Bengal lights, magic boxes, the stamps of long-forgotten countries, Chinese decals, indigo, calaphony from Malabar, the eggs of exotic insects, parrots, toucans, live salamanders and basilisks, mandrake roots, mechanical toys from Nuremberg, homunculi in jars, microscopes, binoculars, and, most specifically, strange and rare books, old folio volumes full of astonishing engravings and amazing stories (Schulz 1963, 56).

Similar objects are found in the rooms of the historical Crystal Palace. More importantly, when Ferber enters the room, he recognizes it as "my parents' drawing room" (Sebald 1996, 176). In Schulz's "Cinnamon Shops," the lost boy reaches the back of his old high school. He spends a few moments inside the room of Professor Arendt, who had taught him painting and engraving. The room holds plastercast heads of Greek and Roman gods, "ashen profiles, and meditations dissolving into *nothingness*" (Schulz 1963, 58 italics added). Ferber, not by chance, paints ashen portraits that are intensely worked over until they are lost in nothingness. The professor is happy, enveloped in smiles, "exuding an aroma of secrecy" (Schulz 1963, 58). Herr Frohmann hovers between the present and the past. The Temple and the teacher's room exist outside of the dimension of time: "[time] ran by unevenly, as if making knots in the passage of hours, swallowing somewhere whole empty periods. [. . .] The night was copying now, at that late hour, the nightly landscape of Professor Arendt's engravings, reenacting his fantasies" (Schulz 1963, 58).

Being out of time is important in political life, as when the Crystal Palace fixes a fantasy in the minds of British citizens in order to justify imperialism. Being out of time is important in Sebald's narrative of forgiveness, resentment, and repentance, for in the face of these emotions nothing is forgotten, at the same time that no hope for a better future is relinquished. On the contrary, Sebald's Schulz is a fictional, semiautobiographical protagonist, a figure out of time, who can weave together language and the ineffable. Sebald's reference to Schulz sutures prosopopoeia and image, and puts the faces back on Ferber's erased portraits. Thus, intertextuality creates tangible negative possessions, and restores innocence to the world, despite the knowledge of the radical evil that innocence must overcome.

Schulz wanders through the halls of his old school, and his descriptions mirror the descriptions of the art gallery that Ferber wanders into:

> Turning the first of these, I found myself in an even wider more sumptuous hall. In one of its walls there was a wide glass arcade leading to the interior of an apartment. I could see *long*

*enfilades of rooms*, furnished with great magnificence. The eye wandered over silk hangings, gilded mirrors, costly furniture, and crystal chandeliers (Schulz 1963, 59 italics added).

In his Crystal Palace dream, Ferber "*walked through the endless halls* containing 16,000 gold framed works of art" (Sebald 1996, 175–76, italics added). In one of the books illustrations, Sebald includes a crystal chandelier and miniatures inside a glass cabinet (Sebald 1996, [Figure 1]). He meticulously refracts the reality of nineteenth-century British colonialism and its delirium of Empire through the most humane, imaginative capacities that Schulz's modernism brings to the literature of the twentieth century. Sebald, who after all lives as an exile in England, exposes the delusion of imperialism at the same time that he transforms the German language, so that it is grounded in Schulz's dream poetics. Sebald installs negative possessions in his mother tongue: a reader who does not know that Sebald left Germany because he was at odds with his country, a reader who does not recognize Schulz in Sebald's "Max Ferber," cannot make sense of the emotions, of forgiveness, remorse, and resentment.

**Figure 1:** "Max Ferber," the room that Ferber dream-walks into.

The ties between Sebald's "Max Ferber" and Schulz's "Cinnamon Shops" become clearer in light of the materials that Frohmann uses to build his diminutive temple: Sebald mentions pinewood, papier-mâché, and gold. In Schulz's story "Treatise on Tailor's Dummies, *or* the Second Book of Genesis" Schulz's father describes the creature he is interested in creating. The father names the materials with which he prefers to work: "We shall give priority to trash. We are simply entranced and enchanted by the cheapness, shabbiness, and inferiority of material. Can you understand' asked my father, 'the deep meaning of that weakness, that passion for colored tissue, for papier-mâché, for oakum and sawdust?'" (Schulz 1963, 33). This list turns the everyday life of mortal Jews into something with metaphysical value. This is the reason that Sebald incorporates listing, and uses the term "papier-mâché," the same term used by Schulz. Frohmann uses "pinewood," while Schulz's father recommends "sawdust" (Sebald 1996, 176; Schulz 1963, 33). Frohmann wishes to create a Third Temple that would fit the measurements and needs of its own human creator.

Frohmann, who is from Schulz's hometown, is an everyday Wandering Jew. The dummy that Schultz makes satisfies the needs of a tailor at work (Schulz 1963, 33) while Sebald's replica of the Temple satisfies the needs of a Jew who travels and wanders in different Jewish ghettos in Europe. These parallels show that Sebald successfully adapts to Schulz's ability to move between deep love of his Jewish roots and his ability to be ironic toward the world of Jewish folklore. Yet they also reinstall Jewish lore and myth in the German language, which did everything it could to demolish the significance of the Jewish culture.

In his introduction to a volume of Schulz's works, David Goldfarb argues that Schulz utilizes both the mythological effects of narrative and the labyrinth that gives an impression of timelessness. He argues that Schulz's choice of elements possesses mythological force, enhancing the presence of the everyday. The fabrics, the dummy, the simple materials used for work, generate a meaningful world in which every object is part of a mythology of daily creation. Even the trash belongs in a masterpiece.[14] This is how Schulz turns reality into myth. The labyrinth makes the story of the existence of this community, these Jews, this archetypal father-creator who is metonymical to the Wandering Jew more mysterious.[15] Schulz tells the story of his inner labyrinth, implanting the labyrinthine experience into his readers. The more we read, the more we become lost in that

---

[14] George Gasyna speaks directly about trash, *tandeta*, as the material of the imagination and mythopoesis. Gasyna understands trash as political resistance, specifically in view of the looming threats of totalitarianism. He relates trash to provincial creation of new archetypes that challenge the literary institutions of modern, cultural centers. The use of trash in aesthetic production and political dissent creates a structure of "pure suggestibility." Gasyna mentions the streets and family apartment as effects of *tromp-l'oeil* and mentions that the stories use a "papier-mâché" modernity (Gasyna 2015, 765–768, 775).

[15] Denis Hollier associates the labyrinth with Georges Bataille and with postmodernism. Unlike Daedalus, who creates the labyrinth from the outside, Bataille is pervaded by the labyrinth within. See Hollier 1992.

labyrinth of modernism, which Schulz shares with Kafka and Nabokov (who are two of the ghosts present in "Max Ferber").[16]

Forgiveness becomes the powerless gesture that connects these diverse people. The need to forgive and repent makes the protagonists and their authors give fictional representation to atrocities too extreme to fit into normal language. Negative possessions transform language and make the reader discover more meanings in the ineffable, uncover silence by creating new images, and take to task old tropes. A dream, like the one in which Ferber meets Frohmann, exists as part of the dialogue between victim and perpetrator.

Schulz pronounces his artistic credo in a violent world that persecutes art and artists, turning them into ghosts. He hopes that his art will survive him, and dreams of a world that recognizes the value of dreams:

> Today those remote dreams come back, and not without reason. The possibility suggests itself that no dreams, however absurd or senseless, are wasted in the universe. Embedded in the dream is a hunger for its own reification, a demand that imposes an obligation on reality and that grows imperceptibly into a bona fide claim, an IOU clamoring for payment.... He [the artist] heard a summons, an inner voice, like Noah did when he received his orders and instructions (Schulz 1998, 271).

According to this allegory, saving the great dream of art from oblivion is as important as saving living creatures from the flood that will destroy them. The artist, like Noah, must be chosen.

Unforgivable crimes can only be forgiven within the realm of ghosts. Forgiveness does not advance redemption. It perpetuates the "hunger" of the dream from which art and the Other emerge (ibid, 271). Sebald fashions a text and an image that make forgiveness, repentance, and resentment forceful. These emotions cannot be reasonably explained. Either forgiveness and resentment are entangled in dialogue, or they arrive into the world as a forceful revolution. To engage in dialogue with the perpetrator requires language that does not depend on the perpetrator's political power. Victim and perpetrator must bridge the abyss between them.

To articulate emotions using dreams – as Derrida does, as Sebald and Schultz, and their protagonists as well, do – is to take radical evil most seriously. The suffering which is encoded in the ineffable calls for a new language, and dreams both protect and forge the new, the inarticulable. Améry is also caught up in a dream, specifically, in the daydream in which he recalls his torturer's execution:

---

[16] It takes Ferber a year to paint Nabokov, "the faceless 'Man with a Butterfly Net.'" Ferber is unhappy with the complete work because it conveys "not even the remotest impression of the strangeness of the apparition it referred to" (Sebald 1996, 174).

SS-man Wajs from Antwerp, a repeated murderer and an especially adroit torturer, paid with his life. What more can my foul thirst for revenge demand? But if I search my mind properly, it is not a matter of revenge, nor one of atonement. The experience of persecution was, at the very bottom, that of an extreme *loneliness*. At stake for me is the release from the abandonment that has persisted from that time until today. When SS-man Wajs stood before the firing squad, he experienced the moral truth of his crimes. At that moment, he was with *me* – and I was no longer alone with the shovel handle. I would like to believe that at the moment of his execution he wanted exactly as much as I to turn back time, to undo what had been done (Améry 1980, 70, italics in the original).

Resentment, like forgiveness, is forceful, yet the roots of both are sunk deep in powerlessness. Neither one has or aims to generate political power. Améry does not seek revenge. He demands that a dialogue remain alive in Germany, to open up the burning questions of guilt and repentance, of forgiveness and resentment. Part of Améry's vision is that the perpetrator recognize his absolute guilt in dialogue with the victim, not only in the face of a firing squad:

The people of whom I am speaking and whom I am addressing here show muted understanding for my retrospective grudge. But I myself do not entirely understand this grudge, not yet; and that is why I would like to become clear about it in this essay. I would be thankful to the reader if he were willing to follow me, even if in the hour before us he more than once feels the wish to put down the book (Améry 1980, 63).

Sebald realizes that, for Améry, the German years devoted to jurisdiction and political compensation left behind a need for "silence," because resentment, like forgiveness, is Other to politics (Sebald 2003, 147). Sebald grounds Améry's resentment in "achieving some ultimate understanding of what it means to be marked out as a victim, excluded, persecuted, and murdered" (Sebald 2003, 148). Negative possessions are traumatic scenes that furnish clear memories, like the ones in Améry's daydream. Sebald feels that all of Améry's work "[is] reconstructing his memory to point where it became accessible to him and to us" (Sebald 2003, 151). He realizes that Améry addresses the intellectuals because they speak truth to power. But Améry also knows that "in the same intellectual process [intellectuals] capitulate to [power]" (cited in Sebald 2003, 155). Yet Sebald acknowledges that Améry chooses to write nevertheless: "Considering the superior force of objectivity, it is even less defensible to refrain from writing than to go on with it, however senseless it may seem" (Sebald 2003, 155). Here, resentment is no less "mad" than forgiveness. According to Sebald, Améry is interested neither in compensations nor in enlightening the hangmen, but in "an attempt to actualize the conflict – which never in the moral sense took place – between the overpowered and those who overpowered them [. . .] The issue, then, is not to resolve but to reveal the conflict" (Sebald 2003, 157–58).

In resentment and in forgiveness, the victim seeks to be released from abandonment. Life must be rediscovered. "Max Ferber" culminates in "shreds and patches, utterly botched" (Sebald 1996, 231). It brings into language three abandoned exiles: Sebald, Améry, and Ferber, while also calling forth the work of the dead Schulz. "Max Ferber" consolidates Sebald's view of suffering: "The destruction of someone's native land is as one with the person's destruction. Separation becomes *déchirur* [a rending], and there can be no new homeland" (Sebald 2003, 160). Yet, the lesson of forgiveness and resentment is that the abandoned victim can be reintegrated into society. When s/he transforms the conversation and the language used in discussing moral emotions, s/he is able to access a sense of moral force free of the need for political power.

# Interchapter 1
# Aesthetic falsehood and emotion – on Bruno Schulz's *The Sanatorium Under the Hourglass* and Wojciech Has's *The Hourglass Sanatorium*

## Foreword: Aesthetic falsehoods in 1937 usher in decent politics in 1973

This interchapter explores how artists deploy time in their work and, in so doing, compel us to reconsider the way we think about morality and politics. My study focuses on works by the Polish-Jewish novelist Bruno Schulz and the Polish filmmaker Wojciech Has. In particular, I examine Has's *The Hourglass Sanatorium*, in which he reimagines the cycle of stories collected in Schulz's *The Sanatorium Under the Hourglass*. By juxtaposing Schulz's unorthodox treatment of his familial heritage against Has's reshuffling of the terms of their relationship, I offer one compelling example of how moral commitments are articulated in the aftermath of the Holocaust.

A central preoccupation of Schulz's *The Sanatorium Under the Hourglass*, which he wrote between 1934 and 1937, is the subversion and manipulation of time. The flow of time, in these tales, is marked by explosions, unexpected events that intrude on and ultimately destroy the conventions of everyday life. In the story "The Dead Season," Schulz focuses on the obsessive thoughts of Jacob about his shop of dry goods, thoughts that are linked with a sense of loss, of continuity, and of heritage. In "The Age of Genius" a similar effect is produced by the train journey undertaken by Joseph, a stand-in for the author, soon after he completes high school, as well as the release of Joseph's friend Shloma from jail. In "The Book," the reader observes Joseph enthusiastically recall himself as a child, drawing pleasure in collecting the colorful images from commercial catalogues and press advertisements that provided an outlet to his budding sexuality. In each case, what is described amounts to an event in time that both provides an anchor in the real world and impinges on, intensifying and defamiliarizing, life itself.

In Schulz's stories events are described metonymically. Species blend into each other as we observe a kind of impossible time flow from present to past and then to an almost surreal future, while the narrative structure plays tricks on the

---

**Note:** This chapter first appeared in translation to Polish in the journal: Schulz/Forum No. 19-20 (2022), 60-86, under the title: **Estetyczne fałsze i moralne emocje w *Sanatorium pod Klepsydrą* Brunona Schulza i filmie Wojciecha Hasa.** Translation, Katarzyna Lukas.

characters and the reader alike. These characters become clear to the reader only when they are removed from the everyday circumstances of their lives and undergo some sort of transformation. In "Spring," for example, in the aftermath of the death of his younger brother, "the Demiurge" Franz Joseph I of Austria forbids the use of the color red for mourning, because, he explains, red is the color of royalty. The story then reveals the proliferation of red in the world, which demonstrates the Demiurge's powerlessness to control how the color is used in the public sphere. The noon sun bathes the world in red, as the reader realizes how red embodies a kind of perfection and liberation:

> Sometimes an entire day goes by vivid explosions of sunshine, in stacks of clouds luminously and chromatically encircled at their borders, all their edges full of a red that is breaking through. [. . .] And suddenly, while they are waiting [the people in the market square], the world reaches its zenith, matures to the highest perfection in two or three final beats. [. . .] The May greenery is foaming and boiling like glittering wine at any minute to overflow its rim. [. . .] Having passed the highest peak, the beauty of the world separates and ascends—with enormous fragrance it enters into eternity (Schulz 2018, 133–134).

"Spring" is imbued with a sensuality that jumpstarts phenomenological transformation, an explosion within the very order of the world, a rebellion against the powers that be: the Emperor and the Law.

In Schulz's *Sanatorium* stories, Jacob, Joseph's father, lives on in a sort of time loop. So do the rest of those who are hospitalized in the sanatorium, all of them dead Jews. Thanks to this time loop they are able to pick up their lives where they left off. This notion of a time lag, which Freud calls *Nachträglichkeit*, is a form of belatedness and a quintessentially human trait. Human beings cannot know the present until it has passed, but only in retrospect, through interpretation and in anticipation of the future.

*The Sanatorium Under the Hourglass* paves the way for the philosophical thinking of Gilles Deleuze and Felix Guattari, who associate multiplicity with a loss of presence and of structural authority over the determination of the temporal relation between cause and effect, the spatial relation between center and periphery, the relation of superiority and inferiority among species. Schulz presents time in jumbled form in order to upend the notion that the past must determine the future. In this way he means to subvert the symbolic, patriarchal, hierarchical order of individuation, nationality, and the Law. Schulz's extraordinary treatment of time encourages a new, shifting relation between man and nature, as well as the radical transformation that leads to the embrace of difference, rather than conforming to the expectations of family, community, or history.

Has's film, *The Hourglass Sanatorium*, is an adaptation of Schulz's cycle. It similarly weaves together a tapestry of fragments, stories, and images, which emerge from jumbled time-sequences to present assemblages that accentuate difference through juxtaposition. The central difference between Has's adaptation and the original text is that his sequences are peppered with traditional, stereotypical images of Polish Jews. Early in the film we see a cemetery. Joseph must walk through the headstones to get to the sanatorium, which contrasts with Schulz's text, where we learn that Joseph must walk through a "park," the "basin of the horizon," and a "forested landscape" (Schulz 2018, 186). Has chooses his different framing images because, by 1973, when the film was released, there was a renewed interest in reviving Polish-Jewish culture and making it part of the modern historical memory of the nation. The film seeks to do this work through its representation of the Jewish life and culture that was lost, in order to further a newfound national commitment to preserve it, addressing the concerns of a younger generation of viewers who were seeking a moral reckoning with the past. This younger generation is Has's target audience. He speaks to them but also for them, in that he expresses their resentment toward Poland for its role in the annihilation of Polish Jewry. *The Hourglass Sanatorium* is art as a form of repentance. It enacts the demand that Polish culture and politics articulate a new moral commitment to recall past atrocities and educate future generations.

The film includes moments of stunted eroticism, which contribute to a cinematic world in which the human flows into the natural world. This is how *The Hourglass Sanatorium* breaks free from convention and becomes a difficult rather than a pleasurable film. Has's sanatorium is "minoritarian," to use the language of Deleuze and Guattari. He seeks to break free from the "majoritarian" social structures which follow in the footsteps of authority and the Law. Yet his film carries a commitment to moral imperatives that society neglects but acknowledges, so that it is subject to the law of the land and to ethics as such. Polish Jewry is dead to the culture and the nation. This death has to be dealt with morally, using images that disclose resentment toward the older generation of Polish fathers who perpetrated the genocide. But unlike Schulz's *Sanatorium* cycle, Has's film cannot completely break free of the Law.

The contrast between Schulz's (post)modernist depiction of the Jewish community, as pulsing with life and characterized by plurality while in the throes of radical change, and Has's portrayal of a Polish world in which the deceased Jews appear as a ghostly monolith, an image of the national Other, can best be understood through a close examination of our ideas about temporality and moral indebtedness. Schulz and Has are caught up in the need to make repetition materialize in such a way that enables the possibility of difference.

Schulz needs to become different from his parental and communal environment. Every repetition triggers an unforeseen event of difference, an active choice to belong to a new phenomenological constellation of matters in the world, which affect consciousness and the body in his stories. "The Book," for instance, revolutionizes the notion that the Bible is ontologically and metaphysically different from every other book, from weekly, popular journals, the discarded pages of which are used to wrap fish. "The Book" contains everything that energizes or depresses the life of the reader, "advertisements and announcements," stories about the gray daily lives of people from other countries: "Engrossed in reading, I forgot about dinner. My premonition had not deceived me. It was an Authentic, a holy original, in such a profound state of humiliation and degradation" (Schulz 2018, 87–90).

Has is also seeking moral responses in politics in order to acknowledge the victims. He frames his film with images of the cemetery, associating difference with an everyday, political reality in which affects, like seeking forgiveness for genocide, showing repentance over annihilation, and expressing resentment toward Poland in the post-WWII era, all come together to form a necessary minoritarian position. Repetition, the emergence of difference, and the process of becoming critical of majoritarian worldviews that justify war and atrocity all happen in relation to the dead. The image of time that is simultaneously ridiculed and authenticated in both these works is what makes Schulz's stories revolutionary. For Has, on the other hand, the issue is one of ethics.

In *Kafka, Toward a Minor Literature*, Giles Deleuze and Felix Guattari define the term "becoming-animal" as an escape from the triangular structure of the family or the nation. According to this structure, the father or the leader exerts the power to restrict and manage desire. In becoming, the human escapes from a structure of subjection to the law, and affirms difference:

> Yet, insofar as the comic expansion of Oedipus allows one to see these other oppressor triangles through the lens of the microscope, there appears at the same time the possibility of an escape, a line of escape. To the inhumanness of the 'diabolical powers,' there is the answer of a becoming-animal: to become a beetle, to become a dog, to become an ape, 'head over heels and away,' rather than lowering one's head and remaining a bureaucrat, inspector, judge, or judged all children build or feel these sorts of escapes, these acts of becoming-animal [. . .] To become animal is to participate in movement, to stake out the path of escape in all its positivity, to cross a threshold, to reach a continuum of intensities that are valuable only in themselves (Deleuze and Guattari 1986, 12–13).

When Deleuze and Guattari speak of becoming they are not interested in the subject. Instead they turn to examining the personal and public changes, which an actor in plurality both contracts from the environment and affects in his contacts within the rhizome. Schulz's stories enact this process of becoming within his own home and community. For Has, becoming is what makes it possible to express his own grievances against his country's policies, and to expose Polish guilt. Has learns from Schulz how to become minoritarian, and in that way create a world of possibilities that can subvert majoritarian systems.

Has's overdetermination of time can be understood through Deleuze's contention, in *The Time-Image*, that film is free from the limitations of chronology, causality, and factual truth:

> It shatters the system of judgment because the power of the false (not error or doubt) affects the investigator and the witness as much as the person presumed guilty [. . .] The point is that the elements themselves are constantly changing with the relations of time into which they enter, and the terms with their connections [. . .] The power of the false cannot be separated from an irreducible multiplicity (Deleuze 1989, 133).

Film is an *event*. A difficult film does not submit to a single, singular truth. It does not follow a linear narrative determined by causal relations between present and past. It is thus not beholden to the kind of meaning we associate with such thinking.

Repetition, a necessary practice in film, is central to Schulz's *Sanatorium* cycle. While dead Jews populate Has's film, most notably in the cemetery shots that open and close it, in Schulz's work we observe Jews who are ill but not yet dead. In *The Hourglass Sanatorium* we observe Jews dressed in traditional Hasidic garb, gathered around the Shabbat dinner table. Has's Jews pray in Hebrew and address one another in Yiddish. All of this is absent from Schulz's stories. Has's moral qualms lead him to revisit the past from a sentimental point of view, as he looks for ways to introduce difference into the future. Time and difference are meaningless concepts unless Has can use repetition to lead his viewers to experience a sense of longing for the traditional Jewish way of life. These feelings do not map on easily to the film's intended audience, the new generation of Polish men and women who have no memory of their country's Jewish history. In its quest to escape the prejudices about Jews, the film embraces Schulz's explosive imagery, his bringing to life the diversity and intensity of his own Jewish experience and the experiences of Jews in his home and community. As Deleuze puts it, "The present is the repeater, the past is repetition itself, but the future is that which is repeated" (Deleuze 1994, 94).

For Deleuze, film as event can break free from habit, and from an unconscious return of the repressed, if it chooses to oppose causal connections and instead introduces a pause in chronological historicity. The difficult film is thus an example of becoming, as it chooses difference and thus motivates social and political action. In the *Sanatorium* stories, Joseph is recalling, and trying to make sense of, his father Jacob. The fact that Jacob is caught in a time loop means that Joseph, as narrator, can depart from linear narrative storytelling, from the oedipal affirmation of continuity and tradition.

In the aftermath of his father's death, Joseph comes to the sanatorium to speak with the doctor, who explains: "You know as well as I that from the point of view of your home, from the perspective of your own fatherland, your father died. That cannot be entirely undone. This death casts a certain shadow on his existence here." The time loop within the sanatorium is an *event*: Jacob is alive and his life in the past is open to change. The doctor continues: "The entire trick depends, [. . .] on the fact that we have turned back time. We are late by an interval whose length is impossible to define. This boils down to a simple relativism. Here, your father's death, the death that already reached him in your fatherland, has simply not taken effect" (Schulz 2018, 188).

In the past, Jacob sits in a restaurant. "All eyes are turned toward him," because he is "animated" and "rapturous to the point of ecstasy." Unlike Schulz's father, who was a thin and quiet man, Jacob, the textual father, is gluttonous and loud. But, before Joseph can comprehend the situation, he is transported back to the sanatorium where he finds his sickly father dozing in his bed. Joseph asks: "How to reconcile this? Is father been sitting in the restaurant, overcome with unhealthy ambition in his gluttony, or is he lying in his own room seriously ill? Is he two fathers?" The doctor responds: "Nothing of the sort. The fault of everything is the rapid disintegration of time that is not supervised with constant vigilance" (Schulz 2018, 195–196). With this temporal interstice, Schulz's cycle is engaged in both a surrealist presentation of Polish-Jewish culture and a depiction of his father's becoming.

Schulz's manipulation of time receives new treatment in Has's *The Hourglass Sanatorium*, which, while it has surreal elements, is also bound by historical causality. Has's frame, which depicts Joseph crossing the cemetery on his way to the decrepit sanatorium, conveys a sense of mourning over the loss of Polish Jewry, including, of course, Schulz and the world depicted in his stories. This means, in the words of Richard Bégin, that Has deploys an "imagination of ruins" in order to capture both the Polish past, with its vibrant Jewish life, and the present, with Poland now a *Lieux de mémoire*, a realm of memory (Bégin 2007, 27, 35). Has is committed to memorialization. He seeks to influence a young generation of Polish citizens, so that they are able to mourn and feel shame and guilt for the past, instead of simply hoping for moral expiation. Poland cannot be allowed to only feel that, in retrospect, it would have liked the Jews not have been dead. The nation must feel guilt and shame, and repent, truly repent.

*The Hourglass Sanatorium* uses the time loop to return to a past in which an "organic" Jewish community still exists. Schulz deploys repetition in order to explore the possibility of introducing difference into the future, in order to show a Jew whose everyday living has never been coterminous with that of the stereotypical, Orthodox Jew. While his memories of his father are not reliable, they nevertheless furnish the context in which an *event* takes place, the transformation of the son into a character and a narrator, into Joseph. Loss of the past energizes both father and son, because in Schulz's narrative a life becomes meaningful when it incurs difference, when it undergoes becoming. Becoming is also refracted through the son's future, in which the father is but an aesthetic falsehood, a fiction, an image belonging to a system of tropes that Schulz the author fearlessly manipulates and controls. Becoming means that Schulz's *Sanatorium* cycle freely contracts and disseminates desire, irony, and pain.

For Schulz the past makes the future possible, a future amenable to and transformed by difference. For Has the past is the foundational trauma. When the distant past surfaces in scenes of contemporary life, Has introduces difference to the subject's moral perspective. He insists on representing the Jew in a traditional setting. Schulz's attempt at reimagining the social structures that organized Jewish life in Poland was rendered moot by the Holocaust. Has seeks to revive that work, by allowing memories of the past to filter into the present. In so doing he alters our moral understanding of politics. As Jean Améry notes, "no one can become what he cannot find in his memories" (Améry 1980, 84).

Améry aims to document the history of persecution, so that the culprits be tried and punished. He insists that artists must create aesthetic, fictive reenactments of genocide in order to compel the reader/viewer/listener to consider their own complicity in these crimes, to accept moral responsibility. For Améry the focus must be on creating a future that is substantively, morally different from the past:

> [Germany] would then, as I sometimes *hope*, learn to comprehend its past acquiescence in the Third Reich as the total negation not only of the world that it plagued with war and death but also of its own better origins; it would no longer repress or hush up the twelve years that for us others really were a thousand, but claim them as its realized negation of the world and its self, as its own *negative possession* (Améry 1980, 78, italics added).

Language is not only and always a positive means for connection and understanding. It has at times functioned as a negative possession. It has helped to facilitate crimes against humanity. The job of the writer is to salvage language from its sordid past. Authors/directors have the tools and the power to restore to language its secret, singular affective dimensions. By disconnecting language from bureaucratic systems, it could be used to signify human singularity. To treat language as a negative possession is to fall back on the notion of the ineffable, that which cannot be rationally explained, genocide in this case.

The aim is to recover the human dimensions of language without losing sight of the fact that language is always under threat, in danger of being used to facilitate murder. Poets, philosophers, and critics contemporary with Améry insisted that a language that had been party to genocide had to remain a negative possession. A new critical language had to be established, one that would not cover up the past, but would instead examine it in view of a future, with the understanding that to use language is to act as an engaged subject. Karl Jaspers understands negative possession to refer to the knowledge that Germans rejected during the war, their choice to turn a blind eye to the atrocities that were being carried out.

As Jaspers and Améry indicate, negative possession can be articulated in narrative and visual presentations of war and annihilation. An artist like Has thus takes responsibility for this negative possession. Works of literature, visual art, and architecture, specifically those focused on memorialization, are always implicated in alterity, which emerges posthumously and is found in articulations that are not reducible to semantic meaning. They keep haunting the writer/reader. Améry proposes that such work can counter the German inclination toward forgetting the past, and thus allow for closure. The "hope" for a future of moral reckoning expressed in such works reveals the importance of such negative possessions, which need not simply be regurgitations of the past but rather modes of becoming in the present and into the future. Améry writes not only as a witness but also as a political actor.

Conversations about forgiveness and resentment that surfaced as early as the 1950s looked not only to remember the past, but also to center human emotions. In the *Sanatorium* stories time becomes unhinged, transformed into a nonlinear labyrinth that allows for the experience of utopia, and of emotions that precede conscious cognition. Such emotions do not bring closure, nor are they realized through practices of reconciliation, which remain bound to the type of *ad hoc* values that liberal democracies generate. Certain emotions are political. Vindictiveness is a good example, in that it corresponds to the notion of an eye for an eye. But forgiveness and resentment are not political per se. They are instead in alignment with the Christian ideal of turning the other cheek. They are as scandalous as love or faith. In art, forgiveness and resentment affect and skirt a given political atmosphere, making politics responsive to the fact that the world is not made of institutionalized humans, but rather of living beings, both human and nonhuman. Indeed, life in the rhizome is a constant becoming-different, different from the structure that majoritarian interests fortify.

## 1 "Somewhere on a distant shore" (Schulz 2018, 189)

In the previous section I showed that a literary representation of contingency introduces difference to the world, in the form of choosing to break free from a majoritarian perspective on time and causality. This activates the process of becoming. A difficult film can choose difference, as when Has affirms his ethical stance by employing familiar images of traditional Jewish life to represent Polish Jewry. In this section, I will examine the literary choices Schulz makes that offer him a way out of a stereotypical representations of Polish Jewry. *Sanatorium Under the Hourglass* remembers and preserves Schulz's father's eccentricity, as well as his cultural heritage. A clash emerges between the rhizome, the field of consistency or contingency, and the establishment, with its powerful institutions that reinforce patriarchal and capitalist control. Schulz seeks to both infiltrate and deviate from the existing structural boundaries by producing a book that is not "hollow," but in which "all things are interconnected, all threads lead back to a single ball" (Schulz 2018, 109, 126). In exposing this clash between becoming within multiplicity and succumbing to established tradition, Schulz resists the institutions of power and embraces what community offers to him as an artist, as well as a Jew who represents alterity.

Early on, Joseph needs to go to the market square to find his father's new shop, assured by his father that "It's hard to mistake it." But he does mistake it, since "it" is not simply the shop but rather a radical temporal transformation. In the fictional market square the father has a different relation to his ruined business than he did in real life. Rather than relate to the past with nostalgia, Joseph chooses to be innovative: "A strange, confusing similarity the market square of our native city!" (Schulz 2018, 190–191). The surprising emergence of difference in-between the recurring moments, recollections, and simulacra of past reality vanish when Joseph evinces "the slightest opposition," "the weakest gust of skepticism" (Schulz 2018, 192). The aesthetic representation of the market square is filled with falsehoods that create new worlds when they are affective, not when they are modeled on a historical truth and repeat the past in search of an unchanging identity.

To portray this change, Schulz uses the metaphor of a telescope through which the protagonist discovers an enlarged image of reality "a labyrinth of black chambers, a lengthy complex of darkrooms inserted halfway into one another" (Schulz 2018, 193). The world of disconnected, labyrinthine images that are imperfectly embedded into one another is conjured via the dream world that Jacob and his son often inhabit. Subjectivity regains force in the realm of exhaustion, where the subject is split between acceptance and rejection of the reality and the pleasure principles, where woman is an example of how to participate in society even though she is kept at bay, distanced from desiring the symbolic ends of the social organization, where the child signifies erotism, because children enjoy the world as radically sensual, where the animal suggests living in herds, not in alienation, so that becomings resonate with unforeseen encounters and departures within the rhizome.

Deleuze and Guattari view these social positions of woman, child, the split and even splintered consciousness, and the animal as rhizomatic. These are vectors that enable and participate in becoming. These subjects signify phenomena that exist and operate in and on society, but whose influence society tries to tame. For beings who instigate a minoritarian mode of action in society, becoming is a rhizome. Chaotic time is where one is both affective and affected, proof that "nature operates—against itself." The tools that society uses to name the mentally ill, the woman, the child, and the animal allow them not to be in the service of conservative institutions but operate in the form of "teeming," "spreading," and "infectious" (Deleuze and Guattari 1987, 242, 244). Deleuze and Guattari refuse to call these agents of radical transformation "subjects" and suggest "haecceity," that is, someone or something that "has neither a beginning nor an end," but is an event, an infinitive: "[not] origin, not destination; it is always in the middle." The haecceity "is not made of points, only of lines. It is a rhizome" (Deleuze and Guattari 1987, 263).

Schulz introduces fragmentation into a reality that seems to be tied up with coherence. In "Deleuze on Habit," in a somewhat abstract formulation of the relationship between difference and repetition, the American scholar Brian O'Keeffe suggests that "[i]f repetition looks like a bland repeat of the same thing, true repetition is made up of a series of meanwhiles, so to speak. Differences rely upon the serial occurrence of such meanwhiles in order to be differences at all" (O'Keeffe 2016, 92). Joseph is able to meet his father as a force of difference because, in the present, the text registers a very personal form of time, a time that envelops and is enveloped. It is expressed in the form of an ex-centric point of view, from which the singularity of disconnected experiences, recollections, and narration emerge. "Deprived of this supervision, [time] inclines immediately to transgressions, to wild aberration, to playing innumerable tricks, to amorphous buffoonery," so that the present time of the son and that of the father's past "no longer coincided" (Schulz 2018, 196).

Thus, the attempt to repeat the past yields difference. Difference comes on the heels of an impossible repetition because, when time is turned back, it does not reemerge "reliable," "fresh," "smelling of newness." Aesthetic time, which is "time somehow unwound," moves between a range of fictional worlds. It is full of potentialities brought about in images, framing, and narrative strategies, like the temporal gap in the work of Russian formalists Vladimir Propp and Victor Shklovsky, where *fabula* corresponds to the thematic content of a story and *syuzhet* to its organizing structure. The *fabula* always complicates the *syuzhet* or the chronological order of events, to the point that from the aesthetic object of the story one cannot extract a plot. Every *syuzhet* is but a skeleton of the full story, the *fabula* in which tropes, themes, motives, and narration strategies are fully developed. Aesthetic remembering can never resemble the *syuzhet* or the skeleton of narrative: "on the contrary. It is threadbare time, worn out by people, tattered time holes in many places, transparent as a sieve. It is no wonder that it is, so to speak, regurgitated time—please understand me—it is a secondhand time. God have mercy!" (Schulz 2018, 198).

Schulz asks to be "understood" because his memories of his father and community are filled with aesthetic distortions, which make the past appear to be oriented towards future differences. This instance of remembering remains "negative," not because aesthetic recollections of the past generate a shadowy unreality, but because such narratives have the potential to diffuse power relations and establish an ontological play of difference. Because Joseph is in touch with both inner and outer stimulations of memory, brought about by his choice to unite with representatives of the minoritarian positions in culture, woman, child, the convalescent father, animal, and the mentally imbalanced, difference does not only establish but also diffuses known- or self-identity in the process of becoming.

Schulz repeats the past while also breaking from it in order to undergo becoming, the salient form that difference takes. We witness this in action when Joseph goes to the market square with his decrepit father in the thick of winter. The atmosphere becomes somber as Joseph realizes that armed civilians are threatening passersby. Refusing to believe rumors circulating about imminent war, Joseph nonetheless observes that even the dogs are "silent, full of intensity, and alert" (Schulz 2018, 199). One is left wondering what is real and what is fiction, given that this was written after Hitler's rise to power, yet refers to war as unimaginable, despite the fact that it was a constant looming threat. Joseph explains that the warriors at the marketplace, who are dressed in black, are actually men he knows from the neighborhood: "They inform us that the invasion of the enemy army emboldened a party of malcontents in the city who poured out into the streets with weapons in hand, terrorizing the peaceful inhabitants." Schulz's unwitting historical prolepsis is remarkable, as if prophesying the events of *Kristallnacht*, carried out by paramilitary forces and civilians, which took place one year after the publication of *Sanatorium Under the Sign of the Hourglass*. We observe the instigators "they were restraining outbursts of laughter" at the sight of the frightened crowd but these paramilitary forces "pass by us without accosting anyone" (Schulz 2018, 200, 201).

Joseph feels kinship with the dogs he finds in the back alleys. A conversation on superstition and prejudices ensues. Joseph understands that sometimes, when the dogs cease to run, they are assessing him. From their "black, wise gaze fury peers out, checked in its intended action only by a lack of time" (Schulz 2018, 200). Later, retracing his steps back to the sanatorium, Joseph focuses his attention on a chained watchdog. Somehow, this animal breaks free and accosts him until he manages to hide inside a hollow tree trunk. Is the dog's rage directed specifically at the Polish Jew? Or, is the lone dog a chained Polish Jew? Trapped in his hiding place, Joseph looks at the animal and, for the first time, sees that this is not a dog but a man.

Becoming-animal happens in this temporal interstice when the narrative moves from a reflection on prejudice to offer examples of possible points of connection between Poles and Polish Jews, represented via the relationships between individual dogs in a pack. Becoming-dog can be liberating, if one is absorbed into the herd and survives, or it can be frightening, if the dog is viewed as an outsider excluded from the pack, as Polish Jews were banished from Polish society. Eventually the dog is transformed into a bookbinder. Schulz suggests that, in the aftermath of this transformation, the man and the dog are not separate entities. Instead, the bookbinder is a man who is enveloped in his dog-aspect. Joseph chastises himself for having misrecognized the bookbinder, for seeing him as a dog. He now understand that prejudice is the antithesis of becoming:

> How great is the power of prejudice! How mighty the suggestion of terror! What blindness! For it was a man. A man on a chain, whom, in reductive, metaphoric, undifferentiated abbreviation by some inconceivable means I has taken for a dog. Please don't misunderstand me. It was a dog, certainly, most assuredly—but in human form. Canine quality is an internal quality and can manifest itself just as well in human and in animal form [. . .] A violent man with dark explosive passions [. . .] he was one hundred percent a dog (Schulz 2018, 202).

Joseph understands that the dogman is his double: "Ah, how this terrible friendship weighs me down. How this weird affection terrifies me. How to rid myself of this man walking beside me, his gaze hanging on my face with all the fervor of his canine soul?" (Schulz 2018, 203). Perhaps the reason that becoming is missing from this passage is because prejudice remains intact in the aftermath of becoming-dog. Indeed, it seems as if the lonely Jew despises the dog because he sees, in the dog, his own reflection. But it is the local folk who are guilty of treating the Jew as an outsider, a stray dog who does not belong among them. To become-dog is to remain subject to majoritarian visions of domesticity and inclusion in municipal activities, for the dog is an oedipal, domestic animal. And yet, to be a bookbinder or a writer is to belong to a minoritarian perspective.

Perhaps what Schulz is suggesting here is that the act of writing dissolves the boundaries that compel us to choose a side. Joseph obfuscates the hierarchical boundary lines that separate human form animal, woman from man, or the Polish Jew from the Polish national. "And on top of all this," narration turns to the potentials of becoming-woman: "Mother's inconceivable appearance, incognito, on some secret mission!" (Schulz 2018, 203).

Woman is the becoming that escapes the grid of majoritarian structures of power and control, and this potential for insubordination causes Joseph to resist confinement: "To flee, to flee from here!" (Schulz 2018, 203). He escapes into the train and never leaves, becoming an obscure nomad: "Ever since that time I have been riding, continually riding" (Schulz 2018, 204). Thus, Joseph could represent the wandering Jew, who substantiates the existing structure of majoritarian cultural hi-stories. The nomadic Jew belongs to the minority and understands that the collective both generates prejudice and opens up routes of escape.

## 2 Forgiveness and resentment: Reterritorializing the life and work of Bruno Schulz

*The Hourglass Sanatorium* deploys surrealist strategies in order to further blur the historical truth. Rather than present a literal representation of Schulz's life story, Has's film considers a range of possibilities and explores multiple variations on the story the text conveys. One thing Has does not alter is Schulz's depiction of the sanatorium, in which the dead go on living, except in Has's vision the dead include all of Polish Jewry. The film thus reterritorializes Schulz's sanatorium when it presents the viewer with images that seek out an ethical resolution. The film is not "purely optical," to use Deleuze's language, nor a "cinema of the seer," where the shocking effect of images quickens in the characters on the screen radical affective reactions of pain which leads to death or love, and which could usher in Dionysian desire (Deleuze 1989, 2). It is in this context that guilt, shame, and repentance come together to overdetermine the viewer's identification with the Jewish characters, with both their past and their future potential, either to belong to cultural difference or remain locked up in a mythic repetition of the past.

Joseph, guides the viewer through the sanatorium, addressing the various characters he meets along the way, including his mother Henrietta, his father Jacob, and Adela. The film thus conveys the story of a patriarchal, Polish-Jewish culture. It is as much about the disappearance of that world as it is about making the past come alive through attention, not just to people but also to objects, places, the language and dreams of the Jews among whom Schulz lived and worked.

The film vacillates between long panoramic shots and fragmented, close takes of the everyday. The former represents majoritarian structures and systems of goals in the realm of work. The market square is the realm of both commerce and sociability, and thus turns into a beating heart, an engine of action and transaction between men, when the panoramic image captures the landscape. Immediately the perspective changes and the camera focuses on fragments of reality, so as to expose the field of consistency where woman, erotism, and the crowds, similar to a herd of animals or to a murmuration of birds, play a more prominent role.

On the one hand, the panoramic perspective, much like omniscient narration, creates a sense of structural coherence, in this case with respect to the imagined Jewish community that continues to exist even after the persecution of European Jewry. This persistence and resilience are portrayed through scenes of Jewish homes, captured in shots that resemble citation or a pastiche. We observe traditional Jewish life unfolding from the Polish perspective.

An example of the vacillation between the continuity of myth and its violent transformation into the personal becoming author/artist is found in "The Age of Genius," in which the boy observes that his room is illuminated, but cannot make the members of his household see this blinding light. Schulz confuses the holy signifiers of religion and tradition with the secular daily newspapers and magazines that signify a trashy contemporaneity. He jumbles these together to create a mesmerizing world of stories and images. Joseph jumps into action, grabs his father's Bible and business ledgers, which glow on the floor, and combines these with newspapers and magazines that his brother and mother bring into the house: "And I sat among these papers, blinded by the radiance, my eyes full of explosions, rockets, and colors, and I drew. I drew hastily, in a panic, crosswise, at a slant, across printed and handwritten pages" (Schulz 2018, 96). It is impossible, Schulz is saying, to portray or understand Polish-Jewish culture without implicating the gaze in the plane of consistency of the fragmented shots of the everyday.

*The Hourglass Sanatorium* replicates and displaces the scene described above with one that depicts the father carrying a big, thick Bible, the pages of which are torn, into the market square. The pages fall from the book to the floor like leaves, and have to be collected from the ground and shoved back into the book binding. The chaos of the market square exposes the tentative value of objects, people, conversations, and meanings that perish by the end of the day. As the film closes in on a particular object or individual, these shots are drowned out by an intensity of emotion. The precarity of the situation is brought into sharp relief. The Bible is a metaphor for the panoramic perspective that wavers in the world of the deconstructed rhizome, where the "original book" is but a scrapbook and the people and the landscape generate noise and vitality.

In "A July Night," Schulz portrays the struggle between the panoramic perspective, which coincides with trust in authority, and a perspective of the use of common discourse, which is typical of the rhizome, when he interrupts a scene that depicts the celestial sublime with everyday prattle: "From the flickering of those distant worlds come the croaking of frogs, a silvery astral murmur" (Schulz 2018, 160). This may be the inspiration behind Has's portrayal of Adela as a seductive woman whose beauty generates much chatter. In "My Father Joins the Firefighters," Jacob is surrounded by his brigade of firemen when he is suddenly thrust into an argument with woman. He scolds Adela: "You have never had any

## 2 Forgiveness and resentment: Reterritorializing the life and work of Bruno Schulz — 53

understanding of matters of a higher order. Everywhere and always you have thwarted my actions with outbursts of mindless malice [. . .] Deprived of a noble flight of fancy, you burn with unconscious jealousy toward everything that rises above the commonplace" (Schulz 2018, 164). Despite his didacticism both reader and viewer understands that the father's scolding adds fuel to the fire, generating the kind of verbiage that cannot transcend the "commonplace."

The film opens with a black bird flying in the gray sky, before we move into the train coaches where we observe crowds of exhausted, or more likely dead, Jews. What is the relationship between the bird and these Jewish passengers? The bird appears to have its gaze turned upward, as if encouraging the viewer to seek out God, or another powerful source of transcendence, which has been rendered obsolete in the aftermath of the Holocaust. The scenes that unfold aboard the train are horrific. They depict the removal of people and of their belongings to a place of no return. Only historical documentation and aesthetic modulation can restore the moral perspective and make sense of this catastrophe. The camera zooms into the coach, suggesting that the crimes of the past cannot be sutured, or turned into a coherent understanding, that the lives of those killed remain valuable, and that it is crucial to keep memories of the prewar period alive into the present.

Yet the bird's flight through a gray and empty sky suggests another possible angle from which to examine the film's moral and temporal considerations. In "The Age of Genius," Schulz tells of the release from prison of his friend, the thief Shloma (Schulz 2018, 99). For Joseph this is a Messianic day, a day of emotional beneficence and social belonging. The Messiah is a signifier of the Final Judgment. Shloma is repeatedly imprisoned and released from prison, he is regularly judged and then, having served his punishment, he is forgiven by society. The Messiah is a figure of human patience, not of divine wrath, signifying everyday morality, not transcendental edicts:

> On such a day the Messiah approaches the very edge of the horizon and from there looks down at the earth. And when he sees it so white, and silent, with its azure and pensiveness, it can happen that in his eyes it loses its boundary, the bluish bands of clouds lie down to form a passageway, and, not knowing himself what he is doing, he descends to earth. And in its reverie the earth will not even notice the one who has descended onto its paths, and people will awaken from their afternoon naps and remember nothing. The entire story will be as if it had been blotted out and it will be as it was in primeval times, before history began (Schulz 2018, 101).

Schulz's depiction of the figure of the Messiah indicates that the Messianic is a force-of-life, a movement, a continued deferral and postponement of judgment. Schulz's Messiah doesn't signify the Day of Judgment but empathy. This becomes evident when the Messiah arrives on earth and mingles with the people and the landscape. The bird's flight intimates closeness to nature and organic life. The bird's perspective, which is synonymous with the eye of the camera and the "looks" of the Messiah, transmogrifies into a perspective from which we can observe the Jews in the railway carts and validate their experiences. In this context the Messiah is a signifier of the hope to restore forgiveness to, and resentment directed at, the criminals. In the aftermath of the Holocaust, the film suggests, no one dares to imagine that the Messiah is present.

But he is present in Schulz's fragment, and is brought back to life in Has's film, much as Schulz and Polish Jewry are brought back to life. The image of the Messiah allows the viewer to imagine that the Polish Jewish community does not have to live in a time loop, because it has been "given" or relegated to an afterlife, a belonging in time-immemorial. This community has become "legendary," to borrow an expression from W.G. Sebald. *The Hourglass Sanitarium* tries to restore the dimension of ethics to aesthetics when Has fragments archetypal portrayals of Polish Jewry and introduces the Schulzian imagination to his film. But while Schulz was an agent of becoming minoritarian, Has is an agent of constructivism. He restores Polish Jewry to a position that propels majoritarian state structures to mourn the Jewish dead, commemorate their cultural traditions, and repent for assisting in their persecution.

Améry says that, in order to enter into a moral discussion about past atrocities, it is necessary to practice "regression into the past and nullification of what happened" (Améry 1980, 68). For Améry, this mode of repetition is the hallmark of resentment, a moral reaction to past atrocities. And yet this practice, which demands that we look to the past when we give a moral image to the present and the future, is also the necessary condition for the expression of repentance in the face of Jewish survivorship. The Schulzian mode of a revolutionary treatment of the past is displaced by a pragmatic vision of repetition, as an opportunity to create a morally better future, in which Jewish people are remembered and their traditions honored.

At the beginning of "The Age of Genius," Schulz underlines the linear historicity that he intends to let go of: "Ordinary facts are lined up in time, strung onto its course as if on a thread. They have their antecedents there and their consequences, which crowd together closely, constantly stepping on one another's heels without leaving a gap. This also has meaning for narrative, whose soul is continuity and succession." He chooses to seek out other such instances when he focuses on the question: "What can be done with events that do not have their own place in time, with events that arrive too late, when all of time was already distributed, divided, disassembled, and now they've just been left there, unclassified, suspended in the air, homeless and errant?" (Schulz 2018, 94). These events allow the author to enter into time and revolutionize it through his writing and painting.

## 2 Forgiveness and resentment: Reterritorializing the life and work of Bruno Schulz

Yet when such "events that do not have their own place in time" occur in Has's film, they reterritorialize Schulz's perspective and return to being "facts." The fact is, "strung onto its course as if on a thread," and facts also "have their antecedents there and their consequences."

Améry points toward the possibility that a negative possession, an aesthetic artifact, is related to historical fact because it is affective. It recalls loss and pain but it remains open-ended. It doesn't advance toward historical healing or aesthetic closure. And it is always part of the ineffable, thus reinscribing deterritorialization in majoritarian practices of historical documentation. Has's film, on the contrary, legitimizes the forgetfulness that systematic and factual accounts of the past generate, because it offers closure when it commemorates Polish Jewry. If one of Améry's hopes is that the Polish people accept emotional responsibility for the crimes committed in their name, and acknowledge the ease with which they continue to belong to a nation with a murderous past, then Has's film propels a rapprochement between memory and judgment. The time loop allows viewers to feel as if the Jews portrayed on screen, their culture and traditions, are immortal. It thus offers a lifeline to contemporary Polish aesthetics and art. This attempt to understand the life and world of the Other, once they have been relegated to the grave, is what makes repentance, resentment, and the quest for forgiveness possible.

Three main scenes demonstrate that the film is not simply reterritorializing Schulz's poetics of revolutionizing time. The film is reterritorializing because Has, a Polish director who is at odds with his country's history, suffers from a guilty conscience or a guilty secret, and wants his film to tell the truth, to evoke the viewers' longing to understand the country's rich Jewish history. When Joseph reaches the sanatorium, he does not emerge from the woods but from the cemetery. The sanatorium appears to be located on the same estate as the cemetery, and thus does not exist inside the time loop. Rather, it is enmeshed with death, a building alongside many headstones.

**Figures 2, 3:** *The Hourglass Sanatorium*, the cemetery shots that open and close the film, DVD screen shots.

At the end of the film, Joseph does not walk from one coach to the next inside the train, as he does in Schultz's narrative. Instead, the character reemerges in the cemetery, where he wanders among the headstones, on which candles are burning. These real candles, a metaphor for the commemoration of the dead, are reterritorializing as they commemorate the souls of the victims. This aesthetic difference offers a sense of a structured, national Polish response to the established Jewish tradition that was lost to Poland, along with most of its Jewish citizens. At the same time, Has's choices enact a refusal to remain caught up in Schulz's imaginative falsehoods. It is important for Has to create a Polish negative possession, by taking responsibility for Poland's role in decimating Jewish life and culture in Poland. Yet, when Has offers closure, through the commemoration of the Jewish dead, film remains a cultural possession, but not an ineffable or negative one.

Second, Joseph reaches the sanatorium by train, and he returns to the train as its conductor, a nomad wearing a torn uniform. Each coach is filled with remnants of the Jewish past, and with Jewish people, including men in traditional Hasidic garb. But the Jews depicted here belong to a world and way of life that Schulz does not affirm. This is the life that Schulz revolutionizes in his writing. When Joseph leaves the sanatorium he is happy that he is finally free from familial and communal obligations: "It's fortunate that Father is, for all intents and purposes, no longer alive [. . .] I board one of them [railway cars] and the train, as if it had been waiting for this, slowly moves off [. . .] Ever since that time I have been riding, continually riding [. . .] The cars, immense as rooms, are full of trash and straw, drafts penetrate right through them on gray, colorless days" (Schulz 2018, 204). Nomadism, movement, the proximity to nature and affect, all introduce a different intensity from the one that is associated with father's world of business, clothes, and supervision of employees. Joseph's desire is imperceptible because it is not complicated any more. It is free. In Schulz, the movement through "colorless days" is a line of flight and a way out. In Has the train is metaphorical, recalling a time that was stopped with the destruction of Polish Jewry.

While the trains in Schulz's work symbolize a desire for freedom or escape, in Has the train is a more loaded image given its resonances with the Holocaust. A train also appears in Schulz's "A July Night," in which the narrator compares night wanderings to traveling on a night train: "long as the world, riding through an endless black tunnel? To walk through a July night is to make one's way with difficulty from car to car, between sleepy passengers, through crowded corridors, stuffy compartments, and crisscrossing currents of air" (Schulz 2018, 159). The metaphor of the train both opens and closes Schulz's *Sanatorium Under the Sign of the Hourglass*, perhaps to suggest that the need for escape is never satisfied, that aesthetic falsehoods never bring closure. In Has's *The Hourglass Sanatorium*, however, the train is an elaborate metaphor, an extension of the Polish Jewish home. In this case the message is that a Jewish person can never break free from their origins, that even as a nomad the Jew remains a territorial, a wandering Jew, with roots in a European Judeo-Christian myth.

The third example of how moral emotions become coopted by national and majoritarian practices of memorialization has to do with the *mise-en-scène* where the town's Jewish community lights the Shabbat candles and partakes of dinner together. The diners greet each other in Hebrew and Yiddish, languages that are inaccessible to Joseph/Schulz. In the background we hear klezmer music. The happier the diners become, the more alive the conversation turns out to be, as if to show that for Polish Jews Shabbat is not just a holy day, but a day in which they are separate from the outside world of the gentiles, true to who they really are, happy to live in the enclosure of a unique tradition. As Adela brings the fish to the table, so does the number of the Shabbat candles increases, which suggests that these are not traditional Shabbat candles—typically the Jewish mother lights only two Shabbat candles—but memorial candles.

When Joseph breaks out of the sanatorium he emerges in an alley, between two buildings, a scene that is critically unlike the scene depicted in Schulz's story. In the text, when Joseph leaves the sanatorium, it is because he goes with his father to the market square and sees that civilians are threatening the passersby. Joseph does not believe the warnings he hears of war, but he is cognizant that something is wrong, and even the dogs are vigilant. In a manner that seems disconnected from the realities unfolding all around him, Schulz describes war preparations while showing us that Joseph trusts that the warriors at the marketplace, armed and threatening remain fellow townsmen who might be discontented but they certainly do not intend to use their weapon to harm anyone belonging to their community.

Has's film, on the other hand, refers to what has become historical fact, the events of *Kristallnacht*, in order to impose the moral emotions of forgiveness and resentment on Polish audiences. The disgruntled civilians, who join the soldiers in Schulz's story but eventually move on, causing no harm to the residents, are reimagined in *The Hourglass Sanatorium*, which portrays scenes of destruction and ruin. Has thus seeks to claim a negative possession as part of his native Polish culture, and thereby engender moral emotions like forgiveness, repentance, and resentment to come to the fore and remain open, not subject to the political reliance on legal and diplomatic procedures.

## 3 Can something new ever happen?

Writing about Schulz for *The New Yorker* in 2009, the Israeli novelist David Grossman discusses the circumstances of Schulz's murder in Drohobycz, citing a well-known but unverified story about Schulz's death at the hands of a Nazi officer, Karl Günther. Grossman associates this story with the psychoanalytic concept of "defense mechanisms," noting that Günther committed the murder because he was competing with another German officer. This second man had close connections with Schulz, and Günther wanted to both hurt his nemesis and defy the possibility that a Jew would be protected by a Nazi. Grossman explains that defense mechanisms are so alienating that they can bring about a murderous hatred of the Other. This assertion is important, because it allows Grossman to ask how becoming and difference can save us from such defenses that enslave us. The time of becoming and difference is captured in Schulz's fiction, his world of imaginative falsehoods that revolutionize time and traditions. Grossman writes: "Did the Age of Genius ever occur?, Schulz wonders. And if it did, would we recognize it, answer its secret call? Would we dare to relinquish the elaborate defense mechanisms that we have constructed against the antediluvian wildness and volcanic abundance of such an age, defenses that have, bit by bit, become our prison?" (Grossman 2009).

Grossman claims that Schulz's Age of Genius is a source of "erotism," to use the neologism that George Bataille (1962) introduces to refer to childish playfulness and aesthetic escape. This is the kind of escape that restores animality to human behavior. It allows for becoming minoritarian and actively pursuing difference, understood as a fulfillment of self and society that rebels against stagnant majoritarian structures, which can only persevere if we surrender to our defense mechanisms. Such becoming is not limited to childhood. It extends to other, numerous possibilities of escape, in recognition of the fact that to uphold identity is to reject difference. Sameness does not leave room for anything new to transpire, while becoming minoritarian fractures the hold of majoritarian systems and furnishes us with a way out, if not with perfect freedom. Only the repetition of this kind of genius can introduce difference into the future, where the will to power does not erase the possibility for singular action. Has's film is territorializing, though it does not coincide with the will to power. Instead, it tries to fashion a negative possession, while resisting indictment and reconciliation, the hallmarks of politics. In this way, the film invokes the rhizomatic diversity and polysemy of an aesthetic that is rooted in opening up rather than narrowing down possibilities.

Early in the film, Joseph asks the blind train conductor: "Can something new ever happen?" The conductor replies "yes and no," because some things are too great, they cannot be summed up in a single event. A negative possession is an aesthetic device that connects to the ineffable. It recalls catastrophic events but does not reduce the meaning of catastrophe to a majoritarian form of reconciliation with the past.

To conclude, I'd like to briefly consider one of Schulz's later works, one that vividly portrays the necessary connection between becoming and difference. In "The Republic of Dreams," Schulz realizes his town is controlled by judgment, capitalism, paternalism, orderliness, and efficiency. To expose this majoritarian perspective, Schulz depicts a social structure that is, in Deleuze's formulation, "arborescent":

> Here events are not ephemeral surface phantoms; they have roots sunk into the deep of things and penetrate the essence. Nothing happens here by chance, nothing results without deep motive and premeditation. Here decisions take place every moment, laying down precedents once and for all. Everything that happens here happens only once and is irrevocable. This is why such weightiness, such heavy emphasis, such sadness inheres in what takes place (Schulz 1988, 217).

To counter and revolutionize this kind of structure is Schulz's genius. He introduces a deterritorializing scheme of space and time into this realm, through a text that examines how a sunny summer day becomes a rhizome. It delineates lines of flight, or a way out. Schulz describes an environment drowning in "weeds," buildings covered in "moss," a town that "from a pinch of chlorophyll it draws out and extrapolates under the blaze of these summer days the luxuriant texture of emptiness." Jacob's shop is immersed in this scintillating, natural surround that emerges from the field of immanence. Schulz wonders how to flee from "the conflagration, from the incubus lying heavy on the chest in a torrid noontime nightmare?" (Schulz 1988, 218–219). The pragmatic response is a vacation in the countryside. But an aesthetic consideration suggests that this past, which defines the child, has turned to a line of flight, a present filled with difference:

> Today those remote dreams come back, and not without reason. The possibility suggests itself that no dreams, however absurd or senseless, are wasted in the universe. Embedded in the dream is a hunger for its own reification, a demand that imposes an obligation on reality and that grows imperceptibly into a bona fide claim, an I.O.U. clamoring for payment (Schulz 1988, 221).

Schulz aims to break free from majoritarian capitalist and juridical practices, so he devotes himself to dreaming and fiction. He believes that the author is one who finds his deterritorialized perspective, "someone ingenuous and true of heart who [understands things] literally, [takes] them for coin of the realm, and treat[s] them as things that [are] plain, unproblematic" (Schulz 1988, 221).

# Chapter 2
# Love and worldliness – on Hannah Arendt

> What is Love? – Ask him who lives what is life; ask him who adores what is God. *On Love*, Percy Bysshe Shelley

Hannah Arendt rejects the possibility that love can be political because she does not consider the libidinal aspects of collectivity. Despite the crucial role that *amor mundi* plays in her work, she does not give a systematic account of the passion inherent in being together in the public sphere. Although Arendt adamantly resents psychoanalysis, in this chapter I would like to initiate a dialogue between Arendt and Freud, for whom love and sublimation are fundamental to worldliness, and central to our understanding of forgiveness.

In Freud's view, love and sublimation expand knowledge, enhance creativity, and enable community building. Love mediates between the private and public spheres. Arendt, on her part, holds that the kind of self-disclosure and acknowledgement of Otherness that abounds in love can bleed into the public sphere. Private love is more than passion or desire. Love's habit to make us more exposed and disclose both our vulnerability and our strength is valuable in the political sphere. Arendt is interested in the ways love teaches us to be open, willing to engage, to connect, to step away from solipsistic self regard and accept when our will is denied. The feeling of being opposed, rejected in the public sphere, as much as the feeling of being respected as an equal, allows for introspection, for self examination, and for change.

The key question, in my view, concerns the relationship between love of the world and its negation by radical evil. When anti-Semitism, or racism, or imperialism produce radical evil, how can love forged in the private and public spheres help the victims of evil face it and defeat it? Answer: by bringing together the multiplicity of disenfranchised groups and individuals, who can join into a body politic, a civil society, grounded in bonds of friendship and respect, legitimately opposed to mainstream politics, yet not excluded from politics altogether. In this context, friendship and respect are forms of sublimated love, which retain the traits of love from the private sphere.

Grace enhances sublimated or universal love. This poses a problem for Arendt, who does not see love of the Other as mediated through the love of God. Love of the Other is particular and differentiated. It is directed specifically at *who* the singular person is. One of the effects of totalitarianism is the destruction of the space for love. Totalitarianism coerces people to live in isolation and fear the Other. Arendt concludes that totalitarian regimes destroy love both in the political and private realms, turning the commandment 'thou shalt love thy neighbor' into its opposite: 'thou shalt kill thy neighbor.' Totalitarianism generates sameness through bureaucratic mechanisms that control individuals, households, and social collectives. Both Arendt and Freud are convinced that love in the private sphere effects scientific, artistic, and political change in the public sphere. Yet they are employing different theoretical frameworks as they analyze the transition of love from worldlessness to worldliness, from private interests to social and political judgments. For Arendt, the splitting of love into private and public divides the *who* (private) from the *what* (public). My aim is to show that the paradox splitting private and public love is the same that splits forgiveness into personal and penal logics.

Love and forgiveness are moral emotions that inform and strengthen each other. Forgiveness is an eminently personal emotion, yet it can move the public sphere into social change and political action. Arendt argues that we forgive the person because of *who* she/he is, not for the *what* of the crime. Much as forgiveness and resentment are bound up together, so too are love and repression. If forgiveness without resentment creates a form of forgetting, then love without repression creates naiveté, the lack of an incentive to self-examine and judge one's desires and reasons for action.

## Private and public love

Arendt was fundamentally skeptical about psychoanalysis, which she found reductionist and solipsistic. According to Arendt, psychoanalysis destroys the world of the in-between – the differences that enable people to form relationships. Rather than encourage revolutionary ideas and actions aimed at making the world better, psychoanalysis instructs us to "'adjust' to those [bad] conditions, taking away our only hope, namely that we, who are not of the desert though we live in it, are able to transform it into a human world" (Arendt 2005, 201). Arendt finds that psychoanalysis and totalitarianism have something in common: they deaden the faculties of passion that could help us change the world. Taking a psychoanalytic approach, or living under totalitarian rule, might, in some ways, lessen our suffering, but at the cost of relinquishing our courage – a courage that allows us to raise society's moral bar.

Arendt, however, wrongly assumes that psychoanalysis pathologizes one's experience of foreignness, promising it can bring about healing through conforming. Arendt argues that people who reduce their foreignness in the world engage in love, in acting and thinking, and in political cooperation through natality – the quality of being born each time the world is renewed through joint action. She accepts Augustine's concern for the creation of *mundus*, but she questions his reliance on neighborly love as mediated by divine love.

In *Love and Saint Augustine,* Arendt differentiates between *eros* (erotic love), *philia* (friendship), and *agape* (love of God). Yet she does not consider the libidinal aspects of collective social and political bonds, or the significance of *amor mundi,* which I understand as the responsibility that people assume and advance collectively for the welfare of the world. Arendt labors to explain what it means to love the Other, not through the mediation of God, but via observing the particularity of this Other. She does not want to betray the world – for to equally love every Other is a betrayal of the world – but neither does she want *mundus* to deteriorate to intimate love, advancing personal and communal interest, losing sight of the importance of universal rules and traditions of government whose implementation can humanize the world.

By contrast, Freud views libidinal and sublimated love as forces that bind people together. In *Civilization and Its Discontents* he presents love as capable of subduing violence and enhancing the separateness of people, enabling relationships to function as the foundation of our joint work and civilization. In this sense, love, or *eros,* is not only discrete, but a cultural and political force, enhancing worldliness rather than withdrawal from the world.

Juxtaposing Arendt and Freud highlights the relationship between love, forgiveness, and *amor mundi.* Love is necessary in enabling people to think. People who are kept from loving will be kept from thinking. Arendt has Socrates and Thoreau in mind when theorizing about thinking. Thinking people are in dialogue with themselves, not just with others, and this inner dialogue informs their actions in the public sphere. Inner dialogue causes the thinker to take conscience into consideration before s/he acts: "[Thinkers] do not say what to do; they say what not to do. [. . .] [T]hey lay down boundaries no act should transgress. They say: Don't do wrong, for then you will have to live together with a wrongdoer" (Arendt 1969, 63).

If, as Arendt claims, totalitarian regimes eliminate love at the same time that they eliminate plurality, we can better understand Arendt's view of *the banality of evil.* Eichmann's crimes against humanity and his failure to understand his guilt are the result of his inability to think, to engage in an inner dialogue that forces him to accept that there are limits to how badly he (or anyone) is allowed to harm the Other. In both Freud and Arendt's perspectives, prohibiting love institutes an incapacity to think and activate one's conscience.[1]

---

[1] A famous paper by the British psychoanalyst Wilfred Bion (1962) explains that thinking is associated with the development of a container for thoughts in the infant. This development means that the infant is able to endure frustration through thinking, for frustration is an undesirable libidinal stimulus and this irritation is checked when the person engages in thinking. The infant first encounters frustration when s/he is suckled, and therefore the development of the capacity

Although Arendt describes the thinker as conscientious, she does not clearly relate the birth of conscience to love, as Freud does. On the contrary, she argues that "the habit of thinking, of reflecting on what one is doing, is independent of the individual's social, educational, or intellectual standing" (Arendt 1969, 65). Arendt neither excludes the possibility that inner dialogue projects love, nor does she affirm the necessity of introjected love for the existence of inner dialogue. I aim to show that, without love, the relationship between humans and the world is swayed by interdictions of the obscene superego, engenders anxiety and doubt. Below, I focus on Arendt's biography of Rahel Varnhagen, as a way to more closely examine the role of both intimate love and love interests in the social sphere of the German Enlightenment.

## Lovers of the world

It is no coincidence that Arendt's and Freud's works on love were written at just about the same time. *Love and Saint Augustine* was published in 1929, *Civilization and Its Discontents* in 1930. Freud's text studies the role of the divine decree, 'love thy neighbor as thyself,' in the formation of communities and nations. Arendt questions "the relevance of the neighbor" (Arendt 1996, x). In a 1946 letter to Karl Jaspers she describes their mutual commitment to philosophy as follows: "what it all comes down to is that we're trying for the first time and in all seriousness to turn the universum into the mundus, if I may go back to the old Augustine once again" (Arendt and Jaspers 1992, 50). I understand this to mean that Arendt's phi-

---

to think is directly related to the formation of the bods of love. Thinking begins in the psychic and somatic healthy relationship with the good-enough mother and, by extension, within the family. The same structure that parents can activate when they teach children to cope with the world through experimentation, playing, and thinking is differently described by Melanie Klein and D. W. Winnicott, but for both of them thinking and love are connected. Klein discusses a schizoid position in which the infant vacillates between envy of her/his environment and gratitude toward the world that sustains her/him. As the child matures, s/he internalizes the love that will enable the adult to feel more integrated, when both envy and gratitude accompany her/him in her/his various social interactions. Winnicott construes a paradox that the good-enough mother accepts without forcing the infant to decide if s/he creates the world or if the world precedes her/his desire and its fulfillment. The infant is allowed to feel omnipotent and creative in relation to objects that s/he finds around her/him, despite the fact that these objects define the limits of the infant's ability to act in reality. Fantasy is of major importance to Klein and illusion/disillusionment is central to Winnicott. Both of these states institute and are equal to checking sadistic impulses and to choosing love, for love facilitates the development of thinking and thereby the integration of the self even under harsh circumstances. See Klein 1975, 1–24 and Winnicott 1984, 140–152.

losophy is focused on humanizing the physics of the universe through love, and through thought that guides action.

In *Civilization and Its Discontents*, Freud says:

> Love with an inhibited aim was in fact originally fully sensual love, and it is so still in man's unconscious. Both – fully sensual love and aim-inhibited love – extend outside the family and create new bonds with people who before were strangers. Genital love leads to the formation of new families, and aim-inhibited love to 'friendships' which become valuable from a cultural standpoint because they escape some of the limitations of genital love, as, for instance, its exclusiveness. But in the course of development the relation of love to civilization loses its unambiguity. On the one hand love comes into opposition to the interests of civilization; on the other, civilization threatens love with substantial restrictions (Freud 1961, 58).

Freudian psychoanalysis presumes that civilization is grounded in love. However, with the development of both the unconscious and the ego, this relation of love to civilization becomes complicated. Both genital love and aim-inhibited love are valuable to the conversation concerning forgiveness and *amor mundi*:

> It [civilization] aims at binding the members of the community together in a libidinal way as well and employs every means to that end. It favours every path by which strong identifications can be established between the members of the community, and it summons up aim-inhibited libido on the largest scale so as to strengthen the communal bond by relations of friendship (Freud 1961, 65).

Civilization deploys libidinal love for its own preservation. But how? How does civilization benefit from the libidinal energy that circulates in culture?

Loving the Other coincides with respect for plurality and is basic to forgiveness. Victims remain capable of love, despite the unforgiveable injuries that brought about their justified resentment. This is at the heart of psychoanalytical and political explorations of "worldliness," and constitute the core of Freud's and Arendt's theories of the private and public spheres. Although Arendt rejects the possibility that love can be functional in the public sphere, I will show that her analysis of forgiveness points otherwise.

Love and forgiveness are instances of sublimation. They enable one to love one's neighbor as one loves oneself.[2] Forgiveness is, in fact, a gift of love, and is

---

2 Although it seems that in Arendt's correspondence with Gershom Scholem she rejects the possibility that love can be functional in the public sphere, I suggest that love is structurally relevant to the public sphere. (Scholem 2002, 394). Love is a primary affect and an event in the lives of human beings. Without love we cannot fully experience ourselves as alive, we cannot reply to the question "am I alive?" with "yes!" Human rights do not subsume only those phallus-oriented rights, such as autonomy, knowledge, and justice, but are also concerned with desires that are fundamental to the development of healthy, socially active human beings. Chief among these desires are love and empathy. Jonathan Lear views psychoanalysis as a system that produces love

split between the unworldly, the transcendental, and the worldly. 'Love thy neighbor' requires human beings to saturate communal ties with aim-inhibited, libidinal love. And yet this decree is perplexing for Freud. He asks, "Why should we do it? What good will it do to us? But, above all, how should we achieve it? How can it be possible?" (ibid, 66). In reply to these questions, Freud argues that people only willingly support laws that enable them to keep nearby the objects of their love. People support laws that increase their sense of safety. Conversely, 'love thy neighbor as thyself' is essentially about creating a new language, a language of sublimation. Culture symbolizes the human desire for sublimated love relations with others. According to this interpretation, sublimation is not a defense mechanism of the unconscious, like repression, but a function of the ego that enhances the availability of *Eros* – desire and love – to consciousness.[3]

Freud's study of sublimation takes into account aggression and hatred of the Other. Freud turns to Hobbes, who famously argues that, because humans protect their solitude, they are inherently hostile to each other, and that, left to our own devices and to our nature, humanity would inevitably devolve into a war of all against all – *Homo homini lupus*:[4] "Who, in the face of all his experience of life and of history, will have the courage to dispute this assertion?" (Freud 1961, 69). According to Freud, civilization inoculates us against our inherent propensity towards oppression:

---

and binds it to sublimation in each and every act of interpretation that the analyst and the analysand undertake. Empathy and love coincide with each other: "It [interpretation] is a conceptualization that is lovingly directed toward and in touch with its 'object.' A good-enough interpretation is thus structured like an emotion. For the interpretation is itself sublimation, an organized manifestation of love, and it is lovingly directed toward the drives which are less organized manifestations. The acceptance and internalization of a good-enough interpretation is part of an emotional reorientation toward one's inner and outer world" (Lear 1990, 213–14).

**3** Sublimation is a difficult Freudian concept. Laplanche and Pontalis criticize Freud's conviction that, "this capacity to exchange its originally sexual aim for another one, which is no longer sexual but which is psychically related to the first aim, is called the capacity for sublimation." They argue that "Freud's formulations regarding sublimation were never very far reaching [. . .] For example, does it include all work involving thought or merely certain types of intellectual production?" They ask if sublimation is given high social esteem or if it covers the realm of adaptive activities including work and leisure. What poses difficulty is "the question [. . .] whether it [sublimation] concerns the aim alone, as Freud long maintained, or both the aim and the object of the instinct" (Laplanche and Pontalis 1973, 432).

**4** "Hereby it is manifest, that during the time men live without a common Power to keep them all in awe, they are in that condition which is called Warre; and such a warre, as is of every man, against every man" (Hobbes [1651] 1909, 96).

> Civilization has to use its utmost efforts in order to set limits to man's aggressive instincts and to hold manifestations of them in check by psychical reaction-formation. Hence, therefore, the use of methods intended to incite people into identifications and aim-inhibited relationships of love, hence the restriction upon sexual life, and hence too the ideal's commandment to love one's neighbour as thyself – a commandment which is really justified by the fact that nothing else runs so strongly counter to the original nature of man (ibid, 70).

It is clear that Freud views psychoanalysis as more than a diagnostic tool for the individual, as a tool capable of engendering an ethical imperative for civilization. As a corollary to this, however, communities and nations must also offer relatively safe outlets for human aggression. It is imperative that people be permitted to *fight* one another. Conflict is necessary.

According to Freud, arrangements that allow for neighborly, reciprocal pestering are often present among distinct communities that have much in common, "like the Spaniards and the Portuguese, for instance, the North Germans and South Germans, the English and Scotch, and so on. I gave this phenomenon the name of 'the narcissism of minor differences'" (ibid, 72). Freud notes that the Jewish people present an interesting phenomenon: dispersed among so many different nations in Europe, they are a unified people. At the same time, as the perceived enemy of Christian Europe, the Jewish presence serves to unify their host nations through their shared hatred of the Jews. Thus the Jews of Europe are the victims of a violence that emerges from the "narcissism of minor differences."[5] Often, social bonds emerge not out of mutual love but out of hatred.

While love is directed at an object, it is also directed at the ego. This triggers conflict between love of the neighbor and self-love. What does one do if the welfare of the community calls for restraining desire in order to win the community's respect? How does one learn to accept another's plan of action, her/his rise to power in the community? Freud stresses that object-love succeeds when the object reflects the image of an ideal ego. Hence, narcissism and object-love have something in common. In the public sphere, an actor who is capable of both love and thinking can acknowledge the superiority of, and collaborate with the actions taken by, the neighbor, the one who, under certain circumstances, is seen as an ideal ego.

---

5 In 1938, before the Second World War breaks out, Freud recognizes that Thanatos too can combine humans into larger units, which can be murderous as well as bonding. But here the death drive is active, not Eros: "We live in very remarkable times. We find with astonishment that progress has concluded an alliance with barbarism . . . It was a real weight off the heart to find, in the case of the German people, that retrogression into all but prehistoric barbarism can come to pass independently of any progressive idea" (Freud, 1939, 53).

Freud insists that "civilization is a process in the service of *eros*, whose purpose is to combine single human individuals, and after that families, then races, people and nations, into the great unity, the unity of mankind. [. . .] These collections of men are to be libidinally bound to one another. Necessity alone, the advantages of work in common, will not hold them together" (ibid, 82). In this context, 'love thy neighbor as thyself' is a means for civilization to provide an outlet for the libidinal bonds of love that pervade society.

Melanie Klein uses the term "gratitude" rather than kindness. In the family and in the public sphere, envy or anger may surface when one is thwarted by another. At the same time, gratitude emerges when one appreciates the increased personal and social benefits of the ties that are forged through accepting that others may justifiably correct one or keep one's selfishness in check. "Love thy neighbor" enforces libidinal bonds, so that the libidinal energy does not turn to violence.

According to Adam Philips and Barbara Taylor, kindness is not sublimated love, but, like love, it is an id impulse that enhances identification with the Other's vulnerability: "When God is dead, kindness is permitted. When God is dead, kindness is all that people have left" (Philips and Taylor 2009, 13). Klein also sees gratitude as belonging to the realm of unconscious emotions. Only later in life does gratitude become a conscious mechanism to help maintain self-integration under trying social circumstance. Daniel Stern describes a range of emotions that the infant has to become acquainted with before being ready to acknowledge friendship, one of the most important attachments that love transforms to in the public sphere, according to Arendt:

> The infant first has to learn to be with someone and to create and share the experiences that a relationship is built on. Beside the gratification of feeding and warmth, these involve the mutual creation of shared pleasure, joy, interest, curiosity, thrills, awe, fright, boredom, laughter, surprise, delight, peaceful moments, silences resolving distress, and many other such illusive phenomena and experiences that make up the stuff of friendship and love (Stern, 91–92).

Though Stern does not mention it, Freud highlights how sublimation transforms infantile love into a love of knowledge and art, which are both practiced in the social and political sphere with friends and peers. As Arendt shows, love of art and knowledge transpires in the public sphere at the same time that it contributes to the creation of the public sphere.[6]

---

[6] See Arendt's discussion of the institution of the "Salon" in *Rahel Varnhagen: The Life of A Jewess*.

I will return to this theme below, when I discuss Arendt's biography of Rahel Varnhagen, for in it Arendt examines the kind of public figure that Rahel becomes once she relinquishes true love, and adopts instead a love that is socially beneficial. Rahel gives up on love in the private sphere because every love is also public, and her true love does not win the public's consent. But she accepts in the private sphere a love that appears socially valuable, because this compromised love brings private advantage. I nonetheless focus on Freud, who recognizes the connection between sublimation and the taboo on incestuous love, where incestuous love defines the very border between what is not yet, and what is already, culture.

Endogamy, which is not necessarily incestuous, is harmful to society, while exogamy is socially and politically valuable. The transition from endogamy to exogamy is a form of sublimation, since sublimation inculcates exogamous sexual bonds. Yet sublimated sexual function can advance culture in the fields of science and art as well. Laplanche and Pontalis suggest that one possible function of sexuality is that non-sexual functions "must serve as paths for the attraction of sexual instinctual forces to aims that are other than sexual, that is to say, for the sublimation of sexuality" (Laplanche and Pontalis 1973, 433).

For Freud, Leonardo Da Vinci was a genius because he "represented the cool repudiation of sexuality" (Freud 1985, 158). In "Leonardo Da Vinci: A Memory of His Childhood," Freud's Leonardo is incapable of *falling* in love. He first carefully studies the object. Only if he knows that the object is worthy is he then able to love it.[7] Freud believes that, if one initially devotes one's passion to knowing the object, and only later to loving it, one begins to love knowledge more than the sexual body. From this logic emerges what I would call "the law of sublimation":

---

7 In Leonardo's case, it would be incorrect to quote Shakespeare who says that "Love looks not with the eye, but with the mind, and therefore is winged cupid painted blind," for using the eyes of a painter Leonardo examines the object carefully before he can love it. See Shakespeare 1997, Act 1, Scene 1, Line 234. Arendt too is pushed to the limit when she allows that love increases our capacity to observe the world, does not reduce our ability to see the different perspectives that each actor holds in the political sphere. If as I argue above, those who revert to inner dialogue are not afraid of civil disobedience because in civil disobedience they use conscience to advance the good of all then dissent is related to sublimated love. The one who undertakes resistance pays with his freedom so that the public sphere will not settle for less than the ethical, good action. Arendt writes: "The civil disobedient, though he is usually dissenting from a majority, acts in the name and for the sake of a group" (Arendt 1963, 76). Arendt does not use the words love or sublimated love but describes the phenomenon of self-sacrifice for the benefit of society based on ethical considerations. I will show that this conduct involves love and that thinkers contemporary to Arendt expose the necessary relation of love to politics in their political interviews and writings. Most famous is the correspondence between Arendt and James Baldwin and her correspondence with Ralph Ellison. The first concerns the place of love in politics and the latter the place of sacrifice in politics. See Arendt 1962 and Arendt cited in Aavitsland 2019, 543.

"the postponement of loving until full knowledge is acquired ends in a substitution of the latter for the former. A man who has won his way to a state of knowledge cannot properly be said to love and hate; he remains beyond love and hatred" (Freud 1985, 165). Such a person is more inclined to extend recognition to the Other, because to acknowledge the Other is a form of expanding one's knowledge of the world. Sublimation ensures that strong affects toward the Other are subordinate to symbolization. Leonardo loves the object through studying it and through painting the object as loved, representing his knowledge on the canvas.

This explains why virtually all of da Vinci's paintings are unfinished. His interest in dissected animals, anatomy, mechanics, flying, and astronomy led him to acquire a thorough knowledge of the subjects of his paintings. This in turn rendered him unable to feel aroused by the sensuality of these objects/subjects, and thus, incapable of completing the paintings. Instead of reacting to a visceral, sensual pull, Leonardo studied the objects with his faculty of reason. His preoccupation with such knowledge affected his ability to create.

In order to elaborate his theory of sublimation, which values symbolic interaction with objects, Freud hones in on a particular memory from da Vinci's childhood, recorded in the artist's diary. By exploring this memory, Freud seeks to demonstrate that Leonardo's libido was enhanced rather than inhibited by his attachment to his mother. Leonardo writes about being an infant in the cradle when a vulture came into the room and struck him several times, cutting open his lips with its tail. For Freud, this recollection is a fantasy that registers the pleasure Leonardo felt while being suckled by his mother. According to Freud, the image also suggests that a penis was inserted into the infant's mouth. Freud's interpretation taps into Egyptian mythology, in which the goddess Mut was represented as a vulture. More importantly, vultures were believed to be exclusively female in Egyptian lore, and that they were inseminated by the wind. Several fathers of the Catholic Church used this legend to show that it is possible that Mary, too, was impregnated by the wind.

Egyptian sculptures depict vultures with both breasts and penises. For Freud, the male child believes that both his parents have penises, and only later in life does he come to the realization that a maternal penis does not exist. The androgynous vulture represents potent maternity. Freud was aware of the fact that Leonardo grew up without a father during the first five years of his life, and assumes that Leonardo's mother would have lavished tender sexual kisses on his mouth, which is why his memory conjures up feelings of being *sucked* rather than of being *suckled*. The infant is passive. He is in a homosexual posture in relation to the vulture, and takes the metaphorical penis or tail into his mouth, enjoying the repeated strikes (or strokes).

This childhood memory/fantasy is fascinating in and of itself, but the reason it is relevant to my argument is that it shows that an unconscious grid enables people to mature along a matrix of intersubjective or relational contacts with the Other. This psychosomatic grid both enhances and limits people's perceptions and, as a result, their actions in the world. The unconscious reservoir of passions and desires can nourish private love and spontaneous action in public. When affects are sublimated, thinking intervenes.

As love is not enslaved by either passion or desire, but operates for the benefit of the family and the council (a political concept that Arendt embraces), it splits into the kind of love that discloses *who* one is and the kind that allows *what* one is to come into effect. In its two different forms, love thereby enhances the creation of aim-inhibited bonds of friendship and respect. Spontaneous action in the political realm is structured by screen memories, not just by conscious thinking. These screen memories produce lucid judgments, but they also set free judgments that are based on prejudices.

When we take into consideration how Leonardo's paintings stage the mouth as the site of enigma, the sensual childhood memory becomes a moment of sublimation. Freud concludes that "only a man who had had Leonardo's childhood experiences could have painted the Mona Lisa and the St. Anne [. . .] as if the key to all his achievements and misfortunes lay hidden in the childhood fantasy of the vulture" (Freud 1985, 230). It seems to me that Freud sees the sexual origin of beauty as the most meaningful aspect of symbolic representation in Leonardo's oeuvre. His fixation on the mouths of women indicates that his symbolic language is aimed towards investigating the secret of love.

Arendt argues that political action is always spontaneous, which leads to my contention that political action emerges out of the possibility that unconscious drives, like eros or thanatos, bear on persons' interaction with the Other. If one's passions and desires are sublimated, then, in their symbolic appearance – speech, forgiveness, making promises, and action – they allow one to critically evaluate the meaning of spontaneity. How we act can change when we speak to people we trust, or when we try to imagine why we do not trust some people. Sublimated love does not lose sight of particularity. It does not destroy spontaneity, while spontaneity does not lose sight of universalism. One's political judgment can change based on trusting in other people's ability to articulate new perspectives on political questions.

## The politics of love

Arendt's most explicit discussion of love occurs in her dissertation on Augustine. Hans Jonas, Arendt's friend and colleague, thought that Augustine appealed to her because "both Heidegger and Jaspers turned to such thinkers" (quoted in Arendt, 1996, xv). It is important to remember the circumstances under which Arendt and Freud were writing their books. Both *Love and Saint Augustine* and *Civilization and Its Discontents* were composed between the two World Wars. Surely, the economic difficulties of the time, as well as the increasingly prevalent nationalist and racist rhetoric, prompted these thinkers to examine love's ability to propel culture and politics.

For Augustine, love is the means of transcendence: humans are estranged from the world because their origin is in God. Through love there is a return to the world. Arendt vacillates about whether or not love can play a constructive role in the public sphere of human plurality. She can accept love when it enhances plurality and protects diversity, but not when love is structurally abused, made to collapse difference into sameness. This is why, as I mentioned earlier, Arendt cannot accept the Christian vantage point that love requires a choice between betraying the world and seeing every Other as equally loved, because God loves all His creatures equally.

For Arendt, "love, in distinction from friendship, is killed, or rather extinguished, the moment it is displayed in public. ('Never seek to tell thy love / Love that never told can be.') Because of its inherent worldlessness, love can only become false and perverted when it is used for political purposes such as the change or salvation of the world" (Arendt 1958, 51–2). When love is only interested in *what* a person is, then the humanity of the Other is at risk. In social life, people can act in concert despite their differences because they choose to uphold the compound structure of love and remember *who*, not just *what*, a person is.

Arendt differentiates between carnal and divine love – that is, between *cupiditas* (passionate love) and *caritas* (love of God). As Augustine examines the world from the vantage point of loss, he finds that love directed at the outward is bound to produce unhappiness. In *cupiditas*, either the lover or the loved one dies, introducing pain to life. And yet the value of *cupiditas* is that it enables human beings to become "lovers of the world" (Arendt 1996, 17). Human beings come to transform the world into an inhabitable place by loving it and by living in it: "So the world consists of those who love it. [. . .] [I]t is the human world, which constitutes itself by habitation and love. [. . .] Love of the world, which makes it 'worldly,' rests on being 'of the world'" (ibid, 66).

Worldliness is tightly related to *amor mundi*, or to sublimated love. Human beings do not exactly fit the world. They are in a state of temporality, not simultaneity, in relation to the world. I understand this to mean that, in the world, desire is neither satisfied nor annihilated, but that, in *amor mundi*, humans recognize that they always remain foreign in the world that they create. In the same vein, the couple in a love relationship are together, and yet infinitely separate and different from each other. Love does not turn two lovers into a single being. Love does not eliminate the lack that emerges from both sadistic impulses and gratitude.

It is important to remember that the body politic is interested in structural, not personal, changes, yet it relies on personal, spontaneous, unique action and thought, not just on the universal law that dictates uniform action.[8] To reformulate what Arendt calls "the worldlessness of love" in Freudian terms: "[A] pair of lovers are sufficient to themselves, and do not even need the child they have in common to make them happy. In no other case does *Eros* so clearly betray the core of his being, his purpose of making one out of more than one; but when he has achieved this in the proverbial way through the love of two human beings, he refuses to go further" (Freud 1961, 65). Once the couple has a child, they are forced back into the social and political sphere (the education system, making a living, etc.), and must contend with the advantages and disadvantages each one of them brings to social and political life.

In *The Human Condition*, Arendt clarifies the moral structure of love and forgiveness. Forgiveness is a faculty that can free the individual from the consequences of a wrong done on purpose or by accident – it relies on plurality, on acting together with others. The faculty of forgiving "rests on experiences which nobody could ever have with himself, which, on the contrary, are entirely based on the presence of others" (Arendt 1958, 238). The structure of forgiveness is caught up in the same complexity as the structure of love:

> Forgiving and the relationship it establishes is always an eminently personal (though not necessarily individual or private) affair in which *what* was done is forgiven for the sake of *who* did it [. . .] and it is the reason for the current conviction that only love has the power to forgive [. . .] love [. . .] indeed possesses an unequaled power of self-revelation and unequaled clarity of vision for the disclosure of *who*, precisely because it is unconcerned, to the point of unworldliness with *what* the loved person may be, with his qualities and shortcomings no less then with his achievements, failings, and transgressions (ibid, 241–242).

The unworldly or transcendental aspects of love and forgiveness affect the world. The personal realization of *who* the Other is transforms the burden of *what* the crime is. Surely, love may fail, and a perpetrator may be denied forgiveness, but the humanity of both can remain. Love and forgiveness transcend the world.

---

[8] For an inclusive study of Arendt's interpretation of Augustine, see Kampowski (2008).

They inspire moral considerations in the social sphere and open potentials for just action in politics.[9]

*Cupiditas* is not of the world. It is the love that will disappear with the death of man. The love that looks for eternal things is *caritas*. It is strange to refer to sexuality as evil and to sublimation as good, yet Arendt understands religion as accepting procreation, not romantic love, for the sake of mutual narcissism. By the same token, *caritas*, good deeds, or the Jewish concept of *tzedakah*, are seen as good because they practice sublimated love in a wholly altruistic fashion. The evil deeds that human beings bring into the world emerge from *cupiditas*, where people become love objects for each other, while the roots of good deeds are sunk deep in *caritas*, where people are pure subjects, despite the fact that both kinds of love emerge from a lack that is exposed to the world when people forge relations of love. *Cupiditas* fuels the human propensity to commit evil because it legitimizes a narcissistic craving for an object-world. In craving one misses one's aim, the self that aspires to unite with God, and thus exist beyond objectivity.

Another name for man's unity with God is "neighborly love" – that is, extending sublimated, ideal love to the neighbor regardless of the neighbor's particularity. Neighborly love substitutes a good will that can grant and attain freedom for narcissistic love. *Cupiditas* is hostile to the good will because it imposes its ego onto the world. A spirit that is interested in objects desires "its own good" (Arendt 1996, 21), that is, sexual desire. A spirit immersed in *caritas* is interested in universal ethics, in the good for all.

Augustine believes that we can love our Creator even if God is outside of us. For Augustine, *caritas* is the only love of the good, "the love that is shed in our hearts" (ibid, 22). We share in Being if we do not share in want, which means that we are fearless. But as long as man is fearful, freedom is "essentially freedom from fear" (ibid, 23). "What do I love when I love *my* God?," asks Augustine. He answers that to love God is to love the essence of being, since God is internal in the sense that God is the good that I lack. Love of God confers being, and the "inner man" loves God "because his proper good is in the eternal" (Arendt 1996, 26). Indeed, to be free is to belong to eternity, but the split between *cupiditas* and sublimated love recurs. In order to love God, man must hate his self, which is attached to earthly objects that are subject to death.

It is in this context that Arendt discusses 'love thy neighbor as thyself.' This is the worldliness important to both her and Freud. Love eliminates the situation of

---

[9] Jankélévitch associates this worldlessness or transcendence of forgiveness and love with a wager on innocence. It is the innocence of the one who loves/forgives despite the wickedness and because of the wickedness integral in the Other. This wager follows in the footsteps of Pascal's wager on faith. See Jankélévitch 2005, 147.

being "godforsaken" in the world. Love that manifests craving can be a vehicle for the attachment of man to God. In love of the neighbor we engage with the questions "Who is my neighbor? [. . .] Who is next to me?" (Arendt 1996, 43). The reply clarifies that my neighbor is a person just like me, which implies that all human beings are siblings. *Cupiditas*, or covetous love, is a necessary evil, which prevails in and defines mortality, if only because covetousness enhances procreation. On the other hand, "the freedom of *caritas* is a future freedom. It consists of anticipating a future belonging for which love as desire is the mediator. The sign of *caritas* on earth is fearlessness, whereas the curse of *cupiditas* is fear – fear of not obtaining what is desired and fear of losing it once it is obtained" (Arendt 1996, 35).

'Love thy neighbor as thyself' also means that the neighbor puts a limit to *amor sui*, or self-love. I must not love my neighbor more than I love myself, which is to say that love of the neighbor is not an end in itself. Rather, the neighbor is my equal and I must love my neighbor for the sake of a higher good, which is love of God. This is also why I must love my enemy, for the enemy, too, is my neighbor, and I cannot choose between people, but must love all my neighbors equally.[10] All of this serves to highlight the fact that love is uneven. Temporality manifests itself as future hope and as recollections from the lost past.

Happiness, however, according to Augustine, is something that each person has experienced in the past. In order to be happy in the future, one must recall the happiness that one experienced before, when the "I" belonged to God. Each person is dependent on God, and because s/he recalls that God is eternal, s/he has a notion of happiness in the world of mortality.[11] The way to discern God is through recollection and not through desire, since God exists in our consciousness: "What ultimately stills the fear of death is not hope or desire, but remembrance and gratitude" (Arendt 1996, 52). In psychoanalysis, remembering is crucial to the development of the subject, whereas repetitive acts are destructive to the individual and to civilization (Freud 1914, 151; 153).

Arendt's, "Report from Germany" and *The Human Condition* promote remembering and reject repeating or acting out. Arendt stood against Germany's attempt to suppress what happened during the years of National Socialism in the 1940's and 50s. She began to offer difficult forgiveness to Germany by the end of the 50's and the beginning of the 60's, when the discussion of German guilt became more

---

10 In *Civilization and Its Discontents*, Freud declares that "love thine enemy" is a greater imposition than "love thy neighbor as thyself" (Freud 1961, 67).
11 In psychoanalytical terms, we might say that this is an instance of original oneness between sexual passion and the divine, which enriches the experience of the sacred or of the love of God. See Loewald 1988, 11.

urgent, in part because of the strengthening diplomatic ties between Chancellor Konrad Adenauer and Israeli Prime Minister David Ben Gurion, but also thanks to the Eichmann trial in Jerusalem and the Frankfurt Auschwitz trials.

In order to attain God, one recalls the past and thus imitates God. Human love is based on imitation, and love of God educates the quality of imitation: "[I]mitation can be actualized explicitly through love: 'They loved by believing; they imitated by loving'" (Arendt 1996, 54). What Arendt stresses in her reading of Augustine is the fact that the human being is a principle of newness in the world, because natality, or being born, means that s/he remembers her/his origins. Each person expresses the principle of natality in interaction with the Other by imparting earthly love. For Arendt, friendship and forgiveness are forms of worldly love. For Freud, they are forms of sublimated love. Regardless, they create the world by encouraging community. This, transforming post-Holocaust Germany into a community, was the all-but-impossible task Arendt, and all of German society, faced in the 1950s and 1960s.

The world is inhabited by those who love it, who keep it going through love. Heaven and earth become the world through our love of the world. But this is not creation *ex nihilo*, for we create with divine material, *fabrica dei*. We use heaven and earth, that is, God's creation, to re-create. There is a Kabbalistic/Chasidic notion that God is constantly in the act of recreating the universe, that were it not for his continuous reiteration of the words that brought the universe into being, the world would cease to exist. The human being loves God through loving the world, even though s/he is a foreigner in the world (Arendt 1996, 66).

It follows from the above that estrangement from the world precedes love.[12] The human being is subject to the law 'thou shalt not covet,' which means that love of the world for its own sake is denied to humans. From this estrangement emerge the politics of love. To be foreign in the world is to realize that one is a soul, or has a spirit, and nurturing that spirit is dependent on denying the passions. While *cupiditas* follows the demands of the passions, *caritas* propels spiritual pursuits. Good deeds project *charitas*, which must remain secret. Socratic civil disobedience is public, and thus it falls under the logic of *caritas* and not *cupiditas*.

---

[12] In a famous passage in *Civilization and Its Discontents*, Freud mentions his friend Roman Roland, who understands the religious *weltanschauung* as an *oceanic* existence where he is at one with the world. Freud interprets this *oceanic* feeling to mean that his friend is absorbed by an infantile, narcissistic fantasy/memory of unity with the mother. I suggest that Arendt's interpretation of a return to God, which love brings into effect, is similarly caught up in an unclear difference between the fantasy and the memory of unity. In psychoanalysis, unity with the mother gives way to frustration when she teaches the baby to contain lack by introducing her/him to a symbolic system of what is allowed and what is not. In Arendt's interpretation of Augustine's system, God supports man by enabling him to learn the difference between carnal and divine love, and thereby sustain the lack that he experiences as a foreigner in the world.

Arendt advances the Augustinian claim that the developed person loves her/his fellow through the exercise of self-denial. In this sense, human beings must betray the world, as they interdict the satisfaction of desire as self-satisfaction, despite the fact that the world seduces all to reach out and satisfy craving. The politics of love is moral when one betrays the world but remains loyal to one's higher ideals. The paradox of love means that the call for betrayal of the world actually testifies to genuine love of the world. Grace enhances sublimated love. This poses a problem for Arendt, who does not see love of the Other as mediated through the love of God.

Arendt conceives of political action in plurality as a complex affair, because people act on the basis of universal principles like justice, freedom, and fraternity, while also driven by personal traits and desires. One individual is more courageous, another is smarter, another is entering the life of friendship and politics – Achilles, say, Odysseus, Telemachus. We remember the differences between these characters, thereby focusing on *who* the individual is and not just on *what* he achieved. Culture remembers singularity, individuality. It does not deny love to the individual, nor does it allow singularity to be consumed by universality.

Totalitarianism denies singularity. It coerces all to deny private and social love in favor of blind conformity to the State. This is the paradox that Arendt wrestles with when she proposes "two questions: first, how does the self-denying person meet his neighbor?; and second, in this encounter, what is the neighbor's role?" (Arendt 1996, 93).

In friendship and in politics, the neighbor is respected, or receives the support of others, because of personal traits that attract others to him. But, according to Augustine, one loves the neighbor because one loves God – that is, one loves neighbor and enemy regardless of *who* they are, simply because of *what* they are, because they are human. The opposite approach is typical of totalitarian states, which reduce individuals to superfluity and deny the sanctity of our shared humanity. Forgiveness can exist only in a democracy, where *who* one is supplements *what* one expresses, in speech and action in the public sphere. Radical evil, which Arendt later describes as "the banality of evil," can come into being when the neighbor has no singular traits, for it is the bureaucratic practices of the State that dictate what it means to be human.

In this context I want to briefly turn to Freud's *Moses and Monotheism*. I want to understand how Freud, in this theoretical, experimental, psychoanalytical historical *novel*, explains the bonds that keep the Jewish people strong as a nation, not just as a religion. Freud does not find sublimated love to be a form of belief in God, but rather a form of neighborly love, or aim-inhibited public love, that strengthens cooperation between people. Freud connects the Mosaic interdiction on the creation of an image to an appeal to a higher, more abstract intellectuality. This interdiction is not related to love of God, but to love of the human numinous, the faculty of thinking.

According to Freud, their symbolic distance from God gave the Jewish people a valuable treasure: "The nation's political misfortune taught it to value its true worth the one possession that remained to it – its literature. Immediately after the destruction of the Temple in Jerusalem by Titus, the Rabbi Jochanan ben Zakkai asked permission to open the first Torah school in Jabneh. From that time on the Holy Writ and intellectual concern with it were what held the sacred people together" (Freud 1939, 114). Not the belief in God but the actual studying of the *Torah*, *Halachah*, and *Haggadah*, forges an intellectual bond of neighborly love between the Jews, who are dispersed among all the nations. This neighborly love restores trust and hope in humankind, for both Arendt and Freud.

I recognize Arendt's serendipitous agreement with Freud in a reply to Gershom Scholem. Scholem feels "rage" toward Arendt after he finishes reading *Eichmann in Jerusalem*, because, he says, she does not love the Jewish people: "what the Jews call *ahavat Israel*, or love of the Jewish people. With you, my dear Hannah, as with so many intellectuals coming from the German left, there is no trace of it" (Scholem 2002, 396). In her reply, Arendt insists that "the role of the 'heart' in politics [. . .] strikes me as highly dubious." On the other hand she affirms her love for the Jewish people, on the grounds that this people know how to love something higher than themselves. This people are not interested in *cupiditas*, nor in God as a symbol of harsh retribution: "the magnificence of this people once lay in its belief in God – that is, in the way its trust and love of God far outweighed its fear of God. And now this people believes only in itself. In this sense I don't love the Jews, nor do I 'believe' in them. I *belong* to this people, in nature and in fact" (Arendt 2002, 399). Arendt accepts that Judaism propels the Jews to trust one another. Neighborly love leads to trust among people, not to blind faith in, nor fear of, punishment from a wrathful God.

## Love in plurality

In *The Human Condition*, Arendt discusses religious love in the context of good works. Religious love is related to Arendt's study of human affairs, specifically with regards to doing good in the public sphere. Christianity ordains that one must perform acts of goodness in secret, for when good is done in public it loses its goodness. Arendt asserts that the doer must not be a witness to her/his own good-doing: "[G]ood deeds can never keep anybody company; they must be forgotten the moment they are done, because even memory will destroy their quality of being 'good.'[. . .] Good works, because they must be forgotten instantly, can never become part of the world; they come and go, leaving no trace. They truly are not of this world" (Arendt 1958, 76). Love's effects, likewise, should not be made public.

Goodness and sublimation are activities that the self performs in the form of an internal dialogue: "The otherworldliness of religious experience, in so far as it is truly the experience of love in the sense of an activity, and not the much more frequent one of beholding passively a revealed truth, manifests itself within the world itself; this, like all other activities does not leave the world, but must be performed within it (Arendt 1958, 77). Paradoxically, true goodness negates the political sphere: "[G]oodness that comes out of its hiding and assumes a public role is no longer good, but corrupt in its own terms and will carry its own corruption wherever it goes" (Arendt 1958, 78). This coalesces with the feeling that forgiveness is not equal to reconciliation, for forgiveness belongs to morality and the good, while reconciliation is political, and structured on agreements and interests.

It is difficult to comprehend why Arendt is inspecting the lover of good deeds from the position of the benefactor – the one who must not know of her/his deed. Unlike *cupiditas*, neighborly love does leave a trace in the world. In psychoanalytic terms, the emotional consequences of good deeds influence the receiver, and s/he is swayed to feel gratitude for the good that is done to her/him.

Peg Birmingham's analysis becomes useful in understanding Arendt's distinction between the transcendental and the historical good. In *Hannah Arendt and Human Rights*, she focuses on the difference between good works and carnal love. Because she wants to articulate what is human in a human being, Birmingham stresses that every person is unique and cannot be subsumed by universal laws. A person's radical alterity is irreducible to either the objective world or to divine, transcendental origin:

> Arendt points out that when Augustine grasps that God is "the essence of the heart," he discovers a radical alterity that marks the self "at the heart of the self, that which is in me but is not me." For both Augustine and Arendt, desire and questioning arise out of a double negative that characterizes the givenness of human existence in time: "This questioning beyond the world rests on the double negative into which life is placed. And this double negative (the 'not yet' and the 'no more') means exactly the same as 'before' and 'after' in the world." This generative origin that cannot be remembered or reclaimed in desire nevertheless gives rise to memory, desire, and meaning. Memory, desire, and meaning are suffused with this generative origin that cannot itself be explicitly recalled or possessed" (Birmingham 2006, 80–81).

At the end of the Second World War, even though refugees or the stateless were deprived of the right to have rights, they remained human. They remembered their lives before the catastrophe, and sought to restructure the German language and give new meanings to law and politics.

Arendt was stateless for a number of years, and this chapter shows how strongly she desired and felt an obligation to change German, to cut its ties to anti-Semitism and racism. Humans who are reduced to the state of bare life may not have the right to have rights, but they can love and be loved. They are capable of forgiveness and resentment, because each one of them is still unique, thanks to her/his memories, desires, and the ability to make the world respond to new meanings. Individual emotions emerge out of a past that cannot be fully explained and, therefore, partially at least belongs to the ineffable. At the same time, memory, desire, and speech, which are suffused with moral emotions, can be made to bear on the new reality, and saturate it with mnemonic narratives, contemporary desires, and speech-acts.

## Radical evil as the absence of responsibility

I have shown that, for Arendt, without thinking there is no love of neighbor, and when there is no love of neighbor there is atrocity. In "Collective Responsibility," Arendt asserts that feelings of the goodness of the self are of consequence in Socrates's proposition "It is better to suffer wrong than to do wrong" (Arendt 2003, 151). Thinking and self-criticism influence social and political decisions and, in this sense, goodness emerges from thinking. Goodness has visible political outcomes. Socrates cannot murder, for he refuses to live with a murderer. Only thinking can yield such a relation to the self. In the following section, I show that the position taken by Socrates in relation to goodness mirrors the position that emerges from the love of Otherness. In Arendt's attempt to elucidate the interconnectedness of thinking, responsibility, and love of the neighbor, she must also speak to the one who lacks the capacity to think, be responsible, or care for her/his neighbor.

Eichmann is the perfect example of a man incapable of self-reflection. Arendt describes Eichmann as subject to a pathological condition that prevents him from engaging in a dialogue with himself. He is for all moral purposes incapable of thought. From this madness emerges the "banality of evil." Although he understands that he is morally wrong, Eichmann rationalizes his actions and claims that he was a cog in a machine, someone who had to fulfill orders, at the same time that he claims that he was more than just a cog in the machine, and was not involved in the Final Solution.

Rationalization is the opposite of judgment. Rationalization is retroactive narcissism, and stems from imposing one's desire on the world rather than judging what is meaningful or right for the world. Eichmann represents an extreme form of conformity. His conformity is a warped love of the Führer, which precludes his thinking and results in radical evil. Arendt argues in relation to mass atrocity that "this is the true hallmark of those offenses of which, since Kant, we call 'radical evil' and about whose nature so little is known, even to us who have been exposed to one of their rare outbursts on the public scene" (Arendt 1958, 241).

Radical evil emerges when a regime turns the commandment 'though shalt not kill' to its opposite – 'though shalt kill' – and thus destroys the realm of human affairs. Totalitarian regimes destroy diversity and do not distinguish between *who* and *what* a person is. They wage a war on sublimated love. Totalitarianism makes people superfluous.

Susan Neiman describes evil as "a way of marking the fact that it shatters our trust in the world" (Neiman 2002, 9). The effects of evil are as crucial as its causes. Under the Third Reich, radical evil included one more perverse imperative 'thou shalt bear false witness.'[13] Radical evil is characterized as that which can be neither punished nor forgiven: it undermines and destroys our very humanity, where humanity is defined by our ability to forgive.

In "Personal Responsibility Under Dictatorship," Arendt argues that "the non-participants were those whose consciences did not function in this, as it were, automatic way. [. . .] Hence they also chose to die when they were forced to participate. To put it crudely, they refused to murder, not so much because they still held fast to the command 'thou shalt not kill,' but because they were unwilling to live together with a murderer – themselves" (Arendt 2003b, 44). In order to live with oneself, one must constantly engage in an inner dialogue, which is to say, that one must constantly make judgments about one's actions, never ceasing to think.

One of the effects of totalitarianism is the destruction of the space for love. Totalitarianism coerces the human being to live in isolation and fear of the Other. It actively destroys the space of intimate love, instituting laws that interfere with the very structure of the family. For example, the Nazis regulated marriage and prohibited "inferior" people from marrying "superior" Aryans. In totalitarian regimes, the relational bonds between people are under constant surveillance and assault. Policing practices force family members to spy on one another, informing

---

13 See also Elizabeth Young-Bruehl, who confirms that totalitarianism "is the disappearance of politics: a form of government that destroys politics, methodically eliminating speaking and acting human beings and attacking the very humanity of first a selected group and then all groups. In this way totalitarianism makes people superfluous as human beings. This is its radical evil" (Young-Bruehl 2006, 39). To deprive people of the possibility to be in relationships is the equivalent of eliminating their humanity. They cannot talk to one another about their world-views, nor can they humanize the world by trying to change it. New perspectives come into existence when people talk about the world and act on their opinions.

on relations and friends alike. Totalitarianism destroys both public space – the political sphere – and private, intimate space.[14]

When the capacity for love in the condition of diversity is destroyed, totalitarianism's subjects are willing to conform, because their love for the Other has been transformed into fear of the Other. This fear fuels an anxiety that laws of action might completely disappear from the totalitarian state. Democratic laws enhance the body politic, just as they enhance friendships, but totalitarianism suspends these laws for the sake of the impersonal, inhuman "law" of history – which Arendt calls "the laws of the desert" (Arendt 2005, 190).[15] This becomes truly tragic when a "wasteland" prevails between human beings who have basic rights and those who have lost them (such as Gentiles and Jews in Germany, or whites and Blacks in the United States). As I mentioned above, the salient example that Arendt uses is the "statelessness" that Jews endured after the Holocaust. In *The Origins of Totalitarianism,* Arendt describes the emotional, intellectual, and active barrenness that rules over the treatment of refugees and stateless people:

> They [stateless persons] lack the tremendous equalizing of differences which comes from being citizens of some commonwealth and yet, since they are no longer allowed to partake in the human artifice, they begin to belong to the human race in much the same way as animals belong to a specific animal species. The paradox involved in the loss of human rights is that such loss coincides with the instant when a person becomes a human being in general—without a profession, without a citizenship, without an opinion, without a deed by which to identify and specify himself—*and* different in general, representing nothing but his own absolutely unique individuality which deprived of expression within and action upon a common world, loses all significance (Arendt 1951, 297–98).[16]

---

**14** Kenneth Reinhard interprets Arendt's analysis of the neighbor in totalitarianism thus: "Arendt's analysis suggests that what is lost in totalitarianism is the spacing proper to the function of the neighbor. To destroy the relation of the neighbor is to eliminate the breathing space that keeps the subject in proper relationship to the Other, neither too close nor too far, but in proximity, the 'nearness' that proximity entails." "Nearness" is the space of both love and action in which the *who* and *what* the agent/neighbor are disclosed. See Žižek et al. 2005, 26.

**15** When Leszek Koczanowicz and I coedited the volume *Democracy, Dialogue, Memory* (2019), he opposed Arendt's claim that love disappears in totalitarian regimes. He related a personal memory: in Poland, under the rule of the Soviet Union, love flourished in unexpected ways. Older people used to stand in bread lines and engage in conversation. These became necessary to both the private sphere, where they helped the working young couples to keep house and raise the children, and the social sphere, where they became instigators of social connections and a source of local, communal news. I associate this memory with Arendt's conviction that a minority of the population remained capable of thinking through perpetuating love relations in the private and the social sphere.

**16** Peg Birmingham underlines the connection Arendt makes between human rights and the creation of a world in which people can belong to a community. By the same token she also explains

Radical evil deprives the individual of the right to have rights. Without being a citizen, one loses both love and sublimated love in the political and in the private spheres. Yet it is clear that, even in a state of bare life, the Other's alterity is preserved. The Other's alterity is not reduced to social or political activity. The Other can love and be loved, can forgive and resent, despite the political circumstances that cut her/him off from cooperation with others. People who are denied the right to have rights do not lose their humanity, only their contemporaries' acknowledgement and respect of the Other's alterity. Currently, European democracies do not necessarily offer asylum to every refugee, but refugees receive homes and schooling for their children while their applications are examined by the relevant institutions. This was one of the achievements of the Universal Declaration of Human Rights, crafted by the General Assembly of the United Nations in 1948 in the aftermath of the Second World War.[17]

## Love, forgiveness, and promises

Arendt relates love to two fundamentally political actions: forgiveness and making promises. Making promises institutes a borderline between the private and the political. Arendt defines forgiveness as "a secular miracle." Rather than retort to revenge and perpetuate violence, the victim declines to nurture negative affect toward the perpetrator, and opens society and politics to new possibilities:

> Forgiving and the relationship it establishes is always an eminently personal (though not necessarily individual or private) affair in which what was done is forgiven for the sake of who did it. This, too, was clearly recognized by Jesus ('Her sins which are many are forgiven; for she loved much: but to whom little is forgiven, the same loveth little'), and it is the reason for the current conviction that only love has the power to forgive (Arendt 1958, 242).

Love and forgiveness enhance each other, so that both of them are transcendent (not necessarily divine in a theological way) and contingent in the world:

> For love, although it is one of the rarest occurrences in human lives, indeed possesses an unequaled power of self-revelation and an unequaled clarity of vision for the disclosure of who, precisely because it is unconcerned to the point of total unworldliness with what the

---

"the wilderness" – the lack of love between people: "For Arendt, more fundamental than the rights of justice and freedom is the right to action and opinion and the right to belong to a political community in which one's speech and action are rendered significant" (Birmingham 2006, 36).

[17] See articles 2, 7, 15, 22, and 28 in the Universal Declaration of Human Rights. https://www.ohchr.org/EN/UDHR/Documents/UDHR_Translations/eng.pdf accessed July 30, 2020.

loved person may be, with his qualities and shortcomings no less than with his achievements, failings, and transgressions (Arendt 1958, 242).

Love is political because it is related to the structure of action. In action, the human being discloses *who* s/he is. One's actions reveal the judgments one makes between right and wrong. In this manner, love is the natural habitat of self-revelation. It co-inhabits action that is grounded in the possibility of self-evaluation and natality. One can change a course of action when, through interpersonal connections with others, one learns of one's mistakes, or simply how to judge situations from multiple perspectives.

Despite the fact that love disregards the *what*, Arendt accepts that forgiveness is implicated in sublimation. She grounds forgiveness in the language of law and in the structure of action, or the *what*. While love disregards the *what* and stresses the *who*, forgiveness stresses both. Throughout her work, Arendt struggles to separate love from politics. Even though love is not a political action, it produces valid political results:

> As long as its spell lasts, the only in-between which can insert itself between two lovers is the child, love's own product. The child, this in-between to which the lovers now are related and which they hold in common, is representative of the world in that it also separates them; it is an indication that they will insert a new world into the existing world. Through the child it is as though the lovers return to the world from which their love had expelled them. But this new worldliness, the possible result and the only possibly happy ending of a love affair, is, in a sense, the end of love, which must either overcome the partners anew or be transformed into another mode of belonging together. Love, by its very nature, is unworldly, and it is for this reason rather than its rarity that it is not only apolitical but antipolitical, perhaps the most powerful of all antipolitical human forces (Arendt 1958, 242).

Arendt imagines sublimated love in the form of raising a family and educating children, not necessarily through social engagement and political wisdom. According to Patricia Bowen-Moore, Arendt's hesitation is grounded in "the promise inherent in natality is rooted in the experience of love which takes into account the world of human existence. Natality's full expression of this type of love – a love open to the world and its promises – is *amor mundi*: love of the world" (Bowen-Moore 1989, 19). For Bowen-Moore, natality is the same as sublimated love. It is intimate loving that educates one's affections, teaching one to love the world rather than be limited to private, discreet love.

Arendt compares symbolic love to respect. She suggests that, without it, action in the public sphere of politics is almost inconceivable:

> If it were true, therefore, as Christianity assumed, that only love can forgive because only love is fully receptive to *who* somebody is, to the point of being always willing to forgive him whatever he may have done, forgiving would have to remain altogether outside our

considerations. Yet what love is in its own, narrowly circumscribed sphere, respect is in the larger domain of human affairs. Respect, not unlike the Aristotilian *Philia politikē*, is a kind of 'friendship' without intimacy and without closeness; it is a regard for the person from the distance which the space of the world puts between us, and this regard is independent of qualities which we may admire or of achievements which we may highly esteem (Arendt 1958 242–43).

The distance that sublimation enables introduces respect and friendship into politics. This is precisely what Freud calls aim-inhibited love. Sublimation is interpersonal. In order to feel respect and friendship in the public sphere, sublimation is necessary. Friendship and respect, in turn, enhance the political world of action. Doing and acting can be affective, when deeds and words proliferate and expand the network of mutual relations between people. People acquire a place in history when their actions and words are acknowledged. To put it differently, people are remembered for being the originators, the carriers of new actions.

I mentioned above that it is curious that Arendt examines *caritas* uniquely from the perspective of the good-doer, for here it becomes clear that the benefactor is a witness and a broadcaster of good deeds, and of the respect the good-doer deserves. If friendship and respect emerge from sublimated love, then acting together increases sublimation in public life. Political decisions and actions, such as forgiveness, are grounded in sublimation.

"The alternative to forgiveness," says Arendt, "is punishment.": "It is therefore quite significant, a structural element in the realm of human affairs, that men are unable to forgive what they cannot punish and that they cannot punish what has turned out to be unforgivable" (Arendt 1958, 241). This means, on the one hand, that one has to ask for forgiveness in order to receive it, but, on the other, that one cannot receive forgiveness even if one asks for it – particularly when the transgression belongs in the realm of radical evil.

Forgiveness can free one from a wrong that s/he committed in the past, enabling her/him to continue living in the present as a participant in a new world. The wrongdoer does not remain tied to the deeds of the past, nor to the guilt that they provoke. However, radical evil, which eliminates the *who*, the humanity of the Other, is neither punishable nor forgivable. Eichmann can be neither adequately punished nor forgiven. This is why forgiveness must transcend the realm of human affairs. Eichmann cannot be the standard or the criterion of forgiveness.

Arendt also talks about the "passion" of making promises. How do we understand this? In politics, treaties are needed to protect us against two threats. The first is the "darkness of the human heart." The second is the unknown consequences of actions that individuals take in a community of peers, all equal to one another in power, action, and speech. Human beings are not masters of their reality. Promises are islands of predictability, guideposts of reliability that the body politic erects: "The moment promises lose their character as isolated islands of certainty in an ocean of uncertainty, that is, when this faculty is misused to cover the whole ground of the future and to map out a path secured in all directions, they lose their binding power and the whole enterprise becomes self-defeating" (Arendt 1958, 244). The future always looks chaotic and uncertain, but the faculty of making promises introduces a degree of reliability to the future.

Arendt discusses this passion in the context of the biblical Abraham (then still called Avram). Making promises institutes a borderline between the private and the political. Arendt asserts of Abraham that "his whole story, as the Bible tells it, shows such a passionate drive toward making covenants that it is as though he departed from his country for no other reason than to try out the power of mutual promise in the wilderness of the world, until eventually God himself agreed to make a Covenant with him" (Arendt 1958, 244). This "passionate drive toward making promises" is related to sublimation, and the need to turn the neighbor into a close ally bound by passion. From Kierkegaard to Derrida, Western philosophy has defined Abraham as the subject of the sacrifice of Isaac. He is a man of faith, since he believes in the need to preserve the law, even when duty resides in obscurity. This culminates in his decision to sacrifice his own son (Derrida 1995, 91).

Arendt, on the other hand, offers a more understanding version of Abraham. She does not speak about the *Akedah*, the sacrifice of Isaac, but instead stresses the passion for making promises. Ultimately, a ram substituted for Isaac as the divine offering. Yet Arendt argues that Abraham is a very particular believer, one who believes in the power of mutual promising. Long before the birth of Isaac, a covenant was made between God and Abraham. It justified his exile from Ur of the Chaldees, and his subjecting his seed to being "a stranger in a land that is not theirs, and shall serve them; and they shall afflict them four hundred years" (Genesis 15:13).

Abraham's passion is the opposite of the desert. Through passion, Abraham realizes that the desert must be humanized, and that making and keeping promises converts the desert into a world. God is the principle of Otherness, beyond the human capacity to understand. Yet the word of God becomes world, is subject to *amor mundi*, it becomes politics, when Abraham forces God to make a contract with him: "In the same day the Lord made a covenant with Abram, saying, Unto thy seed have I given this land, from the river of Egypt unto the great river, the river Euphrates" (Genesis 15:18).[18]

In this sense making promises is related to emotions of trust and love. Promises enable people to trust one another and to trust civilization. Individuals and

---

18 Paradoxically, this covenant disrupts the creation of a common world to be shared between modern Israel and the Palestinians. Israel contends that the vast territory between Egypt and

states know that, whatever the situation is in the future, they can rely on a set of treaties or promises that they made in the past to guide them, to display a known path in an otherwise unknown world. Promise making substantiates the newness that action and speech bring into the world. It introduces something of the present to the future. Forgiveness and promises make the new reverberate in the public sphere and create the body politic:

> The miracle that saves the world, the realm of human affairs, from its normal, 'natural' ruin is ultimately the fact of natality, in which the faculty of action is ontologically rooted. It is, in other words, the birth of new men and the new beginning, the action they are capable of by virtue of being born. Only the full experience of this capacity can bestow upon human affairs faith and hope. [. . .] It is this faith in and hope for the world that found perhaps its most glorious and most succinct expression in the few words with which the Gospels announced the 'glad tidings': 'A child has been born to us'" (Arendt 1958, 247).

Arendt's innovative theory connects hope to birth. She refrains from studying hope in the context of Saint Paul – "And now abideth faith, hope, charity [*agape*, love]" (*Corinthians* 13:13). "With Paul and his successors," according to Alain Badiou, "hope is described as pertaining to justice. Faith allows one to have hope in justice" (Badiou 2003, 93). But Arendt is not interested in hope related to the Day of Judgment, but rather in the hope that emerges from "natality." Man came into the world in order to introduce to it a new beginning. For Arendt, this new beginning is founded on a domestic love, which culminates in giving birth to a new human being, or, alternatively, in the love of neighbor that brings about cooperation. Active love includes forgiveness and the passion of making promises. Hope does not pertain to retributive justice, but to people's ability to trust the effects of sublimated love. These include forgiveness and making promises, which enable political actors to care *who* the Other is, not just *what* the Other demands and thereby turn the desert to world.

## The loophole of existence

Arendt's biography of Rahel Varnhagen is directly related to the question of Jewish assimilation in Prussia and Germany in the eighteenth and nineteenth centuries. Jews who could not assimilate into German society were seen as either socially or intellectually inferior, or sometimes as exotic and curious. Regrettably, to Arendt's mind, only the enemies of the Jews thought that the Jewish question

---

Iraq belongs to it, while the Palestinians believe that the people who have for centuries been living off this land own it. They have been loving it by inhabiting it.

was political, but not their friends. In Rahel's Berlin Salon, there come about brief encounters with those who seek the company of Jews in order to feel that those Jews are truly human. Among the visitors of the salon were true personalities, who "joined a Hohenzollern prince, Louis Ferdinand, to the banker Abraham Mendelssohn; or a political publicist and diplomat, Friedrich Gentz, to Friedrich Schlegel, a writer of the then ultramodern romantic school — these were a few of the more famous visitors at Rahel's 'garret' – [which] came to an end in 1806 when, according to their hostess, this unique meeting place 'foundered like a ship containing the highest enjoyment of life'" (Arendt 1951, 60).

Arendt recounts that artists and politicians alike became anti-Semites at the moment when the laws were beginning to grant equal rights to the Jews. As long as Jews were seen as inferior, "exceptional Jews" (Arendt 1951, 56) like Moses Mendelson or Rahel could be assimilated. But once Jews were eligible to social and political equality, all Jews became "backward brethren" (Arendt 1951, 61). Arendt argues that Jews failed to realize that their predicament was that they were reduced to individuality in their struggle against superstition, and therefore could not act as political agents:

> In order to rationalize an ambiguity which they [Jews] themselves did not fully understand, they might pretend to "be a man in the street and a Jew at home."[19] This actually amounted to a feeling of being different from other men in the street because they were Jews, and different from other Jews at home because they were not like "ordinary Jews" (Arendt 1951, 65).

This situation leads Arendt to the conclusion that a Mendelson or a Rahel can either be a *pariah* or a *parvenu*. As parvenu, in their attempt to climb higher the rungs of the social ladder, they can either leave the Jewish community, and seek the favor of their German fellows, or become *elders* or lords within the Jewish community. As pariahs who are rejected by both communities, they can never be socially and politically active in both German society and the Jewish community, not even if they convert to Christianity.

Two questions emerge: how do Jews give and receive love in its social and political frameworks; that is, when love morphs into friendship and respect of the Other, my neighbor, my peer? Secondly, does this mean that Jews are an apolitical or an antipolitical people? Arendt's *Rahel Varnhagen: The Life of a Jewess* is wholly devoted to the question of how love creates potentials for action in the private and the public spheres.

---

**19** In a footnote, Arendt indicates that the citation that describes the exclusion of the *exceptional Jews* from both the origin and the target communities involved in assimilation is from a much later Hebrew poem by Judah Leib Gordon. This recognition signifies that Zionism is an organized and therefore a political national movement, not a struggle of individuals (Arendt 1951, 65).

Arendt left Germany in 1933, carrying the finished manuscript of her research concerning the Varnhagen estate. As part of her research, Arendt read some two hundred and seventy letters that Rahel and her close friend, Pauline Wiesel, exchanged. These letters had been excluded from the larger collection by Rahel's husband. Instead, he included only sixteen of Pauline's letters to Rahel. He deliberately falsified Rahel's life in order to make her a more conforming figure, in line with the stereotypes and prejudices of the period: "The significant fact is that almost all his omissions and misleading codings of names were intended to make Rahel's associations and circle of friends less Jewish and more aristocratic, and to show Rahel herself in a more conventional light, one more in keeping of the taste of the times" (Arendt 1957, x).

Despite Varnhagen's insistence on "manners," Arendt shows that Rahel succeeds in her desire to "expose herself to life so that it could strike her 'like a storm without an umbrella'" (ibid, xi). In return for this talent to "let life rain upon me," Rahel has to pay with *love*: "to this end, the particular traits one had to have or to marshal within oneself were an unflagging alertness and capacity for pain; one had to remain susceptible and conscious" (ibid, xi).

Love defines Rahel's loyalties as an individual, and delineates the structure of her social desire. Rahel wants both love and a superior social standing, her Jewish origins severely limit her social mobility. If she finds love within the Jewish community, she cannot become close to the Prussian aristocracy. And, if she makes attempts to socially advance through marriage and conversion to Christianity, she would have had to relinquish her roots, and possibly sacrifice love. As a Jew, she is a pariah. As a parvenu she might arrive, be acknowledged as having a high social standing, but will have to relinquish her inner truth. Rahel's state of being torn between the pariah and the parvenu forms a conflict that Arendt stages in psychological and social terms, not in political ones.

Rahel's love of the pariah opens new personal and social options. She marries Varnhagen (who is a parvenu), but she doesn't love him. Through this marriage, Rahel attains enough social power to withdraw from society on a whim, and devote herself to the love of the pariah and to her Jewish friend, Pauline. The pariah loves humanity from the position of the excluded. This unworldly love saves Rahel in her old age, after she is baptized, takes the name Friederike, and marries Varnhagen, a government official. Rahel is also an independent writer who cultivates a correspondence with her one true friend, Pauline Wiesel, who was the mistress of Prince Louis Ferdinand but lost her social power, and ended up broke and alone.

The love that emerges from the correspondence between Rahel and Pauline is the fruitful kind of love that Arendt sanctions, yet it is neither social nor political. Rahel loves humanity by seeking intellectual and social freedom, and in this "loophole of existence" she learns and offers recognition of differences that carry the mark of transcendental ideas. The loophole of existence is a state of mind that allows Rahel to contemplate larger questions concerning human interrelatedness, not just personal love. It is an antipolitical social position. Rahel becomes a hermit who practices the life of the mind. According to Katja Garloff,

> Whereas the parvenu manages to fend off the claims of others and his own impulses, the pariah remains vulnerable and exposed, but for that reason also able to form new bonds with others, including political alliances with other oppressed people . . . The political message of Arendt's biography is that Jews should demand political rights *as Jews* and form alliances with other marginalized groups rather than seek social integration at all costs (Garloff 2016, 179).

Garloff correctly points out that the correspondence between Rahel and Pauline has a political edge, which is similar to the political edge of forgiveness and resentment in cultures that repress or eliminate Otherness. Rahel and Pauline experience the exposure to the Other as both painful and edifying. Emotions like love and pain become tools with which to make sense of how circumstance can cause one to think, enter a dialogue with oneself, and make a choice between conformity and dissent. Arendt expresses resentment when she lauds Rahel's ability to be thoughtfully resentful:

> But officially she [Rahel] wanted to be neither a fool nor a paradox, and therefore she needed Varnhagen to make her in reality Frau Friederike Varnhagen von Ense, to annihilate her whole existence, even including her given name. Secretly, in opposition to him, in conscious revolt against such a condition, she conjured up scraps of her old life, lived her own life '*altogether* inwardly'. The witness of these unofficial machinations was Pauline Wiesel, with whom she had more in common than character traits, for she shared with Pauline, the deeply human love of all outcasts from society for the 'true realities'—'a bridge, a tree, a ridge, a smell, a smile' (Arendt 1957, 171).

Despite Rahel's need to assimilate and transcend her Jewish origins, she attains love of the world only as a pariah. The sublimation of love is central to her biography. Though she starts her journey as an "injured soul," Rahel eventually finds "a place in the history of European humanity" (Arendt 1957, 185). Arendt signals that Rahel was pliant in her dealings with the outside world. Rahel and Pauline, these excluded Jewesses, forge a public life in letters because they discover that to be the member of a minority who has forged closed ties with another is a form of dissent, an assertion of one's own ability to think for oneself. A loophole in Rahel's existence, says Arendt, propelled her search for meaning and her looming death:

> That she succeeded in salvaging her pariah qualities when she entered her parvenu existence opened up a loophole for her, marked out a road toward aging and dying. It was the very loophole through which the pariah, precisely because he is an outcast, can see life as a whole, and the very road upon which the pariah can attain to his "*great* love for free exis-

tence." It is offered to the pariah if, though unable to revolt as an individual against the whole of society, he disdains the alternative of becoming a parvenu and is recompensed for his "wretched situation" by a "view of the whole." That is his sole dignified hope: "that everything is related; and in truth, everything is good enough. This is the salvage from the *great* bankruptcy of life" (Arendt 1957, 174–175).

Rather than become immersed in an intimate love that shuts out the world, the pariah can truly love existence. Love of existence involves the passionate aspect of making agreements with others. It is sublimated, so that the pariah's love appears in the form of friendships and in literary texts. Such love functions as hope. Rahel is hopeful that she can change the world according to her desire to change from a Jewess into a European intellectual.

Rahel finds a way to be *alive*, in the way of sublimated love, and, rather than give up on having a life filled with knowledge, art, and friendship, she institutes a loophole in which she can exist and maintain the hope that love and sublimation are "everything" and that "everything is good enough," even if she remains a pariah. The terms *pariah* and *parvenu*, which Arendt is so eager to use, can be interpreted in psychoanalytic terms, despite her resistance to psychoanalysis.[20]

It is important to note that Arendt finds value in making the interstices of the mind available to the public sphere of friendship with, and respect for, the Other. Friendship begins with speaking to the other about the self, not just about the world, with acting on the basis of sublimated love, not just on the basis of the political cause, and with knowing how to not capitulate, even though one may be exposed and vulnerable in the public sphere. The final page of the biography lists Rahel's personal triumphs: as a parvenu, Friederike Varnhagen had "freedom and equality." As a pariah and a Jewess, Rahel maintained a connection with "true realities" (Arendt 1957, 183). "Only because she clung to both conditions," Arendt concludes, "did she find a place in the history of European humanity" (Arendt 1957, 185).

I would like to return to the two questions above and ask again if this conclusion means that Jews cannot be one's peer in social and political contexts and whether, therefore, Jews are an apolitical or antipolitical people. In many texts

---

20 Arendt makes no secret of her aversion to the ways in which psychoanalysis makes political use of communications between people. For Arendt, psychoanalysis teaches people to resolve unhappiness through conformity. She sees this as harmful to both the individual and the larger community. Arendt views psychoanalysis as promoting the complacency of both analyst and patient: "Modern psychology is desert psychology. The danger lies in becoming true inhabitants of the desert and feeling at home in it" (Arendt 2005, 201). Arendt wrongly accuses psychoanalysis of avoiding the loopholes of existence – for Freud's probing of the unconscious is consubstantial with the assumption that meaning resides within this "desert."

Arendt examines the social and political value of dissent. But can the politics of minorities be boosted by intellectuals? Again, Arendt is split in her opinions, because Jaspers and his wife definitely took a political stand by simply being married to each other, and by publishing his books when the marriage of a German to a Jew amounted to a life threat. Arendt's appreciation and love of this couple comes up in *Men in Dark Times*.

As an American citizen, Arendt also reflected on the relevance of emotions to politics during the Vietnam War and during the struggle for Black Civil Rights. In her writings on these topics, Arendt supports dissent at the same time as she cautions against the use of love. Still, she recognizes that post-Holocaust Jewish thinkers such as Améry and Levi introduced the value of emotions to the political sphere. We can now see that their narratological and historical lessons were implemented in the South African Truth and Reconciliation Committee as well as in contemporary Israel, where a minority of left wing intellectuals and human rights activists sought to establish bonds between Israelis and Palestinians.

## Conclusion

Worldly love signifies the respect owed to the Otherness of every human being. It is therefore indispensable in political life. Arendt believes that action in non-totalitarian societies produces friendship and respect between people. Such action in turn requires forgiveness and the passion for making promises. At the same time, the alliance for action depends on our capacity to have aim-inhibited relations of love, in order to augment interactions that might create new activities and introduce new ideas into the world. In the public sphere, friendship and respect emerge out of action.

For Freud, love and sublimation bring people together in such a way that the individual becomes libidinally connected to others when s/he engages in working together and building the community. Love is sublimated even though the ties between the actors are libidinal. In politics, such sublimated love relationships bring about the birth of civilization. In art, sublimation brings about the expansion of knowledge in aesthetics and also in ethics. Love, in sum, is central to both Arendt and Freud: it exists in both the private sphere and in the realm of worldliness, inciting transformation.

# Interchapter 2
# The necessary fragility of paradox – on Christian Petzold's *Phoenix*

## On the dead and the possibility of a future

> I with what burned down, the candle, I with the day, I with the days, I here and I there, I companioned perhaps—now!—by the love of those not loved, I on the way to myself, up here. Paul Celan, *Conversation in the Mountains*

In *Conversation in the Mountains*, Celan speaks to God the way Moses did before him. At Sinai, Moses received the Tablets of the Law and oversaw the transformation of God's chosen children into a nation ruled by ethical ideals. God compelled the Israelites to accept the Torah when He addressed them with the words "Hearest Thou, o Israel!" and, in response, the Israelites agreed to "do and hear" the Law. According to Martin Buber (who was very much on Celan's mind), it was when the Tablets were given that the emotional bond between "I and Thou" became conscious, became speech. The "I" became aware of its numen and acquired the capacity to be moral, to learn to hear the imperatives of the Divine Spirit, the "Thou." Celan, writing as a survivor of genocide, rejects the potency of those ethical values inscribed on the Tablets of the Law, rejects the authority of the God who gave them to His chosen people, and calls Him "No One."

As Celan rebels against the existing moral order of the world, as he gives voice to the grievances of the victimized, he thrusts a paradoxical state of affairs in the face of his German-speaking readers. During the twelve years of Nazi rule, the very humanity of the Jews was denied. Celan affirms that he knows himself best as the one who, for God and men alike, was left for dead, together with his "cousins" in the death camps: "On the stone is where I lay, back then, you know, on the stone slabs; and next to me, they were lying there, the others, who were like me." How can Celan make God and men listen to him if he suspects that God commands and then turns away? – "Hearest Thou? He says nothing, he doesn't answer." In light of his animosity towards God, Celan changes his approach to nature and to dialogue because, in order to be part of life again, the poet must remain a loyal witness to the exile, alienation, silence, and death that he and his "cousins" suffered when no one thought they were worthy to be addressed as either "you" or "Thou."

*Conversation in the Mountains* unfolds like a folktale. Klein and Gross, Celan's protagonists, come to the mountains and discuss where they were and how they

**Note:** See page numbers of citations on the bibliography.

https://doi.org/10.1515/9783111317694-005

came to be there. But Celan lets them be silent as well. When they choose the caesura over speech, they find intimacy in being exposed to the threshold moment of guessing, knowing/not-knowing the pain each wrestles with. The demise of European Jewry is at the backdrop of the encounter, the schmoosing, between these two survivors. I follow Hannah Arendt when I submit that, in his conversation with "No One," Celan wants to unlearn the commandment "thou shalt not kill," in order to better navigate his private, poetic, and social life after the Holocaust, in order to unearth the silences that surface in the conversation between Gross and Klein. In *Eichmann in Jerusalem*, Arendt says that Nazi Germany lost the call of conscience and, rather than cling to the commandment "thou shalt not kill," demanded the nation's submission to the new imperative: "though shalt kill." My reading is anachronistic and yet to my mind Celan would have concurred with Arendt's phrasing, even though he didn't read this particular text of hers, which was written after *Conversation* was published.

Celan labors to reforge his bonds with his Jewish friends, with his Jewish self, with Hebrew, the Biblical language, and with Yiddish, the Jewish language. He came from a family of German-speaking Jews, who lived in Czernowitz, Bukovina, which then passed to Romania before Paul Antschel (aka, Paul Celan), was born, and never considered that his Jewishness would be the cause of his destruction. He did not assimilate out of fear. He was a European intellectual, versed in German, French, Romanian, and English. Yet Celan's text is dripping with guilt and shame. He feels guilty about surviving the War when his parents did not. He feels ashamed of being twice a pariah: the one who abandoned traditional Judaism, and the one who survived the murderous regime that sought to make Europe free of Jews. Celan sees himself as a pariah because, at the end of the War, when anti-Semitism lived on strong in Europe, he looked for readers among postwar Germans, yet without knowing whether these "new" German readers felt any shame, guilt, or repentance. Celan sought solace in writing and loving in difficult political times. Despite his shame, he remained loyal to the burning candle that commemorates the murdered Jews: "I loved the candle that was burning there, to the left in the corner, I loved it because it was burning down."

*Conversation in the Mountains* puts forth the following question: does Celan want to be strong and active or does he want to be weak and passive? I think he is morally committed to being weak and passive, to promoting the value of *dissesus* in the face of triumphant liberal capitalism. He knows that those who are powerful and active impose their ego on the world of human interaction, a world rife with possibilities, and abuse it, and break it. Celan's wounds burn bright, not because he romanticizes his scars, not because he dwells on his pain, but because they attach the poet to his passivity. He allows love for the dead to fashion his arguments and tropes, as well as this new rhetoric, the rebirth that he has been given. Witnessing is a breath of life in that it looks to the past, anchored to the possibility of a future of remembering the dead.

The dead are metonymic to human frailty. They inspire Celan to mourn, to care, to resent power, to long for a past in which he belonged to a family, a community, a tradition, in which he relied on a sense of identity secure enough to allow him to choose universalism and the life of the intellect over the faith of his fathers. Celan's poetic fountainhead is his love for the dead Jews, the very ones he chose to leave when they were alive. To deepen the paradox, after the War he wrote for the German-speaking Gentiles, the very ones who betrayed him, who persecuted him because he was a Jew. Paradox, it seems, is inescapable. It is as if only love can survive betrayal, and yet betrayal attaches itself primarily to love. If the survivor embraces his love for the Germans, the Romanians, the French who persecuted his people, then he chooses to believe that, in the present, these nations can feel guilt and shame over the destruction of the Jews, a people who were so much a part of European society, language, and intellectual ideals.

From this text arises my interest in the paradox of forgiveness and resentment. Can Celan forgive the mortal crimes that his beloved European homeland and culture committed against him? If Celan the lover forgives, can he not still be resentful of their betrayal? What kind of a person forgives and lives as if the slate were clean again, the love returned to its original state of integrity? Celan's poetry recognizes that this is impossible, that scars will neither haunt nor nourish the renewed bond between lovers, that resentment must arise. These topics are alarming to survivors of the Holocaust like Celan, like Jean Améry, Primo Levi, or Aharon Appelfeld, because they are personal, intimate, and outweigh the political, juridical, and philosophical debates about the meaning of guilt and judgment.

Christian Petzold, a German auteur is the most famous director to emerge from the Berlin School. His films correspond with films from the golden years of Hollywood's melodramas and with the cinematic ideology of the French "New Wave." Petzold's work occurs in the general present because the films always focus on economic practices and neoliberal beliefs. Yet his vision brings back into the frame a cohort of disenfranchised populations that cannot but fall off the conformist grid that is supposed to lead them to success. *Phoenix* (2014), visualizes events that bring about missed encounters between singular people and emotions. The three main characters are family relatives, close friends, they share the same frame and speak to one another and yet they cannot see *who* the other is, cannot feel neither love nor shame to *who* the other has come to be. *Phoenix* deploys the paradox of betrayal and love but as Petzold's images, soundtrack, and script tackle post-War Berlin he intentionally or unconsciously alludes to the most prominent philosophers and thinkers of the 1960s in his attempt to give an image to forgiveness and resentment.

*Phoenix*, Christian Petzold's seventh feature film, features Nelly (Nina Höss), a professional singer and an assimilated German Jew. She is a Holocaust survivor who believes that the love of her Gentile husband, Johnny (Ronald Zehrfeld), made her survival in Auschwitz possible. As the film opens, Nelly has yet to learn that, by the time she was transported to the death camp, Johnny was no longer her husband. He had secretly divorced her and informed on her to the Gestapo, effectively sending her to her death in order to save himself. *Phoenix* explores whether love and forgiveness can exist at a time and in a place where people's most fervent wish is just to be normal again, to see themselves not as victimizers but as victims, helplessly caught up in terrible historical circumstances. The Germans of *Phoenix* are depraved because they presume to fashion a future for Germany by forgetting, by moving on, by disavowing the atrocities they committed.

Nelly returns from the death camp to her hometown of Berlin with a face so badly maimed that she fears her husband will not recognize her. Her plastic surgeon recommends that she choose a new face and start a new life. Her friend Lene (Nina Kunzendorf) seconds this suggestion. Nelly chooses to reconstruct her old face and although an identical replication of the face is impossible the entire process relies on old pictures Nelly was able to save. These images are relics that preserve the past alive in Nelly's imagination. On them her old face is gleaming with happiness, as are the faces of her husband and their German close friends.

Lene, who spent the war years in London, is a stand-in for Jewish survivors who, like Celan, are engaged in both remembering and reminding. As intellectuals, their contribution is in recording what happened in minute detail, in exposing the machine of genocide and thereby indicting the moral depravity of the Nazi epoch. Lene voices her resentment against the new Federal Republic of Germany through her commitment to historical documentation, through her insistence in recovering the names of dead Jews and searching for their despoiled possessions. She suspects that Germany is more interested in becoming a capitalist power than in admitting responsibility for the death camps. Celan brings Lene's position to mind because he complains that Germany is still interested in being victorious, not in the war but in securing that economic prosperity will make Germany respected among the nations despite the war years. Celan was invited to be a member of the famous German literary association of authors called Group 47, in which young authors like Heinrich Böll also participated. John Felstiner cites Celan's explanation to why he didn't like the organization's meetings: "I was really curious about my first encounter with young German authors. I asked myself, what are they likely to talk about? And what did they talk about? Volkswagens." Celan protests that even the German literati and intellectuals need to bolster the feeling that Germany deserves a victory, the country cannot simply seek out moral avenues of existence, live in repentance and shame.

*Phoenix* is premised on the opposition between Nelly – who embraces the visual arts and music, emotion and sensuality, because she trusts that the love that helped her survive Auschwitz will restore her marriage and allow her to restart her life in the new Germany as a stateless Jew – and Lene – who embraces history and consciousness in the form of distorted, torn, and lost documents from the hellish past, and through them faces the real prospects of Jewish life in postwar Germany.

Upon her return home, Nelly encounters Johnny at the *Phoenix*, the nightclub where he works. He sees her but does not recognize her, and decides she must be a refugee who happens to look like his wife. Johnny is no longer an artist (he was a pianist before the War) and has changed his name to Johannes, signifying his membership in the German generation who seek the future by pursuing business and profit. He proposes to the needy refugee woman that she adopt a Jewish name, Esther, and impersonate his ex-wife Nelly, whom he presumes died at Auschwitz. Together, Johannes and Esther will seek to claim Nelly's family money and with it start a new life.

Throughout the film Johannes fails to recognize Nelly, even though "Esther" can forge his ex-wife's signature, even though Nelly's shoes fit her perfectly and she looks ravishing in Nelly's red dress. Nelly, on her part, goes along with Johnny's insane fantasy that a survivor can return from Auschwitz looking like she did before the War. At the end of the film the two sit at the piano and sing together for the last time. Nelly then moves out of the frame and into the off-screen world of actuality, of the future. She understands that Johnny's love for her was always partial and incomplete, that she survived the hell of the death camp thanks to her love for him, as well as her love for Germany, her homeland. At that moment, for the first time, Johannes realizes that Nelly has a tattooed number on her arm. The extent of Johannes' obliviousness is made plain in an earlier scene, in which he takes Nelly to the boathouse where she hid, to the place he brought the Gestapo to find her after he had legally divorced her. Nelly learns from the place's owner that Johnny was there when the Gestapo arrived, that he betrayed her. Yet she is still willing to forgive him.

Anagnorisis, the moment of recognition, occurs at the train station, where Johnny gathers all of his and Nelly's old friends and stages Nelly's return from Auschwitz. Off the coach comes a beautiful, albeit bewildered and introverted Nelly, who of course is Nelly pretending to be Esther pretending to be Nelly. She hugs all these friends but does not speak to any of them. Instead she listens. At the climax of this sequence, Johannes presses his wife against his breast, clueless that this is not a performance but rather a concrete embodiment of history made real: the return of the repressed, the abandoned, the betrayed. Petzold suggests that Johnny is morally obligated to suffer guilt and shame. Except that recognition does not occur, and so neither does acknowledgment of the crimes of the past. Disavowal protects Johnny/Johannes, as well as the rest of the friends who are so blithely happy to see Nelly return.

Nelly's love is a moral force. It takes the shape of a cognitive, material, and historical attempt to redeem the human. In order to make Nelly's quest for love relevant to the question of the possibility of forgiveness and the value of resentment, Petzold uses her experience like a prism for the philosophical arguments articulated by Jewish thinkers, such as Emmanual Levinas and W. G. Sebald, in their quest to reclaim morality after the Holocaust. This extends the moral reach of *Phoenix* and links it to the work of Holocaust survivors like Celan.

## Petzold's Levinas: "Show me your face now"

> Tell me, love, what I cannot explain:
> should I spend this brief, dreadful time
> only with thoughts circulating and alone,
> knowing no love and giving no love?
> Must one think? Will he be missed?
>     Ingeborg Bachmann, "Tell Me, Love"

*Phoenix* opens at night. The film's theme song, "Speak Low" (composed by Kurt Weill), is soothing at this early stage. But the night and the music are overpowered by the image of the blood-stained bandage that covers Nelly's face. She sits next to Lene, who is driving the car trying to cross the border into Germany. The British soldier at the checkpoint is gleeful, inquiring about the make of the car and Lene's country of origin, presumably because he is a young foreigner and because "boys will be boys," always obsessed with cars and with women. This sequence provokes radical alienation. The young soldier sees the bandaged figure on the seat but remains a signifier of the brute force of war. The woman he sees is weak, mortal. Alienation is then substituted by fear when the soldier orders Nelly to undo the bandages and show her face. Lene, protective of Nelly, explains that she has come from the camps, but the soldier is smug and armed so he demands of Nelly – "Show me your face now!" Sobbing, Nelly complies and, although we do not see her injured face, the visibly shocked soldier apologizes.

Alienation, fear, and, ultimately, ignorance usher in the most valuable moral conviction at the basis of Emmanuel Levinas's philosophy. We do not know how badly Nelly's face is wounded, and this ignorance institutes the moral position, the Levinasan ethical imperative that Lene chooses. She is responsible for Nelly although it is not her fault that Nelly is badly wounded. We the blameless are not blameless in a world that sees the atrocities of World War II and continues to treat people like so many objects of bureaucratic efficiency. We must assert the humanity of the Other, the one whose humanity is not seen as equal to ours. We have to assume responsibility for the life of the Other as if it were we who destroyed her face, who accepted a world in which "thou shalt kill" the neighbor was a valid treatment of Otherness. Lene will continue to be responsible for Nelly until the end, when she elects to commit suicide and lets Nelly be reconciled with her own, different choices.

The choice to begin the film with a heroin whose face is the locus of injury, one to whom the armed soldier eventually apologizes, shows Petzold to be working within the parameters of Levinas's moral philosophy. In the encounter with the Other, a sublime moment of revelation occurs, because the face, the moral site of becoming a subject, articulates a commandment: "though shalt not kill." But it is not just that one must not kill, one is also responsible for the other person, the one who is in danger of being killed. One does not have the freedom to ignore the violence to which that face has been subjected, for, in this case, freedom is violence. Outside ethics there is only desolation.

Levinas's philosophy of facial sensibilities restores the importance of an encounter with the *who* or with alterity. Levinas recognizes that the other person always remains foreign and unknown to the "I" and that this is the reason that the other person's humanity is as valuable as mine. This philosophical moral outlook could only come in the aftermath of World War II, under the rule of a Nazi regime where "thou shalt kill" the Other, the different was the imperative, where the encounter with the other's face, the locus of difference signified a license to hate. In the aftermath of the War, the encounter with the face draws one beyond clear bounds, gives birth to the one who cannot kill. "The relation to the face is immediate ethics" Levinas states in his *Éthique et infini* (81, translation mine), and ethics depends on my acknowledgement that "it is I who support the Other, and am responsible for her" (*Ethics and Infinity*, 196).The human, Levinas argues, is responsible to protect the alterity that is inscribed in the face, even though in this responsibility the subject is exposed to danger. At the checkpoint, the rude soldier, who, upon seeing Nelly's face feels the need to apologize, is now "ordered" and "ordained" by the face, responsible for the women's safe return to Germany, to use Levinas's language (*Ethics and Infinity*, 195).

The trope of love and grief that runs through *Phoenix* is tied together with the ethical imperative that issues from the face although Levinas speaks about the kind of love of humanity that transcends *Eros*. Emotions like gratitude, forgiveness, and resentment emerge when Nelly begins to fear the encounter with ill will. She can only use the old pictures that she has saved to remember what her face looked like, and to remember the then-blameless faces of her husband and friends. Nelly knows that the still images from the past signify the death of the past, as much as they move her to forgive in her search for a new future. Against all evidence Nelly keeps hoping that gratitude for the past can return love from, and to, the dead, transforming love itself in the process.

Early in the film, when Nelly is being anaesthetized for her face-reconstruction surgery, her hallucinating mind returns to a boathouse that neither she nor the audience can identify or connect to the story. In the boathouse – which returns in the scene of anagnorsis – she recognizes Johnny's back. He is at the piano. This is the *mis-en-cène* that introduces prolepsis, as a preconscious state or as traumatic knowledge, to the present. Nelly does not understand that she is already seeking out the return of the repressed. Traumatic memory prompts her to reconstruct her old face and, in her vision, the old images become tactile. Consciously, Nelly recognizes faces through her old photos. Preconsciously, she entertains the idea that Johnny has been waiting for her, that he did not betray her. If she is wrong about this, then perhaps she can be free of him and be able to leave and move on. But where will she go?

As Lene inspects the same photographs, the film's score evokes the thuds of a typing machine and the screeches of a fountain pen. Unlike Nelly, Lene is a researcher, motivated by reason, by the need to know and possibly bring the guilty to trial. Lene knows what Johnny did to Nelly in 1944, but Lene remains a mystery both to Nelly and to the audience. She is a fact finder and the facts do not disclose emotions. The facts do not take shape as a comprehensible story.

The focus on Lene's reasoning, on her conscious and mentally composed state, positions her as the signifier of resentment. She resents Germany in the aftermath of the War, and every encounter with new documents, as well as her chance encounter with Johnny, confirm that her moral stance is just. Everyone she used to know is dead or collaborated with the Nazi regime. The postwar Germans are remorseless. *Phoenix* does not choose sides, does not disentangle the paradox of Nelly's forgiveness and Lene's resentment. As Nelly cruises the ruined city of Berlin in search of Johnny, Lene investigates the archives in search of survivors. Forgiveness and resentment join together to restore emotion and cognitive responsibility to the human face. Levinas affirms neither forgiveness nor resentment but upholds responsibility in the face of Otherness for a unique face signifies the infinity of the dimension of morality. Ethical significance appears, "in the fact that the more I am just the more I am responsible; one is never quite without regard to the Other" (Ethics and Infinity, 197). Responsibility, like forgiveness, like resentment, refuses closure it is a relation to the other person and to Otherness *tout court*.

## Petzold's Sebald: "We have a plague of flies"

In *On the Natural History of Destruction*, Sebald criticizes the allies for bombing German cities, but nevertheless cannot identify with those German writers who, after the air strikes, write novels about ideas, sublimation, and transcendence. Sebald prefers narratives that are historically and morally bound, in which writers face Germany's destruction dead on, from the burnt corpses in the shelters of bombed buildings, to the rats, the flies, the maggots swarming all over the city. Petzold has something similar in mind.

Because Nelly's relatives are dead, she is a rich heiress and can afford to live in the nice apartment that Lene found for them, and to continue to employ Elisabeth (Imogene Cogge), the housekeeper who always hated the Nazis. Elisabeth is the one who forbids her employers to turn the lights on or to take the nets off the windows because of flies. Unlike the texts that Sebald praises, Elisabeth is not interested in why the city is infested with flies. "We have a plague of flies," she simply deadpans. Elisabeth, as a "new German," personifies the phoenix of Greek myth, rising out of the ashes of her predecessor. Pragmatic and industrious, Elisabeth offers proper solutions to concrete problems. Her position as housekeeper illustrates a new pragmatic German, who resides neither in the past nor in the future, but works with absolute devotion and precision and earns a living even in the most difficult of circumstances, to then rise from the ashes and rebuild her life.

This scene when Elisabeth forbids Nelly to open the window is important because Elisabeth and Lene are depicted as straightforward and down to earth, while Nelly appears almost unreal. Pragmatism, it turns out, yields limited results in everyday life. Elisabeth fails to mend the historical wrongs that they all experienced, for even she is unable to prevent Lene's suicide.

## Petzold's Paul Celan, I

Nelly, who runs around town looking for Johnny, yearns to relive the past in order to build a better future for them both because she trusts in love and forgiveness. Lene is also attached to the past and, though she obtains visas to go to Palestine/Israel, and insists on the moral obligation to emigrate from Germany to a country in which Jews can be safe and live as a free nation her emotional attachment is not clear. What kind of affective remedy does Lene seek out when she convinces herself that more than anything it is important that she recover the money and assets that Nelly's family left behind in Germany and Switzerland, take everything back from the Nazis, if her grief is too heavy a weight? When Lene goes to Poland in search of more documents, Nelly reminds her that they are not Jewish by which she means to say that they have always implemented universalism in their lives as intellectuals or artists so how can living in Israel or documenting the belongings of those Jews who died help them to build a new life? This is an attitude that Lene cannot accept, for, in the aftermath of the War, assimilated Jews are still Jews, even if, like Paul Celan or Jean Améry, they are pariahs from Judaism as well as from the liberal new Germany and are still committed to universal laws of justice, judgment.

Nelly finds out what Lene knows about Johnny, that he is a traitor who informed on Nelly to the Nazis, but Nelly's smile signifies that she is happy to have news from Johnny. Nelly is committed to love and forgiveness and trusts that the rest will have to be settled between her and her husband when they meet. Nelly does not relinquish her marriage yet. The betrayal is not personal yet, not personally verifiable or affective. Lene is committed to justice and resentment and gives Nelly a gun, although she does not realize that Nelly has already found Johnny, that Nelly collaborated with his plan though he did not recognize her. Lene does not realize that, symbolically, she is asking Nelly to try and kill Johnny, not love and give him a second chance.

Johnny represents another kind of German phoenix. He collaborated with the Nazis but feels no shame or regret about it. Indeed, disavowal of the past energizes him, for he believes disavowal will allow him to prosper. As Johannes, he locks "Esther" in his basement apartment because, if his plan is to succeed, then no one can see her before she is fully trained, transformed into the deceased Nelly. In yet another paradox, Johannes prompts her to become Nelly by imitating an actress from a prewar poster that Nelly, in her old life, used to model her looks after. The actress on the poster is dressed and made up, her hair bobbing in the wind. Nelly, as Esther, imitates the actress on the poster so she can look, dress, and move like the Nelly from the past, who developed her mannerisms by looking at the same poster. Esther complains, in a plea for recognition, urging Johannes to acknowledge that no survivor of the camps could look like the woman in the poster – "You think anyone leaves the camps like that? It won't work. I can't come back from the camp like that." Johannes denies that the camps are at all relevant to the project at hand. He and Esther just need to make the others believe that Nelly is back and collect the inheritance. The phoenix is not a symbol of remembrance in this film. It is not the locus of a moral enigma that needs to be deciphered. Rather the phoenix who rises from the ashes legitimizes disavowal, because it turns towards the future. It signifies not what ended, but only what is about to begin.

And yet *Phoenix* is a film about forgiveness and resentment, and the roots of these two emotions are sunk deep in the wrongs of the past. Nelly goes along with Johannes's plan because she presumes that Johnny will eventually realize that she survived, and will remember, and be overcome by, the love he used to feel for her, and will feel remorse, and repent, and acknowledge his guilt, and give in to the shame that will subdue him.

In another poignant moment, Johannes recounts to Esther his history with Nelly, before she was arrested and deported, but he does not confess the truth, that he informed on her and is, he believes, responsible for her death. His recollections are a mutated form of disavowal. Johannes tells Esther only what she needs to know in order to better perform her role as Nelly. He scolds Esther – "I know you're not Nelly" – when she tries to sit with him on a bench that they shared as a married couple. "It's not me that you must convince!," he insists, and then kisses Esther, just because he wants to hide her face from the people walking on the sidewalk. Nelly remains committed to the past, because she is seeking a moral meaning and an ethical obligation. She is not too weak to explore new connections in her life. "I would not have survived the camp without Johnny," she tells Lene. For her this is the truth, and this truth entails a moral statement that might save her again, help her move into the future with good memories in her mind, not just the memory of genocide.

Lene is resentful. She cannot understand how, although Jews were systematically murdered, one by one and all together the survivors come back ready to forgive. Nelly cannot believe that Johnny betrayed her, and Lene cannot live in a world where survivors forgive their would-be executioners. But without Nelly's forgiveness, Lene's resentment is meaningless, and, by the same token, without Lene's skepticism, Nelly's hope is pure ignorance. Neither one can break free from the trauma of genocide, but each chooses what to express, and how, about it.

The film comes full circle when Nelly goes into the boathouse and realizes that Johnny was there when she was arrested. The hallucinatory images that were roaming in her head while she was under the influence of anesthesia return. In the boathouse she goes into shock, for consciously she cannot cope with the knowledge that she previously held in her unconscious.

## Petzold's Alain Resnais: The railroad and the past

It seems that, because of masterpieces like Alain Resnais' documentary *Night and Fog* (1956), Petzold cannot bring Nelly back from the camp without calling back to mind the iconic image of the railroad. Resnais's film opens with a tracking shot of the rails in 1955, the tenth anniversary of the end of the War. The grass and the iron rails seamlessly come together to form a peaceful natural image. Later he shows the wagons at night during the War years, bursting at the seams with chocking passengers who would have jumped out had the rails not been guarded by armed Nazi soldiers. Petzold must have thought of this images as he puts Nelly, as Esther impersonating Nelly, arriving from the camp at the train station in a fashionable, contemporary coach. Dressed in a red dress, her hair colored a dark brown, wearing shoes from Paris, she is ready to meet the five friends Johnny brings to serve as witnesses that Nelly has truly returned.

**Figures 4, 5:** *Night and Fog*, DVD screen shots.

## Petzold's Paul Celan, II: "I feel more drawn to our dead than to our living"

Just before Nelly arrives at the train station and into the arms of her expectant friends and husband, she comes to the apartment to see Lene, who has, says Elisabeth the housekeeper, shot herself. In keeping with her position as the signifier of resentment, Lene has left two suicide notes behind her. The first is a recommendation for Elisabeth to show prospective future employers. The second is a letter to Nelly, in which Lene declares "there is no way back for us." Lene, it transpires, could not move forward, and her last words echo Celan – "I feel more drawn to our dead than to our living."

To her suicide letter Lene has attached the documents that prove Johnny's betrayal of Nelly. Nelly is overwhelmed with grief but also furious, yet the incontrovertible proof still does not sway Nelly's mind. Although the revolver that Lene gave her is safely tucked in her handbag, although she can if she wishes kill Johnny, avenge herself and avenge the dead, Nelly elects to play her part in Johnny's melodramatic staging of the lovers' reunion. Only at the very end of the film does it become clear that Nelly's reasons for performing in Johnny's deception have undergone a radical transformation.

*Phoenix* is the marriage melodrama that Petzold implicates in the violence of World War II. The violence of history appears on the documents that Lene uncovers and offers so as to obtain a just judgment of the criminals. The violence of the melodrama between Nelly and Johnny never takes place but it is always imminent. In melodramatic form the affects love, repentance, forgiveness and resentment must fall within the structure of paradox for morality to always be forthcoming, not subject or reduced to closure.

The five friends behave as if the War left behind no residue. They missed her – "now here you are, Nelly!" – then they celebrate her. At this moment Esther/Nelly chooses to perform one last time. With her ex-husband Johnny at the piano, she sings "Speak Low." This is a song about a love that ends, about the lovers that are "swept apart too soon." The music does not stop because Johnny realizes that Esther sings very much like Nelly used to sing. It stops because Johnny sees the tattooed Auschwitz number on Nelly's arm. Can it be that this love ends too soon, if the entire time Johnny was blind to the tattooed number on his wife's arm? Can it be that Nelly's forgiveness is nothing but self-deception? Could Nelly have been made whole enough to leave Johnny and move into her future without investigating the depths of his disavowal, the seriousness of her emotional commitment to wager on the good?

The melodrama is left with a vacant center: Petzold stages nothing. The camera pans out and captures a *tableaux vivant* of the five friends, frozen in their chairs, Johnny transfixed at the piano. These figures are as dead to the film and the viewer as Nelly. They signify absolute absence of both affect and cognition. A point-of-view shot captures Nelly from behind, alone with her thoughts. Her blurry back is all the viewer sees when she leaves these six figures behind and enters into an actuality outside of the frame, on the off-screen. *Phoenix* does not provide any image of the future Nelly aims to build for herself. The future that her love and forgiveness aim for is found beyond Petzold's cinematic melodrama. *Phoenix* points at it, but cannot access it.

# Chapter 3
# The sincerity of forgiveness – on Heinrich Böll and Jean Améry

> I do not want to become the accomplice of my torturers; rather, I demand that the latter negate themselves and in the negation coordinate with me. The piles of corpses that lie between them and me cannot be removed in the process of internalization, so it seems to me, but, on the contrary, through actualization, or, more strongly stated, by actively settling the unresolved conflict in the field of historical practice. **Jean Améry**, "Resentments" (1980, 69)

> Forgive me if I laugh. Don't carry the thing too far, with your formulas in your head, don't lose patience and don't accept any favors. We aren't going to eat a crumb more than we get on the ration cards. Edith is agreeable to that. Eat what everybody eats, wear what everybody wears, read what everybody reads. Don't take the extra butter, the extra cloths, the extra poem which dishes up the Beast in a more elegant fashion. *Their right hand is full of bribes,* bribe money in a variety of coins. **Heinrich Böll**, *Billiards at Half-Past Nine* (1959, 143)

Améry and Heinrich Böll belong on opposite banks of the moral chasm that separated Jewish survivors and Gentile Germans in the aftermath of the Holocaust. Yet, as I argue in this chapter, their texts are in conversation with each other. From their opposite sides of the moral divide each puts forward the emotions of forgiveness and resentment; one by articulating the suffering of the victims, the other by insisting on the need for repentance on the part of the perpetrators, their accomplices, and the nation of bystanders who stood aside and did nothing.

Their investigations into the relationship between resentment and forgiveness allow these writers to implicate culture into moral considerations in the process of rendering mass atrocity meaningful. Survivors and offenders often testify that genocide was meaningless, that nothing could be learned from the inhumanity of the death camps. Yet Améry and Böll show that the opposite is true. An open, honest, moral discussion of atrocity can transform victims, from the prosecuted and abandoned to the necessary voice of ethics and action in the community. The conversation between Améry and Böll is a moral demand that Germany acknowledge its guilt and undergo true moral change.

Améry speaks of the distance between himself and those who hurt him. As he examines the rancor that a victim harbors against the torturer, this distance obligates the German Other to learn his language. Améry demands that the perpetrator "negate" himself in the "field of historical practice" (Amery 1980, 69). That is, Germany must bequeath to humanity an indicting, systematic documentation of its crimes. For Améry, personal remorse and future forgiveness neither exonerate the perpetrator nor completely eliminate the victim's resentment. Only national, public disclosure of the truth, in the form of documentary evidence as well as works of art, can attenuate guilt.

A sincere acknowledgment of guilt legitimizes a conversation on forgiveness and remorse. The German nation must "learn to comprehend its past acquiescence in the Third Reich [. . .] as its own negative possession" (Améry 1980, 78). Repentant Germans must accept that the years of Nazism are not an outlier in German history, but part and parcel of Germany's blood cycle. The Holocaust, therefore, must become Germany's negative possession, much like Immanuel Kant is its possession of Enlightenment. Negative possessions cannot be reduced to logical explanations. The shock that remains in the aftermath of the genocide of European Jewry belongs to a future moral language. As of now, only the ineffable can connote the enormity of evil, that which is indescribably inhuman.

The resolution of conflict between victims and perpetrators dooms both parties to be torn by infinite, torturing resentment, by forgiveness and regret, by remorse and shame. Victims and perpetrators are engulfed in a psychological and moral drama that is played out on the stage of history. This chapter examines Böll's novel *The Clown*, the roots of which are an examination of resentment's value and its necessary relation to forgiveness. Böll's protagonists are resentful. They resist the Nazis while enduring the torments of war.

In *Billiards at Half-Past Nine*, the family's father, Heinrich Faehmel, recalls that his wife and daughter-in-law refused to buy in the black market during the War. The children suffered hunger and cold, but the Faehmel family did not collaborate with "the Beast" (the Nazis). Robert, the children's father, remained loyal to the Lambs (those who resisted the Nazis). Lambs who actively resisted the Beast were either sent to concentration camps or immediately shot.

*Billiards at Half-Past Nine* and *The Clown* are Germany's negative possessions, because they reveal the evil operations of the Nazi perpetrators and discuss the kinds of guilt that Germany incurred as a society. At the same time, the novels are caught up in silence and metaphor, which point towards resentment and forgiveness.

In the aftermath of mass atrocity, forgiveness and resentment are tied up with one another. Inner conflict, war, and genocide give rise to forgiveness and remorse only if resentment propels perpetrators to document their atrocities. Resentment is necessary for acts of forgiveness and remorse to take place. The resentment gnawing at those who forgive does not diminish their forgiveness, but rather adds value to it. Améry's resentment always contains a nucleus of forgiveness. In fact, it is his obligation to the possibility of forgiveness that motivates an examination of his resentments.

In Améry's vision, German citizens will rebuild a new and just German society. He addresses those readers who want to participate in the historical moment, when perpetrators and victims probe their emotions and moral structures in order to find a way to rebuild their culture on values of justice and human dignity. Améry opens a dialogue with his German contemporaries because he wants to establish that they are paying attention, that they are human, and that they can be remorseful. The psychological scrutiny of the perpetrator's ability to change points toward a nucleus of forgiveness that energizes Améry's sincere examination of his resentments. If Améry resents his German reader, it is because he remembers a past in which this reader was a kindred soul. During his childhood in Vienna, Améry was "an impressive German youth" (Améry 1980, 82), but in 1935, when the Nuremberg Laws were instituted, he became a Jew "by decree of law and society" (Améry 1980, 85).

Following Améry, I argue that if an individual is not called upon to both forgive and understand her/his resentments, then s/he is not a politically, psychologically, or morally responsible agent. Améry and Böll write on guilt, forgiveness, and resentment in the aftermath of the Holocaust because they envision a return to moral existence. However, this return is dependent upon a structural restoration of the values of forgiveness and resentment.

In, *On Forgiveness*, Derrida asserts that forgiveness forgives only the unforgiveable crimes against humanity and that, in this context, it is pure – that is, it disables practical, political considerations: "forgiveness must remain a madness of the impossible" (Derrida 2001, 39). But is this mad notion of forgiveness possible? My interpretation of forgiveness follows Derrida, taking forgiveness to be political and very much relevant in the aftermath of crimes against humanity. Forgiveness is a madness of the impossible, because it produces an opening for victim and perpetrator to live together as equals in a new society.

Forgiveness remains not pure. It is a moral value, not a political implement. And yet, forgiveness is necessary in practices of reconciliation. In forgiveness, however, there is a kernel of resentment, which enables the forgiving person to remember the atrocities committed against her/him, and allows both victim and perpetrator to undergo moral transformation. At the same time, there remains a kernel of forgiveness within resentment, which allows the victim to direct moral anger toward the perpetrator. This is important for the sake of the new society that the perpetrator and the victim want to build. To forgive a perpetrator is to invest mental effort in overcoming numerous emotions and convictions. Forgiveness cannot occur without great personal and cultural struggle with resentment. If a victim forgives, s/he does so because s/he is obligated to share existence with a changed perpetrator. The forgiving victim articulates her/his feelings of indignation in order to make her/himself known to the perpetrator. A forgiving subject does not feel scorn toward the perpetrator. S/he feels broken by the brutality that was perpetrated.

True forgiveness points to the victim's ability to initiate moral communication with the perpetrator. It is both conscious and unconscious. Interaction with the perpetrator opens up a channel of communication that is based on sincere disclosure of the victim's pain, as well as the articulation of the perpetrator's guilt. Forgiveness is a moral value, but also an intrapsychic state of openness, which enables one to make one's suffering known and listen to the perpetrator's confession. Forgiveness includes a concrete and an imaginary appeal to the human capacity to care for the Other. Forgiveness opens the possibility that trust will arise. Trust, in turn, promotes the creation of a just structure of interconnectedness between victim and perpetrator. Forgiveness envisions crimes against humanity as radical evil that tortures both victims and perpetrators. When a society attempts to renew itself by extending equality to its victims, that society must be critically examined, seeing as this extension of equality dismantles the supposed superiority of the perpetrator. Forgiveness becomes a future in which the victim is in a productive moral relationship with the perpetrator. The value of forgiveness is intersubjective. Agreeing to restore connections with the perpetrator amounts to a moral outlook on the world, even in the aftermath of catastrophe.[1]

---

[1] Here I view forgiveness in the context of mass atrocity differently from Arendt: "It is therefore quite significant, a structural element, in the realms of human affairs, that men are unable to forgive what they cannot punish and that they cannot punish what has turned out to be unforgiveable" (Arendt 1958, 241). Pamela Hieronymi offers a definition of forgiveness in everyday life, but vacillates when determining if the forgiving victim is allowed to hold on to certain expressions of resentment: "Resentment, I believe, should be understood as protest. In resentment the victim protests the trespass, affirming both its wrongfulness and the moral significance of both herself and the offender. The challenge for any account of forgiveness, as I see it, lies in articulating how we can maintain the three judgments enlisted and yet abandon the protest" (Hieronymi 2001, 530). I think that Hieronymi's definition is wavering because she endorses resentment in the form of inner conviction: "You, as the one wronged, ought not to be wronged. This sort of treatment stands as an offense to your person" (Hieronymi 2001, 530). Does Hieronymi consider a memorial day to commemorate the victims as a protest against the perpetrator, or does she understand practices of memorialization to be an inner strength, knowing that one can survive despite the evil that was committed against him? This indecision becomes accentuated when Hieronymi sympathizes with the resentful victim: "But if we understand the event as carrying broader, social meaning, and if we understand one's identity as at least partially constituted by how one is perceived by others, then we can both start to make sense of remorse and start to see why one's repentance and change in heart requires ratification by others. [. . .] If all goes well, the joint action of requesting and granting forgiveness will leave the original meaning of the

The resentful victim is overwhelmed by negative emotions: disappointment, alienation, hatred, a desire for revenge. Yet resentment is both intrasubjective and intersubjective. It entails an unconscious effort to subdue emotions (such as dependence on the perpetrator), and it is also a conscious, public indictment of the perpetrator. Like forgiveness, which contains a kernel of resentment, resentment protects a nucleus of forgiveness.

As a former Austrian citizen, Améry felt integral to German culture, and sought to change it from within. His conviction justifies the kernel of forgiveness within his resentment. After the Holocaust, German intellectuals could accept Améry as part of German culture because during the War few Germans risked their lives to help Jews, and because, after the War, some Germans sought to discover the conditions that allow them to atone for genocide. These Germans took it for granted that Jews would influence the moral restoration of German culture.

Améryy follows in the footsteps of Karl Jaspers, who argues in *The Question of German Guilt* that Germany only has a future if it accepts radical guilt: criminal guilt, political guilt, moral guilt, and metaphysical guilt. Améry compels his fellow Germans to become ethical by acknowledging their guilt, by recognizing the suffering of the persecuted dead and the surviving Jews. He is open to hearing the Germans who committed the crimes. Yet he also requires that they feel the burden of convincing the world that they are morally worthy.

Crucially, Améry is didactic, laying out the terms for the future restoration of Germany. Such a restoration Améry can safely entrust in the hands of German Gentiles, who will respect the interrelatedness of resentment and forgiveness. Resentment pervaded by a nucleus of forgiveness signifies the need to maintain cooperation between victim and offender. Germany must acknowledge its negative possessions by publicly expressing guilt through cultural platforms such as literature, film, and museums. These practices do not make redundant the transcendental guilt that Germany must honestly accept.[2] For the resentful survivor, historical admission of guilt is an acceptance of her/his demands for respect and equality in the new society that victims and perpetrators must forge together.

---

event in the past. This is the first thing forgiveness 'does'" (Hieronymi 2001, 550). Hieronymi demands that resentment discontinues the portrayal of the perpetrator as a present threat to the forgiving victim, but s/he allows the victim to continue to establish her/his identity partly based on surviving the atrocity that victimized her/him. In other words, Hieronymi does not keep the victim from remembering the atrocities that the perpetrator executed against her/his ethnicity or nation.

2 In the context of Améry's resentment, it is important to mention scholars who disagree with my interpretation. See: (Brudholm and Rosoux 2009, 37–41).

In the case of authors who take the approach of pure forgiveness, the storytelling act memorializes and disseminates descriptions of violence. Such memorialization indicates a nurturing of resentment towards the victimizers, making pure forgiveness and remorse impossible. Böll and Améry belong to the European legacy of remorse and forgiveness. Despite the fact that Böll is a Gentile and Améry a Jew, there is a kinship to how they express festering resentment. Böll and Améry reach out to others to listen, to be informed, to condemn the victimizers, and perhaps even rearrange their own politics in view of the harm to which they have been exposed. Böll's fiction, as much as Améry's confessions, constitutes negative possessions that Germans must embrace in order to comprehend their own guilt. Remorse is a sign that Germans have responded to Jaspers' call to "renew yourself morally." Positive narratives of forgiveness necessarily entail bitter resentment, while negative narratives of resentment carry a kernel of healing and correction. Forgiveness and resentment are interdependent, each wrapped around the other.

## Forgiveness, resentment, and madness

A victim who does not forgive is said to be stuck in a state of resentment.[3] American and Continental philosophers write that a resentful individual remains attached to past injuries in order to make moral claims about the future. This suggests that the victim is psychologically damaged or manipulative, not forgiving.[4] But forgiveness and resentment become possible as soon as they appear in the form of an address. A resentful victim who addresses a perpetrator forges a new connection. A forgiving victim who insists on her/his right to remember and commemorate the dead broadcasts the right to remain resentful and to suffer.

Derrida, as discussed, has a different outlook: "forgiveness worthy of its name, if there ever is such a thing, must forgive the unforgivable, and without condition" (Derrida 2001, 39). For Derrida, forgiveness comes into being only when it is impossible – that is, when the power to forgive is equivalent to one's

---

3 See, for example, Jankélévitch 2005, 119–122 and Hughes 1997, 36. For a more inclusive overview of the principles that define forgiveness and foreswear resentment see Griswold 2007, 38–43.
4 Freud's studies "Remembering, Repeating and Working-Through" and "Mourning and Melancholia" are necessary to understand this. Freud shows that a victim who is attached to the past is immersed in mourning, self-loathing, and rancor, which appear in the form of acting out. These resentments disrupt reasonable mental activities (such as remembering and working-through past injuries) and they disable the cathexes of new love objects in the present.

commitment to remember the unforgiveable crimes.[5] I think Derrida is discretely influenced by Améry, and that it is possible to find in his work a link between forgiveness and resentment.

Améry's reflections on resentment provide Derrida with an understanding of "unforgiveable offenses," which help build his theoretical framework. I interpret Derrida to be saying something like this: Améry articulates pure resentment, an emotion that completely denies forgiveness. Derrida then defines pure forgiveness as tied up with pure resentment, reaching a deadlock where only the paradox exists. For Derrida, forgiveness and resentment remain forever pure. Each one of these emotions rejects its opposite, because it is just as valuable as its counter-emotion. Yet Derrida argues that, if pure forgiveness were possible, it would be mad, a madness of the impossible.

Thus, for Derrida, as for Améry, forgiveness is relevant uniquely to the unforgivably evil. Améry imagines that his German readers are interested in his resentments because they conjure truth, albeit painful: "What matters to me is the description of the subjective state of the victim. [. . .] [T]here was much talk about collective guilt to Germans. It would be an outright distortion of the truth if I did not confess here without any concealment that this was fine with me" (Amery 1980, 64–65). Améry is against those who are "trembling with the pathos of forgiveness," and explains the honest demands of his resentment (Amery 1980, 65). "Absurdly," his resentment "demands that the irreversible be turned around, that the event be undone. Resentment blocks the exit to the genuine human dimension, the future" (Amery 1980, 68). For Améry, forgiveness is a process which cannot be fully completed without resentment. His psychological pain emerges as he enacts an "ethics *beyond ethics,*" reaching towards forgiveness at the same time as he holds on to his resentments:

> The social body is occupied merely with safeguarding itself and could not care less about a life that has been damaged. At the very best it looks forward, so that such things don't happen again. But my resentments are here in order that the crime become a moral reality for the criminal, in order that he be swept into the truth of his atrocity (Améry 1980, 71).

Améry is willing to contemplate forgiveness only if he is allowed to publicly explain the moral reality of suffering. He demands that the unforgivable crimes committed against him be made real to the criminal. He is opening a conversation with German readers, who look to the future and seek forgiveness. For Améry, forgiveness is tied up with the perpetrator's ability to "be swept into the truth of

---

5 Derrida insists that forgiveness is "impossible" and "mad" (Derrida 2001, 39) because his essay is engaged in an open dialogue with Jankélévitch (1971; 1996).

his atrocity" (Améry 1980, 71). He trusts there are Germans who are interested in his story and want to know the truth of suffering: "I would be thankful to the reader if he were willing to follow me, even if in the hour before us he more than once feels the wish to put down the book" (Améry 1980, 63). When Germans read Améry's story, they allow for connection between their contemporary, material reality and the ethical consequences of committing unforgiveable crimes.

For Derrida, the history of forgiveness begins with the unforgiveable. For Améry it begins with resentment (Derrida 2001, 37). Forgiveness is an *event*, a "revolution" (Derrida 2001, 39). Revolution, like forgiveness, alters the ordinary course of history and generates new historical conditions[6] (Derrida 1993, 127). When contemplating forgiveness, Derrida dreams of "what I try to think as the 'purity' of a forgiveness worthy of its name, would be a forgiveness without power" (Derrida 2001, 59). What is forgiveness without power? According to Améry, repentance and forgiveness are "without power" if the memory of the atrocities becomes a "negative possession":

> The German people would remain sensitive to the fact that they cannot allow a piece of their national history to be neutralized by time, but must integrate it . . . It would no longer repress or hush up the twelve years that for us others really were a thousand, but claim them as its realized negation of the world and its self, as its own negative possession (Améry 1980, 78).

Améry is arguing that Germans cannot pretend to explain what they did under the rule of the Third Reich. They therefore must document their individual and national actions, so that every new generation of German citizens will continue to accept guilt for the sake of moral rebirth. *These possessions* are negative because they negate every value that establishes human existence. It is impossible to truly comprehend the evil of the Third Reich, so the victim may articulate truths of such magnitude only when s/he is using the language of the ineffable, wherein every description of evil leaves the addressor and the addressee in a state of being "overcome" (Améry 1980, xiv), even if this language does not yield a reasonable state of understanding.

Forgiveness and resentment cannot be separated. There is neither pure forgiveness nor pure resentment. Both Derrida and Améry show how difficult it is to separate forgiveness and resentment in instances of political reconciliation. National memorial practices usher in a process of psychological healing and social

---

6 See the description of "Marxism tomorrow" in *Specters of Marx* (1993, 127). Marx argues that "the bourgeoisie, to be sure, is bound to fear the stupidity of the masses as long as they remain conservative, and the insight of the masses as soon as they become revolutionary" (Marx 1994, 201).

reconciliation, but those are political conditions that profoundly differ from the gift of forgiveness, which is the isolation of resentment.[7] Derrida insists that forgiveness must not advance redemption, normalcy, reparations, an ecology of reconciliation. At the same time, he recognizes that practices of reconciliation allow perpetrators to actively engage with their guilt by expressing repentance in the public sphere. Reconciliation becomes ethical, not just practical.

The guilty declare their accountability and document their guilt as a negative possession. Yet, Améry complains, practices of reconciliation conceal interests: "The social body is occupied merely with safeguarding itself" (Améry 1980, 71). When Germans claim that there is no race hatred in Germany, Améry is wary: "the man tried to convince me that the German people bear no grudge against the Jewish people. As proof, he cited the government's magnanimous policy of reparations, which was, incidentally, well appreciated by the state of Israel" (Améry 1980, 67).

Forgiveness needs social and political practices of reconciliation in order to initiate a public and subjective acknowledgement that "forgiveness forgives only the unforgiveable" (Derrida 2001, 32). However, Améry is not interested in the practical advantages of reconciliation. His resentments point back to psychology and ethics: "at stake for me is the release from the abandonment that has persisted from that time until today" (Améry 1980, 70). In other words, Améry will emerge from his loneliness to engage with German intellectuals, finding meaning in historical and fictional documentation of the atrocities. Forgiveness delivers the victim from loneliness.

Can Améry forgive the Germans while, at the same time, resenting them? This is not a question of forgiving the Holocaust.[8] The Holocaust is larger than a single victim and survivor. It is larger than the German nation. Améry is interested in forgiveness as both a personal emotion and a public value. Despite his resentment, he does not relinquish the imagined consequences of forgiveness. In this sense, Derrida's assertion that forgiveness is mad comes into focus. In the same way that madness gives meaning to reason, forgiveness gives meaning to Améry's resentment.[9] Unreasonably, forgiveness demands interactions with the

---

[7] See Blustein (2014, 147–48, 175) for an opposing argument that in cultures of resentment memorial practices encourage forgiveness.
[8] See Kristeva (2002, 283).
[9] In "Cogito and the History of Madness," Derrida suggests that Foucault is in the wrong when he claims that Descartes uses force to exclude madness from thinking, and to condemn madness to silence, the opposite of work. According to Derrida, sensory error and thoughtful illusion are the conditions of language, structure, and reason. Madness is the caesura in thought and speech that caries meaning and innovation, which reappear when reason overcomes silence through an

perpetrator, keeping the Holocaust on the public agenda. Forgiveness obligates the perpetrator to construe a just, historical, and educational conversation with the victim. However, forgiveness does not bring about closure. On the contrary, forgiveness consists of continuing the relationship between the perpetrator and the victim, achieving greater individual and public clarity, and exposing the conflict inherent in society.

Resentment forces the disclosure of truth, opening a possibility that the culture will be altered in response. Resentment demands an active engagement with guilt, both psychologically and historically. Such disclosure and memorialization of atrocity enable larger conversations. Forgiveness introduces an imaginative, even illusory meaning into such conversations, which are grounded in horrific facts and histories. Forgiveness opens a space between victim and perpetrator. Resentment keeps that space from collapsing into amnesia. Améry will never cease to remember the atrocities or to feel resentment toward the crimes. Yet, within a German culture that implements the changes that Améry articulates, he can feel less abandoned. If Germany and Austria can accept guilt as a negative possession, then Améry can become more than a mere victim in his German tongue and culture. Améry writes *At the Mind's Limit* not just to understand his own resentments, or to sever his relations with Germany and the German language, but to re-establish the sincerity of forgiveness.

## Jewish biography and German contemporaneity

Améry's story of resentment is not a lone voice in the intellectual landscape of his time. It contributes, rather, to a collection of thinkers striving to make clear the necessity of forgiveness in both personal and international contexts. As I have discussed in earlier chapters, I consider Améry's writings to be in conversation with those of Primo Levi, Hannah Arendt, and Gershom Scholem. Each of them contributes to Améry's analysis of forgiveness and resentment. It becomes clear that resentment does not eliminate the sincerity of forgiveness. It calls instead for an ever deeper historical awareness and documentation of atrocity.

Améry began writing his articles on torture after the Auschwitz trials were held in Frankfurt in 1963–65. However, in 1966, he realized that his initial feeling of belonging to post-War German culture was illusory. As he observed Germans'

---

act of force. "The madman is not always wrong about everything. [. . .] [I]t meets the resistance of the nonphilosopher who does not have the audacity to follow the philosopher when the latter agrees that he might indeed be mad at the very moment when he speaks" (Derrida 1978, 51).

worldview changing, he found German guilt to be dissipating. This led him to the conclusion that Germans did not feel remorse. They only wanted to be strong and "great" again (Améry 1980, 66). In the essays, "How Much Home Does a Person Need?," "Resentments," and "The Necessity and Impossibility of Being a Jew," Améry examines feelings like "loneliness," (Améry 1980, 70), "abandonment," (ibid.), a lack of "security," (Améry 1980, 46) and the impossibility of "trust" (Améry 1980, 47) in the other person, and the need to regain "physical and metaphysical dignity" (Améry 1980, 91). These are the emotions that hold sway in the psychic and moral life of the resentful victim. As Améry and his contemporaries demonstrate, resentment neither ceases when the perpetrator acknowledges his guilt, nor can forgiveness be eliminated if the perpetrator remains silent.

In parallel with Améry's experience, Levi discloses the injuries he suffered in Auschwitz and speaks of a "deep wound" inflicted on "human dignity" (Levi 1988, 111). When a generation of younger listeners asks Levi why he did not erase his tattoo from Auschwitz, he replies that "[t]here are not many of us in the world to bear this witness" (Levi 1988, 120). The tattoo is, as Améry describes, a negative possession of Western culture. But unlike Améry, whose works "consist of returning the blow" (Levi 1988, 129), Levi is "not able, personally, to trade punches or return blows" (Levi 1988, 137).

Although different from Améry's, Levi's forgiveness is not without resentment. He knows that expressions of forgiveness and remorse do not bring about understanding or closure.[10] Levi recalls that, as a prisoner, "[German] culture was useful to me" (Levi 1988, 139). Rather than reject German culture, Levi opens a conversation: "Today I, prisoner no. 174517, by your help, can speak to the German people. [. . .] 'I am alive, and I would like to understand you in order to judge you' [. . .] but it will only be an echo; nobody can 'understand' such events!" (Levi 1988, 175–176). No explanation suffices to account for genocide, yet Levi agrees to be in dialogue with German culture, finding an opening. Levi's forgiveness is not without resentment, and neither is Améry's resentment without forgiveness.

Améry and Levi stress the victims' freedom of speech, upholding the need to reinstate dignified communication between Germans and Jews. Améry does not ignore Levi's choice to try to understand the perpetrators. Neither does Levi deny the force of resentment that Améry radiates.[11] At the same time, they open up a

---

**10** Arne Vetlesen supports the opposite opinion: that Levi has no faith in resentment and is therefore unprotected in his conversations with the perpetrator. Levi fears that, under similar circumstances, he could have committed the same crimes. Vetlesen suggests that this lack of protection from imagined culpability caused Levi to commit suicide (Vetlesen 2006, 41).
**11** Magdalena Zolkos is interested in transitional justice, which facilitates reconciliation and the ecology of national healing. However, she needs to closely examine Améry's resentments in

philosophical spectrum that takes into account both individual psychological inclinations and the atrocities committed during the Holocaust.¹²

Likewise, Arendt's reports – from Germany during denazification and from Israel during the Eichmann trial – seek to legitimize forgiveness in the aftermath of World War II. While she expresses resentment toward the state of Germany, she also refuses notions of reform and remorse. In an early text, "Organized Guilt and Universal Responsibility," Arendt articulates resentment towards those German "bourgeois" who ignored the reality of the extermination camps. "In no other country," she accuses, "did private life and private calculation play so great a role" (Arendt 1994 [1945], 130). In 1945, the Allies devised a poster depicting the horrors of Buchenwald. This poster included an inscription directed at the observer: "you are guilty" (Arendt 1994 [1950], 260). Germans looking at the poster claimed that this was the first time they had heard of these horrors. They did not know about the death camps and, hence, could not feel guilty. The poster is a negative possession, rejected by the Germans.

This rejection of guilt upsets Arendt, as it does Améry. It is therefore crucial that, despite validating resentment, Arendt sanctions historical and personal forgiveness for both victims and perpetrators. Arendt views forgiveness as a secular miracle. In *The Human Condition* she writes that forgiving "is the only reaction which does not merely re-act but acts anew and unexpectedly, unconditioned by the act which provoked it" (Arendt 1958, 241). It is true that Arendt wrestles with crimes against humanity: where we cannot punish for a crime, we cannot forgive

---

order to conclude that resentment may be dissipated in time, and then forgiveness might become viable. She notes that "[Améry] theorizes forgiveness as preceded, and even as preconditioned, by the consummation of resentment" (Zolkos 2007, 25). Although Zolkos affirms forgiveness, I understand Améry differently, and show that his text is grounded in a moral, not a temporal paradox. Forgiveness and resentment necessarily appear together. If forgiveness is the threshold of morality, so is resentment. Because resentment is an ethical practice, it functions as a negative possession in relation to a perpetrator who is forgiven once she embraces guilt.

**12** The Fortunoff Video Archives of Holocaust Testimonies at Yale University enabled me to examine testimonies by victims who favor forgiveness, even if they still feel resentment toward the victimizer. I collected twenty testimonies in which forgiveness and resentment appear together, despite the witness's decision to remain within the bounds of forgiveness. Each one of the testimonies articulates different reasons to check resentment, and yet, each witness is afraid that resentment might come back, sway her opinion, and render her more alien in the world. An example is the testimony of June Feinsilver, an inmate at Bergen Belzen and then at Auschwitz. She remembers that the British soldiers gave to the freed people a twenty-four hour window to take revenge on their torturers. Feinsilver tells the interviewer: "I couldn't as much as pick up a rock and throw it. I learned one thing: don't hate because circumstances like that make out of people animals" (testimony no. 2463). Feinsilver foreswears neither resentment nor forgiveness, but she behaves in a manner that affirms human dignity.

it either. If we knew how to punish the crime, then we could hypothetically forgive it. This elliptical reasoning is not satisfying for Améry. He insists that the Holocaust be Germany's negative possession. The magnitude of evil must not be reduced to legal or discursive reasoning, but must leave the victim and the perpetrator in a state of being overcome, hostages of the unspeakable horror.

As discussed in the previous chapter, Scholem reprimands Arendt for not displaying sufficient "*ahavath Israel* [love of the Jewish people]" (Scholem 2002, 396). Scholem wants Arendt to identify with the resentments of the victims. And yet, he struggles to understand why she criticizes the behavior of Jewish committees in the camps. Is this not an excuse to alleviate the perpetrator's guilt? For Scholem, the concern is love, not reconciliation. Love, forgiveness, and resentment, in his view, are simultaneously conscious and unconscious, subjective and public. Dialogue promises not to neglect these covert aspects of emotion. It allows the speakers to remain within the social realm of conscious understanding:

> *Love*, insofar as it once existed, has been drowned in blood; its place must now be taken by historical knowledge and conceptual clarity—the precondition for a discussion that might perhaps bear fruit in the future. If it is to be serious and undemagogic, such a discussion must be approached on a level beyond that of the political and economic factors and interests that have been, or are, under negotiation between the state of Israel and the German Federal Republic (Scholem 1976, 73; italics added).

Any dialogue between Jews and Germans, of course, is loaded with grief. It also forces both sides to inquire who the German Jews really are. Both Derrida and Arendt, as discussed previously, stress that love is interested in who one *is*, not in the assets of *what* one possesses. A dialogue about love between Jews and Germans can disclose *who* German Jews are, and how they created a German-Jewish zeitgeist. This dialogue, made possible by love, need not define *what* a Jew is in a religious or national sense, nor does it need German economic achievements to define *what* a German is. Scholem's assumption is that, even when love fails, it creates an intersubjective field of reference that becomes a public potentiality for rapprochement. According to Arendt, forgiveness, like love, forgives the person because of *who* he is, and does not have to forgive the *what* – the crime. Forgiveness has social value because it brings the singularity of the person to bear on social values.

Katja Garloff well describes the social aspects that love plays in the history of the Jewish-German literati. She helps to contextualize the relevance of forgiveness in social considerations. Garloff suggests that love addresses itself to the very individuality of the loved one, while, at the same time, love restores universal potentialities. Love compels the lover to care about the social context in which the loved one belongs:

> In all of these works [of literature] love becomes socially significant as the figure of a promise still awaiting fulfilment. The simultaneous invocation and interruption of love opens up a space in which German-Jewish relations can be imagined . . . They conceptualize love as a structure of Twoness, an experience of indelible difference. Rather than as a fusion between two people, they see love as an opportunity for differentiation (Garloff 2016, 173–174).

Scholem remains in the realm of conscious dialogue between Germans and Jews. He insists that love can promote differentiation. Through this opening of dialogue, forgiveness and resentment can belong in the public sphere. Scholem, Arendt, and Améry are handling emotions that seem irrelevant to politics – or, worse still, that disappear entirely when they are socially managed. In the social sphere, these emotions produce intersubjective meanings, while remaining an intrasubjective, emotional state.

## Heinrich Böll

The love that institutes difference is found in literature, a conscious, dialogical practice that activates unconscious affect. Forgiveness, like poetry, is intra- and intersubjective: it displaces the logics of retribution, which is grounded in affect, opening the door to meaningful moral change. Because of this, I suggest that the following sentences from Heinrich Böll's 1972 Nobel address be interpreted in the context of forgiveness and resentment:

> May I then not expect that we trust the rationality of poetry, indeed that we reinforce it, not that we leave it in peace but that we adopt something of its peace and of the pride of its humility, which is always a humility directed downward, never upward. Respect dwells within it, and courtesy and justice, and the wish to recognize and be recognized (Böll 1985, 41–42).

Böll concludes his address with the word "resistance," which I see as an asymmetrical synonym of resentment. Améry's resentment toward fascism made him join the Belgian resistance and fight for liberation. Like resistance, resentment is an action directed toward the future, not just a reaction dictated by the past. Böll recounts how "one of these things" he had to omit from his speech "was humor, which is not a class privilege either, yet it is ignored in its poetry and as a hiding place for *resistance*" (Böll 1985, 46; italics added). In Böll's works forgiveness appears together with humor. This is a form of resistance, through which he advocates forgiveness and the disclosure of truth.

Poetic irony is a different logic of truth, the place wherein resistance and forgiveness coexist. In one of his last interviews, from 1985, Böll discloses that:

> [I]t became quite clear that the same old people, in industry, who to some extent owed something to Hitler and financed Hitler, demonstrably in fact, as for instance Flick, had earned their money from the concentration camps, where one laborer, I think, cost 1.50 Marks per day with very poor food and probable death – these same old forces in the economy were starting to make over again, more than in the military (Böll 1985, 24).

*The Clown* exemplifies Böll's interest in German apathy and hypocrisy. Böll's interplay of sincerity and irony leave the novel's reader wondering *who* the Germans truly are. Are they guilty (yet repentant) offenders? Or are they victims of the Third Reich? Do they presume to be hard-working citizens, seeing themselves as beyond genuine moral considerations like forgiveness and resentment?

## *The Clown*

*The Clown* is a negative possession because it does not pretend that reasoned legal and economic discourses can explain Germans' acquiescence to the Nazi regime. Hans Schnier, the novel's protagonist, seeks and fails to find a German who asks to be forgiven, or who accepts the demands of true repentance. Most importantly, *The Clown* is a negative possession because it culminates in the necessity of maintaining resentment. In order for hypocritical, bourgeois Germans to face their responsibility for radical evil, resentment toward Nazi Germany must exist.

As Böll wrestles with his resentments through his fictional characters, he is able to recognize his own guilt. Böll longs for forgiveness, a forgiveness that his protagonist can neither merit nor extend, because, during the War, he was too young to perpetrate any atrocities or help any victims. Emerging from the complacent atmosphere of post-War Germany, Böll displays a resentment that is both interpersonal and allegorical. In *The Clown* resentment is rooted in the generational clash between father, mother, and son, while, at the same time, being directed towards a fictionalized version of 1960's Germany.

The novel examines the relationship between the artistic Hans in his twenties, who is sympathetic to, yet critical of, the political left in the new Germany, and his parents' generation – the majority of whom was loyal to, and benefited from, National Socialism. As a professional clown, Hans has to frequently cancel his performances. His mimicry routines are not as funny as a clown's performance should be. He delivers social and political criticism of the new Germany with great dexterity, yet his audiences are not interested in moral self-examination. They only wish for entertainment. In the political climate of his time, it is hard for him to remain employed, so he returns to his apartment in Bonn.

Hans attempts to open conversations about guilt with his family and friends. Despite their hypocritical denials, he is trying to enable them to acknowledge their responsibility for the twelve years of Nazi rule in Germany, to show them that, albeit guilty of not resisting Hitler, they too were victims of Nazism. Hans's lover and soul mate, Marie, has left him. Most of the novel revolves around phone calls that Hans makes to old acquaintances, who know both the newlywed Marie and her husband, Heribert Züpfner. These acquaintances are a collection of young Germans who supported National Socialism but did not directly benefit from the Third Reich. Now, they dishonestly boast of their courageous opposition to Hitler.

Hans meets face to face only with his father, and they do not agree on a single thing in the world. Despite being a multimillionaire, the father refuses to give his son financial help. Hans remains an unusual voice of self-criticism as he searches for a personal and national acknowledgement of guilt. He expresses repentance, even though he was far too young to have perpetrated any evil deeds. Hans crystalizes an emotional and an ethical position about the value of resentment and the sincerity of forgiveness in his all but amnesiac cultural environment.

Hans resents his affluent family for the same reason that he resents the affluent German nation: neither are remorseful. In Hans's view, Germany has deposited its moral concerns in the hands of religious institutions, relieving individuals of their responsibility. In the same way, Germany has deposited its concern for the population's welfare in the hands of wealthy industrialists, not in the hands of laborers and unions. By delegating moral reparations to politicians rather than to the German people, the opportunity for moral encounters with the victims is stalled. At the helm of this new German society sit the very same people who were leaders under Nazi rule.

No surprise, then, that his relationships with his family and friends are strained. He calls his brother Leo just to ask for money. He calls his old acquaintances only to find out Marie's whereabouts. When Hans's multimillionaire father comes to visit, the alienation between father and son is extreme. As Hans speaks with his mother on the phone it becomes painfully clear how much he detests her for her allegiance to the Nazis. For Hans, his mother epitomizes German falseness. He cannot forgive the fact that she chairs a reconciliation committee. He even blames her for the death of his sister, Henrietta, a sixteen-year-old schoolgirl in 1945, while performing anti-aircraft duty. After all, it was Hans's mother who encouraged Henrietta to volunteer. For each of them Hans maintains an abiding resentment.

Throughout the book, Hans articulates his resentments in a wide variety of tones: at times he is sincere, at times ironic, and at times he is silent. These different manners of expression comprise his *speech*, highlighting the performative nature of speech-acts. Arendt teaches that speaking in the public sphere of human affairs constitutes a political act (Arendt 1958, 179). In all of his various expressions, as he speaks with family members and acquaintances, Hans is initiating political action. While he never forgets that the matrix of resentment and forgiveness appeals at the interpersonal level, he is well aware that his emotions do not alter political agendas.

Hans is loyal to the dead, especially to his sister. So, too, is Améry. Neither he nor Böll is interested in an easy march towards a future of reconciliation and German prosperity. Loyalty to the dead, exposure and documentation of the truths of the War are more than melancholic reactions to loss. They are moral imperatives conterminous with the articulation of negative possessions.

Everything that Hans does is counter-cultural, as is everything that he fails to do. Hans embodies Améry's philosophy, behaving as if time must be set back to enable responsibility for the crimes committed. More radically, Hans resents everything that results from conformism and obfuscation of the truth. His resentment exposes the relationship between rampant conformity and the rise of Nazism. Conformity pretends to "improve" Germans, yet they reject guilt for the crimes they committed, and deny that they are pursuing comfort or self-aggrandizement. Conformity, then, signals a cognitive dissonance in the German people. They are willing to embrace progress while willfully forgetting the past.

As Hans tells his story he feels deep guilt, though in 1940 he was only seven years old. It is his parent's generation who must seek forgiveness, except they do not. They are conforming, successful Germans who do not acknowledge their own guilt. Hans does not accept the common wisdom that is encapsulated in phrases such as *"tout comprendre c'est tout pardonner"* or "let bygones be bygones." He is depressed, an alcoholic, and insanely loyal to Marie. Even though she left him he still loves her dearly, and continues to refer to her as his "wife." This is the reason that Hans's actions lead to social suicide: Hans is non-conforming. His failure to translate the positive emotion of forgiveness and the negative emotion of resentment remains an allegorical inverse to Germany's refusal of guilt.

Hans, who is maladjusted in German society, is not unstable. In 1950, Arendt described the situation of many Germans who, like Hans, were reckoning with guilt against collective amnesia. She writes about "a normal person who happens to be thrown into an insane asylum where all the inmates have exactly the same delusion: It becomes difficult under such circumstances to trust one's own senses" (Arendt 1994, 259). It becomes difficult for Hans to trust his own senses. Around him, Germany bobbles in delusion, his guilty mother reveling in her clean conscience:

> My mother answered the black telephone in her business voice: 'Executive Committee of the Societies for the Reconciliation of Racial difference.' I was speechless. If she had said: 'Mrs. Schnier speaking,' I would probably have answered; 'Hans here, how are you, mother?' Instead I said: 'I am a delegate of the Executive Committee of Jewish Yankees, just

passing through –may I please speak to your daughter?' [. . .] She said: 'I suppose you can never forget that, can you?' I was almost in tears myself and said softly: 'Forget? Ought I to, Mother?'" (Böll 1963, 26–27).

This is a moment of radical resentment. Hans seeks an admission of truth while his mother is unable to give it to him. Rather, she needs to forget, to move on with the times, with her job. Her pretense even clears the path for Hans's grandfather's ninetieth birthday celebration: "these old boys are not bothered by either memories or conscience" (Böll 1963, 29). The phrase "these old boys" is ironic, for the old boys kept Hitler in power, back when they were neither old nor boys. In the 1960s the ironic mode permits Germans to live long lives with their consciences stowed away, working, conforming.

Some critics find that *The Clown* engages too heavily in caricature and hyperbole, suggesting that the novel remains socially irrelevant. A book review in *Dei Zeit*, a weekly German newspaper, cites the influential critic Marcel Reich-Ranicki:

> Marcel Reich-Ranicki is quite right with his unmitigated verdict that it is not figures who populate this novel, but upright names. Some of them are caricatures, like the president of the association Blothert, who stutters his 'Ka – Ka – Ka' to himself, leaving his listeners uncertain whether he wants to say 'Ka – Ka – Chancellor' or 'Ka – Ka – Katholon. [Marcel Reich-Ranicki hat durchaus recht mit seinem ungemilderten Verdikt, daß nicht Gestalten diesen Roman bevölkern, sondern aufrechtgehende Namen. Teils sind es Karikaturen, wie der Verbandspräsident Blothert, der sein 'Ka – Ka – Ka' vor sich hinstottert, seine Zuhörer im Ungewissen lassend, ob er 'Ka – Ka – Kanzler' oder 'Ka- Ka- Katholon' sagen will (*Die Zeit* 14 June 1963; my translation).]

Despite the critical irony, Reich-Ranicki understands the social critique Böll is going for. In his obituary to Böll, published in *Frankfurter Allgemeine Zeitung*, Reich-Ranicki recognizes that the novelist's resentments reached readers who were struggling to cultivate a self-aware German guilt:

> He incorporated as no other writer in our age the German awareness of guilt, but what the world is accustomed to regarding as German: thoroughness, ceremony, ponderousness, sentimentality and monumentality – all these he steadfastly rejected. [. . .] He was a preacher, but with clownish traits, a fool with priestly dignity (Reich-Ranicki 1985, 11).

Böll, like Améry, requires readers, "willing to follow," even if "in the hour before us" they might "wish to put down the book" (Améry 1980, 63). *The Clown* pushes its readers towards discomfort. Reich-Ranicki is the reader who continues to read, and, in the process, articulates his guilt, not only as a personal fault but as a negative possession.

## Resentment and innocence

Forgiveness has the power to turn a guilty person into an innocent one. Forgiveness wagers that *who* the person is amounts to more than just his evil deeds. Forgiveness restores innocence when the victim agrees that the perpetrator can be genuinely remorseful. Forgiveness allows that, if the perpetrator cannot be good, then he can be miserable, not necessarily wicked, and therefore deserving of forgiveness nonetheless.

Hans becomes Marie's lover when she is nineteen. Marie is a Catholic, but her father is a Marxist. Hans feels surprisingly close to the father, an honest shop owner with barely enough money to survive. Hans's family, meanwhile, is immensely wealthy. Hans's relationship with Marie enables him to forge a definition of innocence within a culture that unforgivably betrayed its humanity. Marie sobs after they have sex for the first time, which indicates to Hans that "such a thing as innocence really does exist" (Böll 1963, 42). Marie's emotionality in intimacy shows that she loves Hans while at the same time expressing her separateness from him. The innocence that Hans projects onto Marie evokes the rawness of interacting with the Other. Marie's ability to honestly express her fragility demonstrates her rejection of the socio-economical façade. This disrupts Hans's experience of unbridgeable distance, a distance Hans knows from his German family.

Marie is not an allegory for forgiveness, but rather an allegory for freedom of choice. She possesses, thanks to her loving attachment to various men, the ability to undergo personal transformation. Because of her openness and her moral self-determination, Hans is happy to feel unclean with Marie. For Hans, being unclean does not carry religious, but everyday, connotations. He is unclean because he hates to brush his teeth, or because he seduced Marie before she had the opportunity to complete her final examinations at school. Throughout their life together she feels lonely, all too aware of how different they are from each other. Hans's love for Marie does not cause him to learn from her innocence and accept loneliness in his life. The politics of guilt and repentance engulf their relationship. With her he might have been satisfied and focused on the unworldly aspects of love. But, even in the private sphere, he is mired in constant self-indictment.[13]

---

[13] Concepts such as "unclean" and "sinner" beg for religious interpretation, especially when they appear in the context of forgiveness and resentment. Derrida neutralizes them by elaborating a notion of forgiveness that is un-reciprocal. This brings to mind Kierkegaard's notion of the *infinite qualitative distinction* – the gap between faith and reason – in the creature's relation to reincarnation. Scholars suggest that, just because it cannot be explained by reason, the leap of faith required by forgiveness does not add up to nonsense. Stephen Evans, for example, argues that in the paradox of the reincarnation, passion comes to the fore, not reason. Either passion

After several miscarriages, Marie decides to leave Hans and marry Züpfner, citing Catholic mores as reason. In a series of telephone conversations with Marie's Catholic friends, Hans expresses his resentment towards them and their false ideals. Hans is indicting the Catholics for turning Marie into a sinner: "When she marries Züpfner, then she will really be sinning. That much I have grasped of your metaphysics: what she is doing is fornication and adultery, and Prelate Sommerwild is acting the pimp" (Böll 1963, 84). Marie's marriage to Züpfner would be an act of fornication – alleviating her fear of deserting Catholicism, while allowing her to abandon her love for Hans. Marie, claims Hans, is not being true to her heart. In order to remain a true Catholic she has to enter into a sham marriage. As long as she continues to live in sin with Hans, whom she loves, her Catholics friends ostracize her. Catholicism preaches love, but accepts love only when one conforms to dogma. In order to emphasize the importance of personal choice making – what Arendt calls "judgment" – Hans explains that he hates all religions. Religion cares about dogma and conformity, at the expense of self-examination and singular, moral judgment.

The question remains whether Hans's moral position is constructive. Hans's resentment for his acquaintances exposes the impact of their denial. By refusing to acknowledge Marie's love for Hans, they pressure Marie to give into fear and relinquish her sincerity. Marie becomes a hypocrite, just like those who deny the past and undermine true love, community, and continuity. It is precisely resentment, remorse, and ultimately forgiveness that make possible a connection between the past and the future. Why can't these Catholic friends accept Marie's choice without making her feel like a sinner? Hans's choice to remain alienated from such practices of intimidation on the personal, national, and religious levels evokes the difference that forgiveness and the unforgiveable introduce to continuity and community. He insists that moral family life is like nation building – based on acknowledging self-criticism, guilt, and suffering, while disclosing the truth about love. Böll's critique of Catholicism is aimed at the hypocrisy of a German society that suppresses personal judgment and responsibility.

---

rejects the reincarnation, or passion believes the reincarnation. In both cases, passion communicates with a reason that could either be offended or receptive of the reincarnation. When the encounter of reason and faith is good in relation to the reincarnation, then it means that the person responded in faith: "This requires understanding to 'surrender itself' while the paradox 'gives itself' " (cited in Evans 2010, 209). Hans rejects religious language. It is too materialistic to emerge from *faith,* and it is too blind to be subordinate to *reason*. But, when he accepts Christ as a model of morality, he does so based on passion – specifically, on the kind of passion that emerges in innocence, in dreams, or in the performances of a clown who engages pantomime. Hans's faith in the human is open to paradoxical miracles, to unexpected revelation of otherness.

## Criticizing Catholicism in the open

Böll grew up in a Catholic family, and understands how both German Catholicism and the Papacy legitimized National Socialism during the War. In an epilogue to a Carl Amery volume that analyzes Catholicism's betrayal, Böll resents mostly the comfort with which Catholics speak about the Church as being held hostage during the War:

> German Catholicism is in a congenial situation: if it is asked about its loyalty, it produces the Concordat, the disastrous consequences of which Carl Amery has exactly described; if it is attacked for its loyalty, it produces the Catholic resistance fighters. But I repeat: resistance was a private affair, the official status was that of the Concordat. [. . .] It is a choice between the innumerable nameless ones who put up a resistance and Franz von Papen – a choice that should not be difficult (Böll 1967, 230).

His resentment is just as plain in a letter he wrote to young German Catholics after the War, expounding on the Church's hypocrisy and complicity: "for it is simply embarrassing, nothing more than embarrassing, to read some of the theologians' positions on political questions; they are squarely in line with Bonn, and behind every sentence one feels the desire to make oneself well seen" (Böll 1996, 26; my translation from the French translation and from the original German). ["car c'est tout simplement gênant, rien de plus que gênant, que de lire certaines prises de position de théologiens sur des questions politiques; elles sont carrément dans la ligne de Bonn, et derrière chaque phrase on sent le désire de se faire bien voir" (Böll 1996, 26). "es ist doch einfach nur peinlich, nichts anderes als peinlich, wenn man Stellungnahmen von Theologen zu politischen Fragen liest; das ist stramm auf Bonn gezielt und man spürt hinter jedem Satz einen Eifer, der auf das Schulterklopfen wartet" (Böll [1956–1959] 2005, 452).]

## Forgiveness as rupture

In a culture that has committed atrocious evil, no moral reaction is as radical as forgiveness. *The Clown* must show a deep commitment to forgiveness in order to restore German integrity. The novel poses an urgent moral question: do Hans's contemporaries, who keep apologizing and asking for forgiveness, understand forgiveness? Do these Germans know that forgiveness is a radical recognition of the humanity of the perpetrator at his most evil? Can Germans feel gratitude in the presence of the forgiving victim, who extends a second chance to the perpetrator, so that the hangman might be remorseful and base his future life on respect to the Other?

*The Clown* exposes the irony that forgiveness and apology are implicated in relationships – both between Hans and his childhood friend, Kalick, and between Hans and his father. In their encounters, the semantic field of forgiveness disrupts the fluency of both political and economic discourses. In the words of Sigrid Weigel, the text "situates forgiveness as a rupture in political discourse" (Weigel 2002, 320). Herbert Kalick wants Hans's forgiveness to normalize his political shift, from Nazi to democrat. When Hans visits Marie's Catholic friends, "[Kalick] asked my forgiveness, even knelt down to ask me for what he called a 'secularized absolution'" (Böll 1963, 174). When they were still in school, Kalick demanded that a pupil by the name of Götz Buschel bring proof that he is Aryan. He was of Italian descent, and the papers were difficult to obtain during the war. This gave him and his family weeks of great difficulties.

Memory overtakes Hans. Rather than offer forgiveness, he reacts with extreme resentment: "And I simply hit Herbert Kalick right in the face, threw my champagne glass into the fire, and the cheese knife after it, and pulled Marie after me by the arm, out" (Böll 1963, 175). Hans recalls the small acts of devotion to the Nazis, including spying on people whose loyalty to Germany was considered suspect. Kalick's request for forgiveness remains insufficient, because he is not remorseful. The reader, like Hans, recognizes Kalick's double-talk when he asks forgiveness from the wrong person, Hans, and not from his victim, Götz. Clearly forgiveness remains a topic most suitable to speakeasies and party babble. Kalick seems not to know where Götz and his family are after the War, what happened to them. Are they human for Kalick in the aftermath of this insincere request for a "secularized absolution" (Böll 1963, 174)?

Hans's father's visit is likewise contaminated with insincere requests for pardon. The father arrives primarily in order to talk to Hans about his "future" (Böll 1963, 138). But, for Mr. Schnier, talk of the future is a euphemism for talk about money. The conversation devolves into the father criticizing his son's way of living. When forgiveness comes up in the conversation, it only expands the distance between father and son. These empty motifs make it clear that the relationship is beyond emotional and moral repair. What is lacking is an encounter based on recognition and responsibility. Rather, the discussion between father and son is transactional, much like that between Germany and the victims of the War.

"Forgive me for being so frank," Mr. Schnier says, "I detest, as you no doubt recall, any evidence of sloppiness" (Böll 1963, 133). In these words, forgiveness is misplaced. Why should one apologize for being frank? Hans responds with the words, "excuse me," and this expression, too, is misplaced (Böll 1963, 133). Hans excuses himself for eating in front of his father. But, again, why should he apologize? Is eating an action that should be avoided when one's father comes for a visit? Forgiveness and apology stress the artificial and impersonal nature of their relationship. Hans resents his father's need to hide behind conventional expressions of politeness. Hans's father enjoys the privileges of a patriarch, in the family and on a national scale, but he is unable to make good on the promise to act on the emotions inherent in paternity and in his position as a leading industrialist in post-war Germany. Respectable Mr. Schnier is a hedonist and a conformist, albeit a hardworking one.

He also has a second family, a dear blow to his respectability: a lover of many years and a son by her. Hans happens to think that his father's lover is much more loving than his rigid mother. What is the commitment that Mr. Schnier undertakes when he does not understand why Hans continues to be unforgiving toward his mother? Is it the position of loyalty to the wife that he deceives or the more prevalent desire to conform to the German norms of marriage ignoring the failure of the marriage? The Schnier family does not understand concepts such as catastrophe, guilt, truth, remembering, love, loyalty, resentment and forgiveness. Hans has to be ironic, and in so doing, shows his resentment:

> "It's a very good thing that racial differences should be reconciled, but my idea of race is different from the [mother's] committee's. Negroes, for instance, have become the latest thing—I wanted to offer mother a negro I know well as Nativity figure, and when you think that there are several hundred negro races. The committee will never be out of a job. Or gypsies," I said, "Mother could invite some to tea some day. Right off the street. There's still a lot to be done" (Böll 1963, 136).

Hans's mother is remote and cold to her husband and children. In public, she wears a mask of openness to the Other, profiting from the categorization of Black people. Instead of actually taking responsibility for the harms of racism, Mrs. Schnier orchestrates social and international symposia about the reconciliation of differences.

The language of forgiveness and pardoning comes up yet again when Hans's father is chastising him. The father sees himself as an integral part of the German economic miracle. He couldn't care less if some people are struggling in this prosperous economy. Mr. Schnier advances the German attitude that Jamkélévitch and Améry reject when they caution that "business isn't everything" (Jankélévitch 1996, 271). Hans half-heartedly listens to his father's irrelevant homily about Genneholm, the theater critic:

> "I beg your pardon," I said, when I could be sure my yawning fit was over for the time being. "What did Genneholm say?" My father was offended. He is always offended when you let yourself go, and my yawning pained him objectively, not subjectively (Böll 1963, 140).

The father is unaware of Hans's political shrewdness. He does not recognize his son's genius. The famous theater critic matters to the father because of the father's need to conform. Thus, he can neither judge his son's art nor access trust in him. Genuine forgiveness rests on the ability to see radical otherness, even when blind trust in future potentiality is required.

From this encounter Hans gleans that his father cannot acknowledge his needs and emotions: "With money it was like with 'desires of the flesh.' Nobody really talked about it, really thought about it, it was either [. . .] 'sublimated' or considered vulgar, never as the thing it was at the moment: food or taxi, a packet of cigarettes or a room with bath" (Böll 1963, 156).[14] In his world of obscene wealth, money is, for Mr. Schnier, an ideal that propels people to work harder. It is not a tangible resource for meeting needs. Hans is committed to the opposite opinion: that people must constantly manifest and tend to basic human needs. Money must be fairly and equally allocated to support those people who are in need of food, medicine, a steady job.

Within this argument about money Hans's father represents Germany itself. Post-War Germany is invested in abstract capitalism, forcing it to suppress the pain of the victims: be they Jews or impoverished Gentiles. Blindness to human fragility enables Germany to suppress its guilt. Forgiveness does not apply where there is such a willful obliteration of the past. Rather, it emerges specifically from radical truth telling, recognition of the crimes committed, and acknowledgement of the suffering of the victims.

Hans refuses to compromise for money, which means that he struggles to survive in the new Germany. He commits professional and social suicide when he refuses Genneholm's advice and his father's two hundred Marks a month. He becomes morally independent, however, protecting his right to remain resentful and abandoned. When Hans chooses abandonment over conformity, he affirms the value of forgiveness and reconciliation. His father's misuse of these emotions shows that Hans's commitment to genuine forgiveness and the value of resentment is premature. Most Germans can only broach these concepts when they are tragically out of place.

Is there a world elsewhere for Hans to be socially involved? A world where forgiveness and resentment propel society to achieve respect and equality in the context of social diversity? Presumably, Hans could emulate his mother: "I could

---

**14** Hans's resentment of Catholicism is also related to money. Those Catholics speak about poverty, but they are very urbane and tell jokes about money: Kinckel, among Marie's Catholic friends, tells the joke about the man who got along fine on five hundred marks a month. He began to earn a thousand and it became more difficult to live on such a measly amount of money. He had real trouble living on two thousand but when he reached three thousand life became very easy again. The punch line is, "Up to five hundred a month one can manage quite well, but between five hundred and three thousand is utter misery" (Böll 1963, 13).

go to America and lecture to women's clubs as a living example of the remorse of German youth" (Böll 1963, 214). Such lectures would be fraudulent, of course. Whereas Hans's mother was a Nazi sympathizer, "I [Hans] had nothing to be remorseful about, nothing whatever, and so I would have to pretend remorse" (Böll 1963, 214). The mother plays at remorse because it is the fashionable thing to do. It is worth her while to conform to the norm. Hans's remorse can only be fabricated. He remains abandoned, once again unable to conform to normativity.

Améry and Böll set their sights on the hypocrisy and complacency of 1960's Germany. German complicity was eerily similar during the Adenauer administration of denazification as it was during the twelve years of National Socialism. In the 1960's, Germans preferred displays of power to displays of feeling. They chose capitalism over respect and equality within social diversity. Thus, the last paragraphs of Böll's, *The Clown* are critical of German apathy. Hans makes up his face in clown makeup, and leaves his apartment to sit on the stairs leading to the train station. In putting on his clown persona, Hans is one with the victim, "that was no longer a clown, it was a corpse acting a corpse" (Böll 1963, 217). Hans's suicide becomes metaphorical, and the rhetorical trope of prosopopoeia points toward the emotions of forgiveness and resentment. Hans is Germany's social conscience. As he waits for the passersby to stumble over him, see him begging on the stairs, recognize his abandonment, and throw him a dime, he becomes the victim waiting for those around him to be awakened to guilt, to responsibility, and to repentance.

## Afterword

One of Böll's German critics states of *The Clown*: "Der Roman versackt im Ressentiment" [The novel is sinking into resentment] (Sieg 2017, 171; my translation). Böll's entire ethics rests on making forgiveness available through the recognition of unforgivable offenses. Similarly, Améry's address to the German intellectuals is a sign of his renewed trust in the future – in both forgiveness and resentment. For, as I have argued, forgiveness is the inner lining of resentment.

*Billiards at Half-Past Nine* recounts the multi-generational saga of a family of civil engineers and their wives. Literary critics see this earlier novel as a forebear of *The Clown*, for it too features resentful protagonists who destroy German culture from within. Forgiveness, in both novels, necessitates resentment. Forgiveness begins with resentment. It does not treat atrocity lightly. Resentment affirms two things: first, the resentful protagonist is not a conformist within his culture; second, resentment becomes genuine only if the protagonist trusts in forgiveness – i.e.

trusts that his resentment can cause his fellow man to deny conformism and become an agent who advances respect for the Other.

In *Billiards at Half-Past Nine,* it is too early to celebrate reconciliation and compensation. The Faehmel family wants to commemorate its commitment to resentment and forgiveness. The family history shows that the elder Faehmel was resentful when he won the contract to build the abbey despite being very young, too innovative, and without connections within the provincial administration. He bequeathed his resentment to Faehmel Jr. He showed his devotion to forgiveness and resentment when he destroyed the abbey built by his father, to show that Germany betrayed its loyalty to justice and faith in a benevolent God. The example of Faehmel Jr., in turn, needs to be taken up by his son, Faehmel the third, who has to find access to the emotions of forgiveness and resentment at the end of World War II, as Germany seeks a new direction.

> So let's not celebrate any reconciliation. Sorry, Reverend Father, you'll have to make the best of it, you won't miss us. Hang up a plaque: [the abbey was] built by Heinrich Faehmel in 1908, in his twenty-ninth year; destroyed by Robert Faehmel, in 1945, in his twenty-ninth year—and what will you do, Joseph, [the grandson to Heinrich and Robert's son] when you're thirty? (Böll 1959, 235).

Before the War, belief in shared ethical values caused the senior Faehmel to build an Abbey as a monument to German work ethic. But after the War trust in the shared values of the Lams caused Faehmel Jr. to destroy the abbey, and thereby erect a monument to Germany's betrayal of humanism.

Acknowledging guilt through forgiveness is integral to Böll's major works. All Germans must understand that the ethical basis on which Germany may be rebuilt necessitates resentment. Hans's resentment, and the resentment of young Germans like Hans, will force the conforming Germans to admit that recognition is necessary.

Améry is aware that resentment means to nurture past pain. He can be accused of living, in Nietzschean terms, in "bad faith" or being absorbed in the vicious cycle of "eternal return." Améry is interested in the value of eternal return under specific historical circumstances – when calling equals to discover the truth, not for the sake of being sentimental: "He [Nietzsche] must be answered by those who [. . .] were present as victims when a certain humankind joyously celebrated a festival of cruelty" (Améry 1980, 68). Eternal return is integral to the strong spirit and the morality of the master. Améry's resentments may destroy him, but his commitment to truth is an active force. This commitment achieves active negation in German culture. If Germany acknowledges its negative possessions, ceasing to buy off guilt with compensations to the victims, then Germany can ignite a moral revolution that points toward new potentialities of forgiveness (Améry 1980, 78).

Améry, like Nietzsche, is interested in the truth "at whatever cost" (Vetlesen 2006, 31). Améry's resentment is conscious, not uniquely unconscious. It is active, not only reactive, revolutionary, or disobedient. It is therefore not permeated by sickness, but is a power that uses the past in order to change the future.

# Interchapter 3
# Negative possessions – on Wladislaw Pasikowski's *Aftermath (Poklosie)*

## The everyday life of disavowal

> Edward Sleszynski: "In the barn of my father, Bronislaw Sleszynski, a lot of Jews were burnt." Jan T. Gross, *Neighbors*

> Harrowing obligations. Rene Char, *Hypnos*

Wladyalaw Pasikowski's film *Aftermath* (2012), tells the story of the two brothers Kalina who find out that their neighbors in a remote village in the norther border of Poland murdered, burnt their Jewish neighbors during WWII and seized their lands, these are the lands that Josef, Jozek, (Maciej Stuhr), the younger Kalina brother currently farms and grows wheat on. It is in this field that Jozef creates a cemetery to the deceased Jews using real headstones, (*Matzevot*), that remained after the Germans destroyed the synagogue and the Jewish cemetery. When after twenty years of absence the elder brother Franciszek, Franek (Ireneusz Czop), arrives from America to visit his younger brother Jozef who can read the Hebrew names on the headstones he chooses to assist him to collect all the headstones that the villagers still use to fortify roads and buildings and as working surfaces. The villagers harass and aggress the brothers when they spray the farmhouse with anti-Semitic graffiti, slash the throat of Jozef's dog, stone the house, burn the harvest in Jozef's field but pragmatically, and meticulously Franek studies the history of the land and the relationships between the Polish Jews and their Polish neighbors and helps Jozef to discover, and at the end of the film expose, dig out, exhume the bones of the murdered, burnt Jews from the mass grave in the marshes. The final images in this tormenting film show Jews from many different nations standing around a newly erected monument to memorialize the murdered Jews of the village and say Kaddish on the Kalina field, where Jozef had the original cemetery, where he is burried. When this comes to pass the villagers have already crucified Jozef, nailed him to the door of his barn but as someone in the crowd suggests that Jozef committed suicide, no *neighbor* will be brought to justice for this additional crime.

The everyday life of disavowal is the reason that the Polish neighbors are willing to do everything, including murder in order to protect their guilty secret: the villag-

---

**Note:** See page numbers of citations on the bibliography.

ers don't want the younger generations of Polish nationals and the entire world to know that they, not the Germans, not the Soviets, burned twenty six Jewish families who were indigenous to the place, owned and farmed lands. If the guilty secret is exposed life in the everyday will change in the village and presumably this change will affect the country and its diplomatic relations with other nations. How does this film mobilize affect so as to differently, uniquely apply the paradox of forgiveness and resentment to Poland in the aftermath of WWII? It is both the script and the dialogues that disclose well organized information to the viewer and allow the viewer to participate in this suspense movie, try and solve the main riddles in the film which are who burned the Jews, the occupying German forces or their Polish neighbors; why were they killed because of anti-Semitism or for capitalistic reasons, in order to overtake their plots of land located on more fertile ground? And yet the images, the *mis-en-cène*, the lighting, the tracking shots of the camera, and the editing do more important work than does the narrative. Rather than allow the viewer to focus on the storyline, the *fabula*, Pasikowski uses the medium to incite the viewer's affects into action and make affect invested in the connections between suspense, premonition and fear, anagnorisis and acknowledgement, guilt, shame, resentment and repentance the form that forgiveness takes in the offender. When everyday disavowal of an orchestrated crime cruel beyond imagining collapses then it feels as if it were this film's main effort to establish a body of works defined as a *negative possession* of the nation, to use the language of Jean Améry and show a history of evil deeds which were committed by the Polish nationals against their Jewish Polish neighbors even if this is a fictional, not a documentary film. *Aftermath* consciously functions as a *negative possession* in Polish culture, it does something similar to what investigative journalism does when it publishes an article about how badly Poland treated its Jewish population during WWII but rather than disclose the facts and bring the guilty to answer for their crimes in a court of law, the film uses falsehoods and the imagination when it opens a space for the viewers in which they experience affects: acknowledgement of guilt, shame, resentment against forefathers who committed heinous crimes and concealed the murder and the burning and reacted violently when the younger generations and professional historians tried to expose the truth. Pasikowski deals in affects, he both allows his viewrs to feel the pain of being descndants of a long history of people who committed racial violence, concealment, and lying and allows the audiences to feel that in order to belong to, and change their national treatment of different nationals they must be able to create an aesthetic archive of *nagative possessions*, acknowledge the evil that was committed in the name of belonging to the national and political majority; own their own affects of regret and repentance; feel the need to offer structural justice and equity for all and allow the Jewish survivers and their Jewish bretherns to mourn the murdered Jews and commemorate their lives in the place where they were born and burnt.

Critics often mention that *Aftermath* doesn't focus on any but deceased Jews. Baker complains that in this films the Jews remain haunting ghosts, but don't appear in the flesh as real beings engaged in living, working, having families and she continues to argue that this state of being living-dead perpetuates the Otherness of Jews which in turn allows the Polish nation to be both anti-Semitic and filo-Semitic in modern Politics and cultural production. "Fueled from the film's opening by tracking shots that stalk Józef's 'long-lost American brother' through the Polish forest as he investigates a strange noise from within the camera itself becoming the undead subject, Pasikowski immediately alerts his audience to the fact that this place is imbued with some intangible yet omnipresent form of life," she suggests. Although I agree that the no living, particular Jews appear as full characters in the film, the criticism misses the point of the film for *Aftermath* doesn't pretend to correct the history of the persecution of Polish Jews; it creates a *negative possession*, an aesthetic object that focuses on the responsibility of the Polish community to the fact that the Jews are no longer part of the Polish culture; the film uses an aesthetic *negative possession* to counter everyday disavowal, demand accountability. A *negative possession* doesn't need to nostalgically turn back to the Jews who used to live in Poland and commemorate their traditional garb or their holiday rituals as does a museum. On the contrary a *negative possession* demands that the Polish viewer remain within the bounds of a paradox, how can I be resentful toward my country, my elders because of the murder and concealment of historical material rather than continue to be loyal to them and perpetuate concealment? How can I sincerely experience guilt and shame over crimes that I didn't commit and be repentant not within the safe bounds of my community but on the international stage by admitting that this dark chapter belongs in my national history, Poland's history? How does *Aftermath*, a realistic film achieve such a strong physical and affective reaction using the language of film, accessing the affects more forcefully than reason without putting to task living Jews, creating a performative Jew so that the film could lure the viewer to feel empathy toward the living while all the time continue to disavow the responsibility for the catastrophe?

## The irreducible difference of two traumas: Victim and perpetrator

> In almost every situation in life where there is bodily injury there is also the expectation of help; the former is compensated by the latter. But with the first blow from a policeman's fist, against which there can be no defense and which no helping hand will ward off, a part of our life ends and it can never again be revived. Jean Améry, *Torture*

According to Jean Améry, a *negative possession* keeps a *moral chasm* open between the perpetrator and victim because torture eliminates the victim's capacity to have trust in the world. *Negative possessions* pronounce that the "pile of corpses [that] lies between them [perpetrators] and me cannot be removed in the process of internalization, so it seems to me, but, on the contrary, through actualization, or, more strongly stated, by actively settling the unresolved conflict in the field of historical practice," referencing both the past and future in order to foster a dialogue. I place the work of Améry in dialogue with specific sequences from *Aftermath*, although Améry is a Holocaust survivor while Pasikowski is a descendant of the Polish nation which he criticizes, as a means of exploring the particularity of *negative possessions* in the Polish, not German historical and national framework. According to Améry, a *negative possession* introduces a new voice into the public sphere, and propels individuals and nations to create change, rather than endlessly rehearse the performance of existing cultural and political identities, loyalties. I understand Améry to be saying that resentment and repentance propel offenders and victims to enter into a dialogue concerning the past, most important this dialogue doesn't reach historical closure. Instead, a negative possession could displace and decenter identity, ideology, and nationality, and introduce difference, making accountability relate to an unforeseen event. Améry's effort to grapple with his resentment begins with a request for the impossible, namely, that the catastrophe be undone so that the dead victims will be among the living when forgiveness or repentance is at stake. Améry construes a strange amalgam of time, memory, and speech. On the one hand, he calls on Germans to accept their history as a negative possession that forces remembrance of the atrocities and captures the fact that existing moral language cannot articulate the evil that was perpetrated. On the other hand, Améry claims that perpetrators and nations can only generate new desires, meanings, and connections to a future in which singularities and communities are transformed and infused with difference through negative possessions. This conflict begs the question of how a negative possession can project the writer/ director into the future and turn him into a being in a continual process of becoming different – even as this being remains accountable vis-à-vis the past. I suggest that more than anything *Aftermath* wants to find a way to influence the future but the film remains obligated to exposing and mourning the political and communal crimes against Polish Jewry that belong to the past. How does *Aftermath* make accountability emerge in the encounter with an unforeseen *event* when on the one hand it realistically traces the legal bounds of the lands' original Jewish owners and flushes out the guilty villagers, and on the other hand instigates in every viewer a personal affective reaction to the events of the theft, murder, and concealment of a terrible guilty secret, a horrific truth which is five decades old. How does the film give form to knowledge and affect through which a future personal and national change in speech and deeds is refracted?

## Tracking shots: A recent archeology of the land

> The sum of thoughts unthought, of unfelt feelings, of works never accomplished, of lives unlived to their natural end. Jan T. Gross, *Neighbors*

In the citation above the historian Jan Gross refers to the 1600 Jewish victims of all ages who were beaten and burnt to death by their Polish neighbors in the town of *Jedwabne* in the summer of 1941 when he both argues that the truths that his historical study brings to the light of day is of major, national importance and mourns those people whose lives were cut short, never accomplished. Gross asks his Polish readers to be accountable to the truth of its history, assume responsibility for the events that took place in Jedwabne at the end of the German occupation in that territory. The crux of negative possessions is that they do not offer a satisfying explanation to the brutal facts of history, and don't explain either the suffering of the victims or exonerate, or articulate the remorse of the perpetrators. Rather, they open questions that reside beyond the realm of meaning. By bringing the projects of Améry and Pasikowski together, I hope to show how negative possessions lead to a materialization of the silence, and the passivity or patience that the Polish families and nation must acknowledge when they seek out genuine personal and national change, open a road on which people move from racism to embracing difference. In an interview with Leonard Quart, Pasikowski suggests that his film might move some Polish people to "be inclined to search for more accurate historical records to discover their own past, even its disgraceful side."

The two brothers Kalina meet for the first time after twenty years and this meeting in the aftermath of many personal upheavals in both of their lives and in the political regime in Poland explains the film's title—the meeting occurs in a comfortable moment in time, after many important alterations, many harrowing events have already taken place. The elder brother, Franciszek (Franek) Kalina, has been living with his family in America for the past twenty years and just recently, Jola and her children, the children of Franek's younger brother, Josef (Jozek) Kalina have left Poland to stay with Franek and his family in America. Franek left before Jaruzelski announced martial law in Poland and comes back to Poland to see how his brother Jozek is doing; Franek can make this visit materialize in the twenty first century, the diegetic time in which events take place in the film, in the aftermath of the death of both their parents, and in the aftermath of a regime change it is possible to visit Poland and not be thrown in jail or disallowed to leave again. In this sense, aftermath signifies a historical moment in which in a democratic environment the brothers have to leave behind their titular relation to life in Poland and in the absence of oedipal, authoritarian figures and tyrannical institutions they must must be the judges of every aspect of their comportment including their moral relation to everyday life and the challenges that crop up and call for attention. Aftermath is a kind of word that brings accountability to mind almost instantaneously, as if it were always the case that once the catastrophe is over, for the first time the survivors cognize what has happened to them and as they begin to assess the damages they also assume responsibility for the new circumstances to which they belong, and labor to find who is guilty of atrocities that came to pass, who is accountable for the crimes that were committed, incurred, and suffered.

When Franek is in the taxi on his way to his brother's village we clearly understand that although the film title is *Aftermath* nothing has really been overcome or forgotten or cognized defined as over and done with and accomplished. On the contrary, everybody is a busybody in this place, people gossip, want to connect Franek, the guest who they don't remember to his family, his genealogy and the archeology of his brother's land. People find reasons to hold a grudge which is why everyone who will meet Franek will first demand to know why he didn't come to his parents' funeral. The Kalina brothers live among conservative neighbors but they represent a young generation which is not intolerant, they are loyal to knowing the past and are affected by sameness when like the other villagers they repeat their habits in order to feel safe in their everyday conversations and silences. Franek has to walk a long way from the godforsaken bus stop to his brother's farmhouse and this walk is an opportunity for the camera to closely track the landscape: there is a road, there are woods, there is a river, and marshes, and there are farms on which a relatively small population grows various crops. This landscape or more precisely the genealogy of the landscape, who owns the different plots of land on this landscape and the landscape's archeology, what is buried under these lands are questions at the epicenter of this film. And yet the film revolves around the question who is guilty of the disappearance of the village Jewish population at the end of the German occupation and it infringes on a second, closely related question as well: what good does it do to speak and think about guilt? What is the value of flushing out the ones who are guilty of acts which were committed two and even three generations earlier? When Franek is walking through the landscape to his brother's farmhouse someone is following him, someone is stealing his duffle bag. At the eleventh minute of the film when Franek and Jozef speak about the past, "ancient history" is how Franek relates to the past, someone throws a stone and breaks the kitchen window. The question of surveillance and punishment in a small village, the fact that a neighbor can become the victim of minor demeanors and of much more serious crimes inflicted by his neighbors are at the very core of this film. *Neighbor* ceases to be a noun, the film transforms this word to a transitive affect so that when a neighbor is friendly to his neighbor positive affects ensue but when the neighbor is alienated or violent negative affects envelope the viewer. If I suggested earlier that *aftermath* is a word that signifies a hiatus in an ongoing catastrophe which allows one to take comfort in reflection and making decisions about the future than the film complicates this definition. As events progress the brothers Kalina become more closely acquainted with the landscape, with the neighbors and the secrets that the village hides while the viewers receive new information which suggests that the catastrophe has been suppressed and disavowed but is all but finished, the catastrophe has morphed, taken a new form of existence; it reappears in the form of a series of aftershocks, which affect the present lives of older and younger neighbors in the village, neighbors who trust in free speech and democratic institutions. The film stages a paradox, it shows neighbors who trust in free speech and deny free speech at the same time and for the same purpose, to better conceal the truth. We viewers know this affect very well, how do we tell the truth and accept the shame that we feel for if we don't tell the truth there will be no end to our shame, no opportunity to fully assume responsibility and become accountable for the shameful action we committed. More disturbingly we feel that admitting the truth and feeling shame impedes the love we could have felt for those we harmed. Although *Aftermath* is a suspense movie that seeks to give moral restitution an aesthetic image this conflict is tinged with a melodramatic treatment of affects and the passion of melodrama lingers with the viewer to the end of the film.

The brothers meet under the sign of radical difference; Franek is dressed in a suit and tie and Jozek, like a farmer is in his undershirt and filthy pants. And yet from the first words between them Jozek comes through as a dreamy, feeling, caring, and generous guy while Franek is impatient, a pragmatist who thinks about action as does every other immigrant in America. When Franek visits the local police office he is not interested in filing a complaint about his stolen duffle bag but wants to know if his brother is liked in the village. Franek observes that his brother is the butt of many obnoxious, hostile actions and the chief of police discloses that a complaint is pending against Jozek, he stole stones from the old tannery road and various other places in the village. Franek speaks to Justyna (Zuzana Fialova), the granddaughter of the old Sudecki (Ryszard Ronczewski), who almost drove the villagers to lynch Jozek because of the theft. She belongs to the enlightened young generation in the village; a physician, and she drives Franek to see the part of the road where the stones are missing. No one understands why Jozek would do such a thing, but the camera yet again tracks the surface, investigates the land as if a long, close look can drill into and uncover what is on or under the surface. For the first time we see the old cottage in which the brothers grew up before they moved to where Jozek currently farms. This ruined house appears in daylight at the nineteenth minutes of the film but it will return at nighttime toward the end of the film; the house frames the limits of the factual and moral accountability the film undertakes to investigate and disclose. This house that signifies the pre-history of the brothers' lives, when they were children, is the locus of the *return of the repressed* and yet the secrets that emerge are of a much more social and political nature because they are shared, belong in a dialogue between Franek and Justyna. These secrets are structured as a *negative possession* and every explanation will fall short, fail to explain away the events that took place on the basis of a better understanding of affective family and neighborly relationships or economical aspirations. It is important to mention that from the beginning the conversation refers to the Yids, an anti-Semitic appellation of the Jews but Jews don't appear in the film only referred to or narratively pointed at. Franek knows wealthy American Jews because he works in the construction business which is headed by Jews with property, and Jozek hasn't seen Jews in the village because he is too you but he keeps insisting to refer to Jews by the correct name, not by the Polish derogatory Yids. A negative possession begins to form when no real Jews are captured by the camera and yet these people are the subject of every conversation, they populate the film with missing images of missing Jews; the film refers to the atrocities that occurred, not to the fact that currently Jews are not under threat, they live in America, Europe, and Israel no less safe than are members of other nationals.

Another good example comes up in the twenty second minute when the brothers go to the regional city to borrow money at the bank. Jozek offers his farm as a solid collateral but the bank manager (Zbigniew Konopka), refuses to give him the loan on the grounds that the title or the deed to the property is not legally his so the farm cannot legally be used as a collateral. Jozek, feisty but congenial gets into a fit of rage because his father received loans many times so what right does the manager have to refuse him a loan? The pragmatist Franek wants to understand the problem, and how it may be fixed. The land came to your father after the agrarian reform but without proper paperwork, says the bank manager. The issue of the title has to be clarified with the office of the municipal registry. At the bar, where Jozek is waiting for Franek to come back a group of farmers severely beat him up and break his nose presumably because he has always been voting for Lech Walesa. The film engages the utilizes editing and fragmentation to create two different spheres, the two resisting poles of the paradox of truth and guilt: Franek cannot be stopped because he is a foreigner in the village who seeks the truth but Jozek has to suffer greatly, consider to relinquish the search for the truth because he belongs to the landscape and society in the village and feels too ashamed to expose the guilt of his forefathers.

Only in the twenty eighth minute of the film a cluster of meanings begins to shape up and we realize that the bothers don't know what to do with the fact that these issues that are now raised are unexplainable, enigmatic, haunting, attached to frightful crime and guilt. Only when Jozek feels protected enough by his brother's presence he takes Franek to the field and shows him the stones that he has been stealing from the old road or buying from people. Jozek explains that after WWII the Germans tore down the synagogue and the Jewish cemetery and began to use the gravestones to reinforce the road. Polish people then followed their example. The *mis-en-cène* is surprising but mostly it is full of pathos for Jozek plants in his field some three hundred and twenty eight headstones engraved in Hebrew letters as if this is the one Jewish cemetery which is indigenous to the village, seamlessly growing on the land among the wheat crop. Franek is amazed that Jozek has learned the Hebrew alphabet and in a clear voice he reads the Jewish names on the gravestones but the only excuse that Jozek gives to the question why he collected and bought the stones is that when he found the stones he felt that it was the right thing to do: "I had to, they were human beings," Jozek says without using the word *guilt* and without explaining why the more he succeeds in finding all the stones the more his neighbors hate him and threaten his life. In the thirty second minute of the film it becomes clear that Jozek is not naïve, he is resentful toward his Polish neighbors who keep on desecrating the headstones, he is judging the new priest in the vicarage because there headstones are also incorporated in the structure, and he feels that an unforgivable cruelty motivates his Polish neighbors to block his way to the truth. Franek is till pragmatic, not ready to think about the difficulties in a moral way, he argues that the Kalina family never had anything to do with the Jews and both implies that he cannot be guilty of harms that came to Jews and that therefore Jozek must not feel so strongly about the headstones, the Jews who used to be foreigners even when they lived in the village. Nonetheless Franek pays a visit to the older parish priest to ask about his brother and the headstones that he wants to take from the vicarage. The parish priest (Jerzy Radiwilowicz) supposes that the Germans came and the Jews were deported. Forgiveness comes up in the conversation between the two because Franek feels guilty that he didn't come to his parents' funeral. The priest suggests that in order to be forgiven a person needs "a conscience . . . above all." Franek who doesn't feel guilty about the disappearance of a community of elders, Jews who belonged to the village does feel guilty that he didn't give his last respects to his elders, didn't come to his parents' funeral. At the end of the film Franek will learn that his father was one of the main instigators of the pogrom of the Jews and he will feel shame and practice repentance toward the brothers of the murdered Jews. The cluster of guilt, resentment, forgiveness, and the unforgiveable is installed in the film both using images—the tracking shots of the road, the old cottage, the headstones in what looks like a cemetery in the middle of a wheat field—and using the narrative and dialogues in which people on the one hand specifically use words like forgiveness, and on the other hand refer to the terrifying diction of lynching.

*Aftermath* is a detective story but what the camera and the narrative are looking for is a way to represent absence, silence, enigma, moral depravity, and moral rectitude or repentance. Jozek and Franek need to learn how to make use of the threats of the old generation of fathers, and rather than be scared find clues that can explain to them what it is that they are looking for. Franek knows that they have to harvest early; because the county refuses to give Jozek the harvester that he orders Franek feels that the crop is in danger. Franek knows that someone tried to throw him off the road when he was driving the tractor and that the young priest has to be on call at the local hospital when he and Jozek take the remaining headstones from the vicarage or else the hostile priest will incite the crowds to a riot. Franek looks for outsiders among the old Polish members of the village, the excluded ones may agree to speak the truth about what happened to the Jews. Franke realizes that not all the grandchildren are willing to keep silent and protect their grandparents and that he and Jozek must cooperate with younger men and women, with those who were seen as mad or as nomads that are irrelevant to the life of the community.

## Difference: The old; the madwoman; the nomad; the crucified; the Jew

> How does one give form to such a searing flame? Where does one start? How does one connect the links? What words does one use? Aharon Appelfeld, *The Story of A Life*

Interpersonal meetings clarify that the secret that Jozef unwittingly threatens to expose is to do with both the history of unimaginable cruelty and the history of everyday capitalism. The words that Holocaust survivors like Appelfeld miss are to do with how the unimaginable evil committed and suffered could be seamlessly woven into the patterns of daily living as a perpetrator and a victim. I mentioned that the difference between victim and perpetrator is irreducible and it is important to know that the *negative possessions* that the perpetrator has to acknowledge and record or broadcast using judgement and aesthetics and the imagination are different from the speechlessness of the victims. Appelfeld is shocked because all the words that might be used to describe his war experiences seem irrelevant, too overwhelming or underwhelming, and incommunicative so that in the aftermath of war radical evil and the experience of abandonment remain in the backdrop, overpowered by words that in order to be heard must be accessible and readable and in these senses those words are conciliatory. Aharon Appelfeld, who was seven years old when WWII erupted, fled with his father from Czernowitz through the Ukrainian steppe, but was incarcerated in a labor camp. He managed to escape, reaching Italy and then Palestine. In Appelfeld's memoir, *The Story of a Life*, traumatic memories undergo a transformation, becoming a constant search for words which compel the writer to move away from a sense of "chaos and impotence" and find the potential for a future existence beyond what can be articulated. As Appelfeld writes: "There were atrocities that were beyond words, that remained dark secrets." Ultimately, the author creates "the language of the persecuted." The memoir, says Appelfeld, lacks an adequate vocabulary because the attempt to dialogically comprehend the Holocaust furnishes language with new words and ideas but fails to explain the catastrophe, as these verbal encounters cannot reach closure. He asks: "How does one give form to such a searing flame? . . . What words does one use?" Appelfeld argues that recognizable words are nothing but clichés used to block the exit to the beyond, the *event*, where disaster looms. I suggest that for the perpetrator, *negative possessions* plumb the wound that exists beyond speech, stimulating transformation and a refusal to reaffirm personal and national oedipal and patriarchal ideology and territory. The survivor asks what words does one use to explain that currently the continued concealment of a guilty secret enables the murderers and the bystanders of the past to know full well their moral depravity and continue to engage in it in the twenty-first century, as they disavow the crimes they committed for the very same reason: concealment facilitates existing patterns of everyday living. Those who are excluded from the daily, majoritarian practices of everyday living nonetheless introduce difference to the community, to conventional patriarchal and national narratives and institutions. The survivor, the ill, the madwoman, and the nomad give eyewitness testimony of the events; they use painfully simple words to articulate terrible memories and furnish *Aftermath* with the vocabulary and images needed to affect the viewers, prepare them for the ultimate, shocking image of Jozef, crucified, nailed to his barn's gate.

At the regional registry office Franek is an outsider because viewers are used to identify him as more American than Polish and only when his addressee, the old archivist (Stanislaw Bruhs) suggests that it would be easier for a Polish national to understand the materials does Franek enlighten the old man that he was born here and is able to visualize the materials that he studies. Franek discovers the discrepancies in Jozef's current plot number compared to several earlier entries and finds out that his father inherited a different plot from his forefathers which is close to the river and the marshes; it is the plot on which stand the ruins of the old cottage. The deed of ownership that the brothers Kalina currently have was signed after

1945 when the agrarian reform simply confirmed the status quo in the aftermath of WWII. The previous owners of Kalina's current field were Jews. The camera, the cuts, the hectic moves from Franek's intense consultation of documents at the registry to Jozef's intense reading, touching and cleaning the gravestones in his field are transforming reasoned information to affect, something cannot be said but can be assumed or guessed at when it takes the form of a *negative possession*, content that seeks no clarification but cannot reach closure: these lands remain a sufficient cause for anti-Semitism in modern-day Poland. According to the registry the current plot of the Kalina family used to belong to Awraham Wimelman but rather than explain this information the camera cuts to Jozef who reads out loud the names on the headstone he is touching: "Itzhak Akiwa, son of Reb Awraham Wimelman." The very fragmentation of the film's images and soundtrack pushes the viewer to experience the tension, and make visual connections before there is a fully developed narrative line with a proper organization that infuses the images with the correct order of cause and effect, earlier and aftermath, pogrom and institutional interventions. Franek continues to examine the discrepancies in the plot numbers for the Sudecki and Malinowski, families which are headed by violent old fathers to this very day, these are the fathers who might know how to explain the inconsistencies but at this point the camera cuts back to Jozef who in his field reads more names on the headstones: Simeon son of Benjamin Zelig blessed remembrance Hirshbaim and this cut brings to mind the possibility that Sudecki and Malinowski perpetrated crimes against the deceased Hirshbaim and then took his land. The archivist uses redundancies when he suggests that the Germans, who everyone is convinced deported the Jews, couldn't take the land and the Jews had no heirs so the local villagers took it. Franek will soon tell his brother that "all these were Jewish farms, from the woods down to the river." Property values poisoned the relationship between the Jewish and the Polish neighbors because the Jews had good plots to farm while the Polish nationals had plots on marshland that doesn't yield good crops and yet these commonplace words don't explain the pogrom. This difficulty is never fully articulated but in the fifty eighth minute of the film, after the discoveries at the registry Jozef's farmhouse is sprayed with a yellow Star of David and his dog Burek lies dead with a cut throat to show that *Aftermath* installs a *negative possession* in a culture that has no words to articulate the anti-Semitism that it still practices, let alone to repent for the crimes that it committed during WWII. The camera makes it clear that on top of gossip, surveillance, and trespassing the cruel villagers might commit murder again. An hour and four minutes into the film, on the same night of the brothers' return from yet another visit to the old ruined cottage to inspect the terrain the unharvested field is on fire as if this were the punishment exacted by the villagers. The camera, the editing, the soundtrack teach us to suspect that this is arson, although there is no proof of such malefaction yet; the camera teaches, educates our affects and we feel that the headstones in the field are on fire again, for the second time, the way the Jews were on fire when they were still alive, but for the moment these are but conjectures, instinctive premonitions. Although the brothers, not the arsonists spend the night in jail Franek assumes that the villagers are hostile because their ownership titles are not legal, they are afraid that someone will take their lands from them but being an American pragmatist Franek who ignores the affects and seeks out facts, still cannot lay the blame for past and present violence in his neighbors' lap.

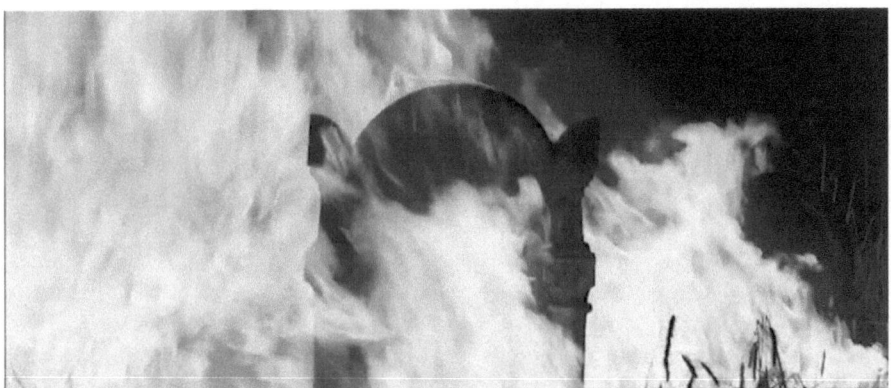

**Figure 6:** *Aftermath*, the burning field, DVD screen shot.

The second decisive meeting in pursuit of historical truths occurs at the hospital where the old Mrs. Palka convalesces. Palka (Maria Garbowska) labors to remember Franek but remembers his older brother who drowned and then she remembers that Franek stole her rabbit because he didn't want the animal to die. This dialogue is so intimate when at the backdrop of the film appear nothing but deceit and past and imminent acts of violence that we immediately trust the information that Mrs. Palka discloses despite that she is old, ill and has always been called "mad." We even suppose that in her heyday she was already different from her other neighbors, feeling, and protective. Palka remembers the Jews, some of them she remembers by name. Palka cannot explain how the Jews died but she is convinced that after the Germans arrived the Jews were gone. She never betrayed the Jews as did their other neighbors but she never helped them either—Palka was not courageous enough to become one of the Polish citizens who were later remembered as belonging to a group of people called *the righteous of the nations* who risked their lives trying to help Jews, to hide them and enable their survival —"for people talk . . ." she says. This meeting convinces Franek to speak to Mr. Sudecki despite that his granddaughter thinks that Franek is a "contrarian," and I would call him resentful, the one who seeks out the proofs of truths, and justice for all. But when Franek speaks to Mr. Sudecki the historical injustice related to the land is confirmed; furthermore Franek begins to feel that the Jews never left the village; they are still here, buried someplace and it is most logical to dig into the ground where the ruined cottage is and see what the brothers find.

## Inspect the old cottage; don't speak to the people

> Hail Mary Full of Grace. The Lord is With Thee. Blessed art Though Among Women and Blessed is the Fruit of Thy Womb, Jesus. Josef, *Aftermath*

**Figure 7:** *Aftermath*, digging into the ground, DVD screen shot.

Resentment reaches its peak one hour and twenty two minutes into the film when in the middle of the night, equipped with digging tools the brothers go to the old Cottage and dig anywhere into the ground until water from the near stream flood so that they stand in water. A cut brings the viewers into the vicarage where the old parish priest undergoes terrible pains in his chest which will kill him prematurely. And the suture of these images of water in the digging grounds and torrential rains from above brings to the fore an ethical affect; the images usher in an inevitable diction: the words that are missing here are related to God and his divine order so that the mark of Cain has to be seen by all while the bones of Able have to be found. One hour and twenty five minutes into the film the brothers exhume skulls and disconnected bones and pile them on the edges of this mass grave to show that all the Jews were burnt and killed and buried there and make the argument that many people know what happened. At dawn, the madwoman (Danuta Szaflarska) appears from the horizon with her walking cane like a nomad who carries a message, who can never be too early or too late in arriving to seal the truth, "found them at last, poor souls," she says, and affirms that she knows everything from beginning to end by suggesting that the brothers bury these bones in the cemetery that they created on their field. The madwoman who has always been an outsider in normative society, the majoritarian organizations of religion and the economic system lives in the woods and has seen what happened well enough to fearlessly assert: "everybody saw it." The villagers, "herded" the Jews into the Kalina cottage and set fire to it. Laughing, drunk with Vodka the villagers pretended that what they are doing is vengeance for Christ's death on the cross. Franek cannot accept this testimony and suggests yet again that the Germans did all this but the madwoman is adamant that the villagers committed all the atrocities including to beat up the women and children so badly that women tried to drown their babies before they are either beaten or burnt. The brothers insist that soldiers in black uniforms, the SS must have done this but it remains the fact that the madwoman is a trustworthy eyewitness and her simple, uncompromising words are truths. The SS spoke to Malinowski and affirmed that the Germans are leaving and the Polish nationals can continue on their own. According to the madwoman all the village participated in this pogrom and she was right there, watching and yelling, asking the villagers to let the Jews go until someone knocked her down with a beating to the head and suggested that she suffer together with the Jews if she feels so sorry for them.

**Figure 8:** *Aftermath*, the madwoman screamed to let the Jews go, DVD screen shot.

One hour and twenty nine minutes into the film the brothers go to see old Malinowski (Robert Rogalski) who refuses to admit to his guilt in the murder and burning of the Jews. He is alone, his son and other family members avoid him so he cannot understand why a full confession and investigation of the crime matter.

The Kalina brothers remain convinced that sixty years after the crime has been committed, the Jews deserve a proper burial but Malinowski feels that in the aftermath of sixty years this burial is even less necessary. The brothers insist that these Jews deserve burial because they are not "cattle," and thereby echo the simple words of the madwoman who said that the Jews were "herded" to the cottage. Jozef shouts that he knows that the entire village aided in collecting the Jews and beating them but only Malinowski torched them. "Dream on Kalina, dream on," is the reply from which there is no return. Malinowlski gives testimony and hopes that the brothers "choke on it," when he tells them that their father held the second torch because one person could not burn the whole cottage alone with all the Jewish families in it. When the brothers call him a liar Malinowski violently and yet with ample justification shouts: "who was there, bastard, you or me?" On top of the beating and the burning Malinowski recalls the outstanding violence that old Kalina inflicted on a Jewish woman who refused his sexual advances. Malinowski denies that he ever treated neighbors badly, but the Jews weren't neighbors. This testimony is so nakedly evil and remorseless that Jozef feels that the brothers have to rebury the truth and leave the bones where they found them or else worse trouble will come to the village; Franek promises that not just the village but the whole world will know about this. The reason that Franek cites when Jozef asks to bury the truth is that he knows he cannot make the world a better place but he will not help to make it worse. In these few words Franek sums up the reasoning that necessitates discovery and broadcasting of a *negative possession*, the world has to see the truth, and practices and rituals of morning and memorialization have to exist so that evil will be known, cognized, and cease to remain the hidden trauma of the few.

**Figure 9:** *Aftermath*, Jozef is crucified, DVD screen shot.

The film only ends when Jozef is crucified by his neighbors, nailed to the door of his barn and then buried in the Jewish cemetery that he built in his plot. Joining together the Christian figure of death with a Jewish figure of commemoration to the victim means that *Aftermath* seeks an affective sublimation because it cannot give to the historical catastrophe a moral closure. In the aftermath of the historical crime, Jozef's graves and the gravestones of the dead Jews come together in the form of a *negative possession*, a memorable albeit ineffable ending *in media res*.

# Chapter 4
# From emotion to national renewal – on J.M. Coetzee

## Normalizing emotions?

The novels of J. M. Coetzee translate Western epistemology to the consciousness of South Africa. *Disgrace*, Coetzee's most controversial work, questions the merits of English by asking if the language of the colonizer could ever tell the story of the colonized. Coetzee rebels against the epistemological colonialism that the use of English embodies in the aftermath of Apartheid. Yet Coetzee is not the first to take up this question of translation. It is asked by Paul Celan, by Jean Améry, and many others. *Disgrace* utilizes the complexity of emotions to show how love, forgiveness, and resentment inform South African politics. These emotions do not seamlessly migrate from the personal to the social and political spheres. South Africa is an example of how a vast range of emotions is at stake during a process of reconciliation. As *Disgrace* demonstrates, these diverse emotions can be misunderstood and abused; as when governments appeal to morality to forge a false normalcy in the name of national healing.

The works of Améry, Vladimir Jankélévitch, Hannnah Arendt, and Jaques Derrida are all focused on forgiveness and resentment for this very purpose: to shed light on how governments distort emotions. In relation to post-war Germany, these thinkers argue in favor of an ethics that denies both the moral relevance of forgiveness and the moral depravity of forgetting the crimes of the Third Reich. In *Disgrace*, both the use and value of forgiveness are under investigation, and subject to translation. Coetzee is plotting forgiveness in two different forms: at the beginning of the novel repentance is political; at the end forgiveness is personal.

Translation from political to personal forgiveness invites difference to emerge from repetition. Coetzee aims to be a harbinger of South African memory. His reflections collect ideas about male and national chauvinism, the superiority of urban over country life, racial inequality, and the cultural and political demands of the colonized. Coetzee prefigures how these contradictory values are politically repressed and marginalized. His novel suggests that the colonized can aesthetically define and articulate their agenda, plunging moral ideals right back into the center of the public sphere.

The main protagonists of the book, a father and his daughter, question the role of harm in their lives. Could ruminating on harm facilitate forgiveness, restore normalcy to post-Apartheid South Africa? This question is invaluable to articulating the epistemology of the Truth and Reconciliation Committee, which pursued restorative justice, not simply allowing victims to undergo personal, sentimental transformations. Difference is implicated in translation because the political discussion of moral emotions in South Africa does not begin a new discourse. Rather, it deterritorializes a Western conceptualization of emotion.

Is it possible to address the evils of colonialism with the encyclopedias of language that Eurocentrism still spreads in South Africa? In an attempt to answer this question, I revisit the Eurocentric political systems and cultural texts that were the educational bedrock of the second and third generations of Jews after the Holocaust, the children and grandchildren of the survivors. This chapter engages with the reciprocal influence between Western epistemology and its translation by new languages, which area studies both exposes and creates. "Area studies" is comprised of cultures whose consciousness emerges from the intimate self-knowledge of violated bodies and borders. New literary, theoretical, and political languages have emerged in South America, South Africa, and India, as well as among certain social groups in the United States and Europe. For my purposes here, South Africa's experiments with the imperative of remembering revise or introduce the option of moral *dissensus*, a minoritarian moral outlook to the European experience.

Every chapter in this volume explores the ambivalence of Western epistemology towards the role of emotions in the public sphere. How can emotions resist becoming bargaining chips in a political sphere that caters to national and economic interests? Emotions can be expressed in order to allow the Truth and Reconciliation Committee to reach its decisions. They then become political, not genuine. Emotions have the potential to propel both victims and perpetrators to remember atrocities and, in this way, although emotions play a political role, instigate long-term commitments to care and acknowledge the suffering of the victims. This process then produces a historical, educational, cultural, and psychological reservoir of what Améry calls "negative possessions." Under the fiercest strictures of memory, Améry hopes, solidarity can consolidate the individual's right not to devote life to mourning, to commemorating evil. Rather, the individual is allowed to cease ruminating on the wounds of suffering, and forgive, forgive as a means to finding a way out of abandonment, and towards rebuilding life.

In Coetzee's post-Apartheid South Africa, forgiveness and resentment are not privileged emotions. They belong to a pattern of shame, regret, revenge, and reconciliation. The love and hate that create the emotional habitat in which friendship, respect, and reconciliation flourish are also necessary to forgiveness, resentment, and revenge. Is a perpetrator feeling regret when his regret influences his judges to offer him amnesty? Is a Black victim truly forgiving the torture s/he suffered? Is the murder of a loved one truly reconcilable in the presence of a Truth Committee?

*Disgrace* does not offer a straightforward answer. It suggests that emotions are lost when they are repeated and reified by an excess of rationalization. Emotions are revived when they are acted on, and undergo translation in different psychological, historical, ecological, and political spheres. Forgetting is valuable because it allows difference to repair emotions. While *Disgrace* is not a political manifesto, it is impossible to understand the novel without translating emotions; that is, going beyond seeking punishment towards justifying social solidarity. *Disgrace* confronts Western virtues, like retributive justice, with interpersonal structures of communication, which stress the social function of emotions in the native languages of Sotho and Xhosa, and examines their efficacy in the public sphere.

In *No Future Without Forgiveness*, Archbishop Desmond Tutu translates forgiveness to both *restorative justice* and *Ubuntu*, or *botho*. Ubuntu is an African concept that encompasses a large scope of moral emotions, including neighborly love, the humanity of the Other, reciprocity, and recognition. Tutu is looking for a concept that is indigenous to South Africa, and which connotes emotional activities that the Western examination of forgiveness doesn't append. He claims that restorative justice is characteristic of African jurisprudence, a jurisprudence that is not primarily concerned with punishment. He explains that the European veneration of punishment belongs in an epistemology that imprisons national history in a cycle of reprisal and counter-reprisal: "and that the only way to [break the cycle] was to go beyond retributive justice to restorative justice, to move on to forgiveness, because without it there was no future" (Tutu 1997, 197). In contrast to retributive justice, "in the spirit of Ubuntu, the central concern is the healing of breaches, the redressing of imbalances, the restoration of broken relationships, a seeking to rehabilitate both the victim and the perpetrator, who should be given the opportunity to be reintegrated into the community he has injured by his offense" (ibid, 46). Combining the rhetoric of restorative justice and Ubuntu, Tutu argues that "the humanity of the perpetrator of Apartheid's atrocities was caught up and bound up in that of his victim whether he liked it or not" (ibid, 80).

It does not follow from Tutu's moral understanding of Ubuntu that one must unconditionally pursue pure forgiveness. Rather, the suggestion is that victims receive a moral response when they accept a political system that encourages perpetrators to regain their humanity through confession and admission of guilt. Ultimately, this encourages a broader cultural remembering, which publicly broadcasts the negative possessions of the collective. In courts of law that seek a verdict, the victim-witness and the perpetrator-defendant are never directly in touch with each other. Their words are mediated by the legal institution. Retributive justice severely cripples the victim's and perpetrator's ability to transform traumatic knowledge into an experience of healing.

Améry acknowledges these complexities when he focuses on the necessity to address, not just try, the perpetrator:

> I speak as a victim and examine my resentments. [. . .] Resentments as the existential dominant of people like myself are the result of a long personal and historical development. They were by no means evident on the day I left the last of my concentration camps, Bergen-Belsen, and returned home to Brussels, which was really not my home. [. . .] I preserve my resentments. And since I neither can nor want to get rid of them, I must live with them and am obliged to clarify them for those against whom they are directed (Améry 1980, 63, 64, 67).

Even within attempts at forgiveness and reconciliation, resentment can linger. Resentment only seems inextricable from a national history of extreme violations of human rights.

Yet, South Africa's turn to restorative, as opposed to retributive, justice suggests that, within the framework of Ubuntu, the humanity of the Other is immediately at stake. The perpetrator's goal might be to achieve amnesty, while the victim might want the Committee to mete out a guilty verdict, but these ends are among many other considerations that make up the process. The conversations between, first, the Committee and the perpetrators and, next, victims and perpetrators, demand that traumatic knowledge be the necessary reference point. Nothing but a disclosure of the ultimate, exposed truth is admissible as a worthy account of what happened.

The victim always attaches the words of the perpetrator to her/his pain and resentment, while the perpetrator invariably connects the response of the victim to the evil that s/he inflicted, to the guilt incurred, to the shame. The conversation between the two hinges on their willingness to trust each other, to truthfully address hurt and injustice, and to forge a new commitment to attachment based on mutual respect. Those who participate in the meetings of the Committee impart knowledge linked to moral emotions like regret, repentance, shame, forgiveness, resentment, and mourning. The Committee uses restorative justice to enhance national healing, to entice the participants to wrestle with their emotions and prejudices towards one another.

Expressions of shame and pain deterritorialize political pragmatism. The hope for possible healing unconsciously brings resentment and forgiveness to the surface of the interaction between victim and perpetrator. How can emotions attain clarity, unless they are present in a conversation where both victim and perpetrator stand a chance of undergoing transformation, at the same time that they effect radical social and political change? How can victims and perpetrators avow their crimes and suffering without assigning emotions to traumatic experiences?

Because traumatic wounds are at stake, language becomes entangled in unconscious facts, memories, and fantasies that seek clarification in terms of difference, and actions of solidarity captured in structural change.

*Disgrace* is a story of sexual assault and patriarchal manipulation embedded in racial and political conflict. It belongs in the reservoir of negative possessions that Apartheid has bequeathed to South Africans. Instead of centering the moral values of forgiveness and resentment, the story pivots around emotions that Western epistemology completely neglects. With *Disgrace*, Coetzee pushes against the conditions of meaning acceptable in his culture, and inserts mysterious potentialities to a reframing of colonialism and Apartheid in South Africa. What does it take to introduce difference to identity, subjectivity, and sociability in totalitarian régimes, or, for that matter, in so-called democratic societies, which perpetuate racial and gendered insecurity and inequality?

*Disgrace* met with a great deal of criticism from both white and Black audiences in South Africa. Readers understood it as a historical document, rather than as a *literary speech act*, when it is actually a bit of both. It orbits around the tension between David Lurie, a fifty-three-year-old divorcé and professor of Romantic Poetry at Cape Town Technical College, and his daughter Lucy. Lucy is a lesbian farmer living on her own small tract of land in the town of Salem, on the Eastern Cape. The plot follows a series of psychosomatic, social, and economic changes in both Lurie's and Lucy's lives, which force them to contend with inner and external evil, react to violence, and undergo physical, emotional, and moral transformations.

Early on Lurie searches for sexual outlets; between passion, stalking, rape, and love, he has ample opportunity for confusion. He relishes sexuality, desire, and violating the Other. Yet he also displays paternal love, love of nonhuman animals, and the love of wisdom and poetry. This conflation of love and desire dissolves love as a pure emotion that subsists even when sexual tensions are satisfied. Coetzee wants his reader to question the meaning of love, and the other emotions usually associated with it – forgiveness, resentment, regret, guilt, and shame – especially in the face of moral atrocity. In this chapter, I will continue to develop my initial hypothesis: that humans will do everything possible to enhance trust and love in the private and the public spheres. Love may fail Lurie and Lucy, but this means that love itself must undergo revision and translation.

## Emotions do not have an essence: Conflating love and desire

In search of the sensual, Lurie the professor initiates an affair with Melanie Isaacs, a Black student half his age. He cannot bring himself to break it off, even though he knows that Melanie is "too young," that "he ought to let her go," that she is *"No more than a child!" "What am I doing?,"* he demands of himself, of an act that is perhaps "Not rape" but "undesired to the core" (Coetzee 1999, 18, 20, 25). When Lurie corrupts the concepts of trust and love, he pretends that, in the throes of passion, he is also giving Melanie fatherly love, mentoring, and sexual experience. In this context of clear sexual abuse, respect acquires an ironic tinge. Melanie's father contacts Lurie to say that his daughter is unwell and wants to quit school, but could Lurie speak to her, for she *respects* him more than her other professors. In the past, Melanie had approached Lurie in difficult moments, because she respected him. Lurie suggests that the father is, in fact, not aware of certain new developments, and should speak to his daughter again. The irony is painful: Melanie respects Lurie, even while he takes advantage of her. Initially she approached him when she was in distress. But, at this trying moment, Lurie chose to corrupt the meaning of trust, respect, and love – a failure that Mr. Isaacs cannot imagine could occur in a respectable university.

The corruption of love and respect occurs repeatedly, most strongly through the dissolution of language. When Lurie is called in for questioning by an inquiry committee of his peers, the terms "confession," "guilt," "apology," "sincerity," "humility," "regret," "repentance," and "forgiveness" are all jumbled up, demanded. The committee is tasked with resolving Melanie's complaint of sexual harassment. They suggest that Lurie give a full confession, admit his guilt, and repent in an overt fashion, otherwise the university will dismiss him with no benefits and his academic career will be over. The committee expects that Lurie will take practical actions to "minimize the damage" or "reach some arrangement," so that the committee can "pass sentence" and "make recommendations." The language that Lurie uses in his responses is more tidy. He declares himself guilty and states that he acted on an "unforgiveable impulse" (Coetzee 1999, 52). Yet the members of the committee feel that Lurie expresses "subtle mockery" (ibid, 51) and demand that, in addition to admitting guilt and accepting punishment, Lurie show vulnerability by signing a public statement that he is both sorry and regretful.

What does this moment make of forgiveness and resentment? Are they symbolic or material emotions? Lurie's resentment appears when he refuses to sign the public statement of repentance, rejecting its religious overtones. He leaves the school and goes to visit Lucy. The dissolution of emotions is so thorough that it seems that love, trust, rape, repentance, and resentment do not have the power to instigate action. The committee doesn't understand why Lurie associates emotions with a right to privacy. His admission of guilt cannot move members of the committee to either empathy or protest. The members of the committee assign an essential, fixed, pure meaning to love, desire, repentance, and sorrowfulness, a pure meaning that amounts to presuming to have common knowledge of what love, rape, repentance, and resentment are in every context. Since Lurie rejects the notion of emotional essence, when he acts as if love changes from one moment to the next in differing circumstances, he poses a threat to orderly life in the community, and on the moral consensus that the community imposes on its members. Yet emotions cannot be contained in a static structure of common knowledge. They do not become strong by appealing to the consensus. Feelings are meaningful only when they propel action and promote change.

When individuals and societies rethink evil and good under dire circumstances, it becomes clear how the emotion is not pure, pervaded by clusters of meaning, some of them disharmonious, as are forgiveness and resentment, or repentance or shame. For example, when Lurie cites from Byron's *Lara* that love is the same impulse that "would in tempting time/ mislead his spirit equally to crime," he is adducing to the impurity of love (ibid, 33). Love is not a pure emotion. It has the potential to contain desire, hatred, and other inexplicable impulses. Love can easily be collapsed and, although desire can be a healthy impulse, Lurie acknowledges his treatment of Melanie was wrong. Meanwhile, the committee assumes that an honest, responsible professor would have known the clear difference between love and desire. When the committee insists that Lurie compose a public apology, it deprives both love and desire of their most valuable trait: the suddenness and inexplicability with which emotion and desire transform relationships and lives.

The committee demands humility through repentance and confession. Yet Lurie feels that repentance and confession bring about pride, not just humility, for these acts are implicated in the creation of a self-indulgent scene of self-accusation, a satisfying performance in itself.[1] Alternately, confession can lead to false accusation and to strengthening guilt. The more one confesses the more in-

---

[1] A relevant example of this performative humility can be found in Paul de Man's famous examination of the "public trial" in Rousseau's *Confessions*. The trial, which is really more of an attempt to settle a domestic feud, involves the question of who stole a pink-and-silver ribbon, Rousseau or Marion the cook. Rousseau lies, accusing Marion, while the truth is that he stole the ribbon and intended to give it to her. De Man suggests that, rather than show how confessions enable one to disclose the truth and cling to humility, Rousseau is enjoying his confession. Because he cannot undo the damage that he inflicted on Marion – he cannot cleanse the guilt – he can at least express his regret verbally, protract his suffering, and satisfy his desire to be seen as ashamed, guilty, and penitent. Self-accusation takes the place of a clean conscience, because Rousseau's performance cannot release his victim form the effects of his crime, a crime that is rendered in a factual utterance. The confession keeps intact the gap that exists between the utterance of fact and the performance of guilt. Confession does not absolve Rousseau. It only highlights the centrality and moral value of his guilty conscience. A guilty secret always desires exposure. The guilty conscience is proud and exhibitionistic. See de Man 1979, 287, 288, 194, and 199.

sistent one's guilt becomes. Is it appropriate then to conclude that emotions are useless in the social, legal, and political spheres? Does Lurie's immediate resignation and dismissal allow the community to forge a productive and helpful closure and rebuild trust? Is it politically significant that Lurie declare his guilt, accept responsibility, and resign without satisfying the committee?

I will return to these questions. For the moment, it is important to realize that Lurie belongs to a society that views rape as a radical evil. I want to connect Lurie's unsatisfying explanation of the rape of Melanie Isaacs, which he defines as *love* and *attraction*, to the moral role that love, confession, and forgiveness play in South Africa's Truth and Reconciliation Committee. I view the inquiry committee that condemns Lurie as analogous to the Truth Committee, which exposed the guilt and offered amnesty in the aftermath of the extreme evil of Apartheid.

## A historical precedent: The truth and reconciliation committee

In the meetings of the Committee forgiveness, resentment, repentance, and shame were not pure, yet neither were they completely warped by political interests. The personal aspect of emotions can be read in, and extrapolated from, the public confessions of perpetrators, when they faced the prosecutors' interrogations. In addition, the attitudes of the offenders came around again in their conversations with the victims' family members. The place and role of emotions was not legally binding, because the Committee made its decisions based on the truthfulness, fullness, and value of the information that the confession disclosed, not on the basis of how genuine the regret was. And yet a wish hovered over these confessions: that they would reveal the humanity of the defendant and his ability to empathize, to feel the pain of his victims, even though he committed the heinous crimes to which he was confessing.

In this sense, emotions unsettle the fluency of political discourse, a discourse interested in the restoration of normalcy to a nation shattered by trauma. Derrida suggests that love and forgiveness interrupt the order of law and politics when they are not caught up in conditions: "Must one not maintain that an act of forgiveness worthy of its name, if there ever is such a thing, must forgive the unforgivable, and without condition? And that such unconditionality is also inscribed, like its contrary, namely the condition of repentance, in 'our' heritage? Even if this radical purity can seem excessive, hyperbolic, mad?" (Derrida 2001, 39). Yet, in the meetings of the Committee emotions appeared side by side with political conditions, and political conditions quickened the rise of emotions. Derrida severs forgiveness and repentance from their corresponding political actions. He thereby declares the purity of these emotions.

When emotions are pure, they are not automatically expressed in, or subsumed by, democratic institutions. Victims forgive because of their humanity, not out of a political calculation. When emotions become conditional, tied up to a penal economy and political benefits, they lose their meaning. Derrida's convictions are challenged not only by Lurie's inquiry committee, but by the Truth and Reconciliation Committee itself. In the meetings of both bodies, a useful, conditional image of forgiveness and resentment meets penal and political goals, while the perpetrator and the victim become irrelevant. Everyone becomes a symbol. The utilitarian image of emotion substitutes for interpersonal communication, which renders the victim and the perpetrator comprehensible to each other. Yet, I will show that Derrida's arguments are not fully convincing. Even though emotions are not pure when revealed to the Committee, when South Africa turned to transitional justice it achieved a juridical, political revolution, because the Committee did not agree on terms and conditions unless emotions transpired in the confessions, both consciously and unconsciously.

The Truth and Reconciliation Committee was established in 1995 to investigate gross human rights violations. Archbishop Tutu, as its chair, oversaw the work of sixteen commissioners who headed sub-committees including the Amnesty Committee, the Reparation and Rehabilitation Committee, and the Human Rights Violations Committee. The Committee did not institute conditional forgiveness. It asked those who perpetrated atrocities to give a full account of the crimes they committed during Apartheid. The Committee facilitated face-to-face meetings between defendants and victims, where those present could express repentance and ask for, or grant, forgiveness. Regardless of these procedures, the members of the Committee decided what reparations each victim received, what punishment each defendant served, and who was granted amnesty. Derrida argues that legal scenes of confession, amnesty, reparations, and encounters with victims become moral only because they are associated with emotions like forgiveness and repentance, not because love and forgiveness engender action:

> At least this, which does not simplify things: if our idea of forgiveness falls into ruin as soon as it is deprived of its pole of absolute reference, namely its unconditional purity, it remains nonetheless inseparable from what is heterogenous to it, namely the order of conditions, repentance, transformation, as many things as allow it to inscribe itself in history, law, politics, existence itself. These two poles, the unconditional and the conditional, are absolutely heterogeneous, and must remain irreducible to one another (Derrida 2001, 44).

Conditional forgiveness and repentance are utilitarian modes where what one can achieve in and for society becomes the central question. Even if this utilitarian or economic basis determines positive political actions, the purity of forgiveness and repentance becomes occluded. Derrida states that the clash between who and what a person is must remain alive if forgiveness and repentance are to have value.

This paradox concerning forgiveness and resentment comes to light in the political and intra-personal encounters of *Disgrace*, which defies the existing social conditions at the same time as it shifts the boundary between social and political emotions. Once Lurie, Lucy, and Petrus, Lucy's Black neighbor, mix ethics with economic, utilitarian thinking, their emotions become more acute.

Emotions become a valuable force if they are sanctioned by state institutions that deal in amnesty, reparations, restorative justice, and national healing. Within the political context, emotions like forgiveness and resentment, or respect and solidarity, recall the traumatic wounds inflicted on the victims and the materiality of the language used to accomplish political goals. Emotions propel the divided subject to action, because s/he is caught between lack in the form of pain or the death of desire, and the wish to accomplish political transformation.

Julia Kristeva stresses that "[b]oth desire and practice exist solely on the basis of language: desire is 'produced by an animal at the mercy of language'" (Kristeva 1984, 131). Love cannot be reduced to desire. Emotions emerge in response to the interdependence between the subject and the Other. Language propels action, and thereby the subject and the Other rebuild relationships in the form of family, community, and nation, at the same time as they remain cut off from traumatic knowledge. They cannot heal the real. To extend forgiveness and repentance while holding on to one's resentment is, as Kristeva puts it, "a punctual position" (ibid.). It is a position of social responsibility that forces the subject to be cut off from her/his traumatic wounds.

Gene Sharp discusses the same phenomenon, the emergence of emotions in a political context. She explains that, when grievances are presented in written statements or in an official context that declares an intention to change the future situation for the better, then the document "becomes influential in influencing people's loyalties and behavior" (Sharp 1973, 123). The Committee was the context that gave a face and a story to each perpetrator and victim. In this context, people react with active emotions of love, hate or sympathy because the audiences remain nonviolent, and, although desire on both sides is subjective, it is bound by language. The traits of the subject and the context succumb to constant change. Sharp suggests that "such change takes place to a much greater degree and more quickly than it does in struggles in which both sides use violence" (ibid, 527). By extension, restorative justice blocks the way to violence and opens the way to transformation, because it includes confession; that is, it endorses the language of traumatic knowledge.

The historical fact is that some victims agreed to become speakers, with the moral power to forgive, while others did not, declining to forgive even during the personal meetings with their assailants.² Some victims offered forgiveness and

---

2 See the film *Long Night's Journey Into Day*, which depicts four stories examined by the Committee. Its focus is on the meetings between the victims' families and the perpetrators. I cite from the film and explain the meeting between the families of those four young men who died in the murders known as the "Guguletu 7 Incident." The Committee invited nine policemen to serve as witnesses to the incident. There was also video footage of the killings. The mothers of the murdered young men saw the mutilated bodies of their sons, in the same room as the witnesses and the perpetrators. They broke down, so that the video had to be stopped a few times before the audience could see it to the end. The mothers later said that, despite the traumatic effect of the horrific images, they felt better, because they learned the truth of their sons' deaths. Two police functionaries asked for amnesty, one Black and one white, but they told different versions of the incident. The Black constable, Mbelo, confessed that he shot the man in the head while he was lying on his back. He explained that he was asking for amnesty because he wanted to bring the truth of the incident to light. He added that there had been a previous inquiry commission about the incident, but the perpetrators had all lied then. Mbelo clearly states that the acting members of the police force had no feelings, they were completing a day's work. When feelings catch up with the perpetrator, he drinks and stays drunk. This Black perpetrator shows very clearly that he is "not a monster," to use the words of Pumla Gobodo-Madikizela in the film. He is repentant, but more clearly, he suffers from his crimes. He experiences regret on a daily basis. A context in which the perpetrator could ask for forgiveness is directly related to his need to express emotions, extend respect to the victims' families, and restore new moral potentials as a speaking, active member of the Black community of South Africa. The camera follows Mbelo's meeting with the families of his victims, during which he calls the victims "my parents." One mother declares that she has no forgiveness for him, while a second forgives and calls the perpetrator "my son." Here is a quote from the footage: "My name is Thapelo Mbelo. I am ashamed to look you in the face [. . .]. And I want to say to you as the parents of those children who were there that day, I ask your forgiveness from the bottom of my heart. Forgive me, my parents." Despite the sincerity of the repentance, which the camera amplifies with a close up on the speaker's face one mother is resentful. She asks the perpetrator how did he feel when he killed a boy who was surrendering to his attackers. She accuses the perpetrator that he devoted his life to compromising the lives of Blacks, like him, just for money. Another mother of another murdered man asks, "what does your conscience say to you? When you really look at it, my son." This mother's resentment is mitigated by Mbelo's choice to address the victims' families using the language of love and deference to his elders. The mother does not relent and adds political causes to withhold forgiveness when she says that the state refuses to give her pension but her grandchild has no father to support him, because the father was murdered, while she cannot find work. A third mother states, "I have no forgiveness for you." The perpetrator's silence strengthens the feeling that he is acknowledging the suffering of the mothers, and that he is regretting the murder he committed, the life he led as a policeman during Apartheid. At the same time, the perpetrator's silence makes the voice of the mother's resound with great force as they negotiate with emotions, tether emotions to concern for the Other, *who?*, and social responsibility, *what?* One of the mothers adds, "Speaking as Christopher's mother, I forgive you, my child. [. . .] and the reason I say I

later regretted their benevolence, appealing to resentment to explain their change of heart. These different attitudes exemplify how victims can forgive while still nurturing resentment. Even the perpetrators who did not ask for forgiveness were affected by the translation of history into negative possessions. Perpetrators are influenced by moral and political changes, and begin to feel shame in altered moral and political climates. Shame propels the changed perpetrators to assume responsibility for the wrongs they committed, by offering respect and equal treatment to their former victims, their current fellow citizens.

*Disgrace* brings Lurie together with Melanie, and later with her father, Mr. Isaacs, in order to show that Lurie's attraction and finally his love for Melanie cannot be separated from the political context responsible for enforcing a ban on sexual relationships with students. Lurie never questions the validity of Melanie's complaint against him. He stresses her right to demand justice in relation to his sexual harassment. In his encounter with Mr. Isaacs, Lurie affirms the right of this Black high-school teacher, who is a deeply religious man, to refuse to sepa-

---

forgive you is that my child will never wake up again. And it's pointless to hold this wound against you. God will be the judge. [. . .] I want you to go home knowing the mothers are forgiving the evil you have done, and we feel compassion for you. . . . So Jesus told us when he was on the cross, forgive those who sin against you. Because we want to get rid of this burden we are carrying inside, so that we too can feel at peace. So for my part I forgive you, my child. Yes, I forgive you. Go well, my child." The film segues to photos of the murdered men but the sequence is paced by returning to the room in which the perpetrator shakes the hands and hugs the mothers and other family members of the victims (Directors Deborah Hoffmann and Frances Reid 2000, 1:20:39–1:28:13). My discussion of this long excerpt from the film aims to show that emotions like forgiveness and resentment do not exist independently of the context in which they appear. One mother refuses to forgive, but she takes advantage of the right to voice her resentments in a political context, while the second forgives but her forgiveness is tied up to her religious faith and to her analysis of the political structure in which the murder and the reconciliation occur. The repentant perpetrator accepts forgiveness and a refusal to forgive, and, although he replies to the questions of the mothers, he does not show emotions, but instead appears to be in great physical discomfort, and his face contort with self-disgust or pain. These images are pressing because they show that forgiveness, repentance, and resentment are emotions that can never be pure, but are translated and reshaped during interactions with the Other. Interpersonal relations are always implicated in both *who* one is and in the fact that the *what*, the context, affects the *who* from the beginning. One therefore learns to forgive when one learns that trust and politics translate forgiveness into a secular hope and action for a better psychological, social, political, or economic situation. *Who* do we love if we love the one outside of any context? *What* do we know of the one we love if we never contextualize the loved one in our daily living, or daily expectations and hopes? To accept that *who* and *what* are relevant to each other is to allow the criminal to show his humanity and the victim to embrace the right to recover form relentless pain and become attached to the world again by using her/his voice, elaborating her/his feelings of forgiveness and resentment and acting on the basis of clearer moral reasoning, moral demands.

rate the interpersonal moral understanding he has with Lurie from politics and everyday interests. Mr. Isaacs extends hospitality to Lurie. He engages in a painful conversation with him about the events that Melanie and Lurie deal with, from different ends of the divide between them: Melanie is the victim, Lurie is the rapist. Isaacs accepts Lurie's expressions of repentance, regret, shame, and his description of himself as a man who is "living it [disgrace] out from day to day, trying to accept disgrace as my state of being" (Coetzee 1999, 172). At the same time Mr. Isaacs suspects that Lurie has ulterior motives that propel him to broadcast his moral blame. Isaacs asks Lurie point-blanc if he confesses in the hope of receiving a reward: "To reinstate you for instance." But Lurie, who is a transformed man, chooses to remain loyal to emotions when he sincerely replies, "The thought never crossed my mind" (ibid, 174).

Once radical evil has been unleashed, it is not enough to indict those who lost their capacity to act morally. Culture must allow victims and perpetrators to express emotions in two contexts: interpersonal encounters and political displays. Lurie rejects the university committee's demand that he issue a public statement of repentance. He is committed to guilt and shame when he chooses to resign, and shamefully leave Cape Town rather than reach a mutually beneficial arrangement with the university. Yet Lurie undergoes transformation throughout the novel. His experiences force him to leave retributive justice behind and trust in Ubuntu, in restorative justice. His behavior is closer to the ideals of the Truth and Reconciliation Committee than it is to the demands of the university committee, because he never expresses repentance in public. In the second half of the novel, Lurie discloses his pain, regret, shame, and disgrace as well as his love, repentance, forgiveness, and acknowledgement of difference with both his assailants and his victims. Lurie undergoes transformation and changes from a white, masculine, privileged intellectual to an attentive, effeminate father and neighbor, who chooses an ascetic life close to nature, in order to affirm the knowledge that the body obtains and seek emotional release.

Jill Scott suggests that, when forgiveness and repentance are embodied in speech, it is inevitable that a poetic meaning transpires, so that the repentant and the forgiving are spoken by unconscious, traumatic forms of empathy. This traumatic empathy process re-humanizes the Other, even as it re-shuffles our understanding of forgiveness: "Forgiveness arises as a product of the creative (over)production and (over)interpretation of the poetic meaning . . . therefore all human communication potentially elicits forgiveness . . . if we accept this then the TRC potentially bears the signifying fruits of forgiveness" (Scott 2010, 147).

Archbishop Tutu preferred to rely on Ubuntu rather than forgiveness. Heidi Grunebaum trusts in Tutu's words as they appear in the Committee's report:

> We must break the spiral of reprisal and counter-reprisal . . . I said to them in Kigali "unless you move beyond justice in the form of a tribunal, there is no hope for Rwanda." Confession, forgiveness, and reconciliation in the lives of nations are not just airy-fairy religious and spiritual things, nebulous and unrealistic. They are the stuff of practical politics (Cited in Grunebaum 2002, 308).

Mark Sanders clarifies how Ubuntu is not exactly a translation of Western forgiveness, but a transformation:

> [In *No Future Without Forgiveness*, Tutu argues *that Ubuntu* means the following] "My humanity is caught up, is inextricably bound up, in yours." [Sanders elaborates] We belong in a bundle of life. We say, "A person is a person through other persons." It is not "I think therefore I am." It says rather: "I am human because I belong. I participate, I share" (Cited in Sanders 2007, 95).

Scott adds that, because in Ubuntu, "I am who I am because of who you are," it is germane to associate Ubuntu to unconscious meanings that shape one's connections with other people (Scott 2010, 149). For both Sanders and Scott, forgiveness appears like a gift, even in the context of the Committee. The perpetrator is locked in the admission of guilt and shame, while the victims are offering their nonsymmetrical gift of Ubuntu, a continued shared humanity, practicing neighborly love through empathy and the process of re-humanizing the victim and the offender.

Forgiveness is a gift only if the forgiving victim freely acts on the moral recollection of evil that tethers her/him to their own resentment. Jeffrey Blustein points out that forgiveness "does not disable protest against wrongdoing, or against forgetting wrongdoing, but can in fact coexist with a readiness to protest wrongdoing if and when the need arises" (Bluestein 2014, 171). I understand this to mean that the Committee could designate a victim who has a stake in structuring the country's political institutions, not just in protecting memory. Impure forgiveness looks both to remembering past atrocities, and to receiving the political respect one needs, in order to become an actor with the power to call out the moral and structural transformations required of the new society. Those who were helpless do not forgive magnanimously. They forgive because the new regime treats them as responsible agents of change, who view forgiveness, resentment, cultural memory, and personal forgetting as necessary processes to bring about that change.

How does Ubuntu translate or naturalize the need to be personally exposed in the public sphere, either as a perpetrator or as a victim? Furthermore, how are these processes of translation and naturalization productive, in regards to the need for moral healing in the political circumstances present in South Africa?[3] The structure of forgiveness keeps resentment articulable, while the structure of resentment demands that perpetrators expose their emotions in public, and thereby acknowledge the respect for the victims. Social and political difference emerge to shape the personal and cultural relation to memory and moral transformation. The example of South Africa upsets the Western cleavage between memory and forgetfulness, between forgiveness and resentment.

## Emotional and social transformation

When normative rules propel politics, decisions and actions always serve the interests of those in power, even if these interests happen to yield good judgments or better social conditions. In contrast, emotions emerge from a radical disturbance of normality. They institute the urgent need to question sovereignty, to transform existing political power, and to disrupt the institutions that tether ethics to interests.[4] When forgiveness and repentance block the articulation of resentment in interpersonal and public encounters, then this feigned normality obscures ethics. Remembering is tied up with the moral right to forget. Repetition is valuable if it is curtailed by difference, if the repetition does not seek to enhance the identity of the self, but instead embraces a self that is split between memories that repeat the past and forgetfulness of that past.

Later in the novel Lurie confides to his daughter Lucy that, when the committee recommended "counselling," he felt as if they recommended he be re-formed,

---

3 Jill Scott explains what it means to interpret texts from the hearings of the Committee when she examines the famous testimonies of Du Plessis and Van Wyk. When these two appealed for amnesty and testified in front of the Committee, they were already serving prison-time for robbery and murder. Scott shows the gap between the symbolic meaning of the apology and the semiotic attentiveness of the victims. An unconscious enigma remains inarticulable; yet it yields the necessary meanings that allow speech acts to have the power needed to induce healing or activate moral emotions.

4 Catherine Malabou (2017) argues that human beings emerge from repetition. Without repetition, the individual has no biological clarity, no memory, not even the quality of agency. In repetition we have the capacity to change and transform what we repeat. Malabou suggests that Derrida understands political scenes of forgiveness as a refusal to change what we repeat: "Questions of memory, ancestrality, and genealogy are acute today, as if what comes back, what returns, what needs to be repaired and restituted, were the most urgent of all problems. As Derrida notes, the urge for repetition, for forgiveness and repair, for repentance and redemption, for remembrance in order to forget, to repeat in order not to repeat, has become so strong that it has become transgressive."

re-educated, turned into an obedient conformist (Coetzee 1999, 66). To Rosalind (his ex-wife), Lurie explains that he lost the favor of his peers at the inquiry because, "I was standing for a principle [. . .]. Freedom of speech. Freedom to remain silent" (ibid, 188). Lurie made the wrong choices, but this does not mean that forgiveness and resentment, freedom and silence, remembering and forgetting, are *a priori*, not affected by human interaction. On the contrary, dialogues and relationships must seek to constantly transform emotions in order to make them relevant to the changing lives of persons and communities. Lurie's declaration of guilt and resignation are performative. While Lurie, the offender, is punished for his wrongful behavior, he does not share repentance, confession, or forgiveness with any community. The implications of this decision appear in the second part of the novel, when three Black men assault him and Lucy on the farm. Lurie must reacquaint himself with his daughter's opinions, which are different from his, and with his own clinging to known languages, traditions, and assumed laws of normality.

Lurie's insistence on the possibility that humans have an inner moral compass is tied up with repetition. The more one is compelled to repeat a traumatic past, the harder it is to reproduce sameness. One is exposed to the visible power of difference, the inevitable veering away from the known, conscious, to the unknown unconscious realm. The philosopher Catherine Malabou suggests that Friedrich Nietzsche's "overman" is flexible in repetition, because he ceases to seek revenge against things that happened in the past, or against the very passage of time: the overman can let bygones be bygones because past wrongs cannot be avenged. The overman does not seek to redress past offences, neither in face-to-face interactions nor in legal and political procedures. But, deploying forgetting, the overman can lure redemption and the materialization of difference at the expense of repetition.

Lurie's behavior addresses and translates Nietzsche's theory because, although the loss of sovereignty is typical of his new life, while repetition aims to suppress the alterity of the Other, it also establishes the perfect conditions in which difference is pressing, insisting. It has an opportunity to surface. Lurie transforms into a person who, because he is reduced to a state of recollections and powerlessness, remains devoted to discovering difference. This devotion is tantamount to resentment, forgiveness, and repentance, not through state institutions, but through translation, or acknowledging the irreducible difference that pervades the self, extends to the Other, and guides one's responsibility to the relationship with the Other. Thinking of the limits of repetition, the insistence of difference, and the role that emotions play in propelling transformation the novel, revolutionizes readers' tendency to accept received ideas. *Disgrace* wants readers to question whether political forgiveness, confession, and amnesty really promote equity and human rights, or whether they enhance morally justified political interests.

## The translation of emotions

Coetzee willfully challenges known definitions of love and forgiveness, of guilt and of shame. He positions these emotions in circumstances that are not necessarily dialogical, intersubjective, or moral, as a means of expanding and better investigating if and where emotions are valuable. He implements translation in ways that bring to mind Walter Benjamin's notion that a good translation connects different language-environments.

Translation takes part in the afterlife of a work of art. *Disgrace* uses concepts and metaphors that have a purpose in the original Eurocentric texts, or the original language-environment. To translate a text is to reveal its meanings without submitting to the desire to make semantics materialize, congeal, or become realized in exact resemblance to the original.[5] *Disgrace* is pervaded with difference – the difference that translation instills in the original text. Coetzee's translation of the original text – and, remember, the original text is Western epistemology itself – carries repetition at the same time that it activates difference. I want to show that the original text that *Disgrace* translates is Western ambivalence about the function of emotions in the political sphere.

In the second part of the novel things change for the worse. Lurie suffers a horrific experience alongside his daughter. His existence is tied to "neutering" (84), "sterilization [and] euthanasia" (91), scapegoating (91), resignation (63), "disgrace" (85), "coup de grâce" (95), "yielding nothing" (99), "pity and terror" (98), and "murmur" (97). These terms all project a frightful lack of personal security. The rural area where Lucy lives is communal: Africans and Boers must trust and help one another at the same time that they suspect one another of betrayal. They help each other farm, but they keep weapons in their homes. These are emotions and behaviors that Lurie, the city dweller, dismisses because he cannot understand them. In this world, where Africans and Boers live and work together, Lurie feels that he is a vein (89), "denounce[d]" (69), fugitive, in a "refuge" (65) city, who seeks "asylum" from being "burned, burnt" (71).

Lurie behaves like a Western foreigner. He clings to his knowledge of nineteenth-century British Romanticism, to the poetry of Byron and Wordsworth. His expertise in Romanticism, his mastery of Western epistemology, are useless in this new world, where Sotho and Xhosa are necessary languages. In the epistemology of nineteenth-century England, the important languages are Italian (the language spoken by Teresa, Byron's lover), French (the language that Wordsworth

---

5 Benjamin (1996) asserts that the afterlife "could not be called that if it were not a transformation and a renewal of something living-the original undergoes a change."

relates to in his *Prelude*, when he reflects on the French Revolution), and English (the colonial language). Lurie experiences Lucy's world through a thick veil of colonial Western epistemology. He is not becoming a willing participant in Lucy's life.

Translation is relevant to literary subversion in *Disgrace* because the Black and white protagonists share neither knowledge of a common language nor common emotions. Rather than serve as moral compasses that guide behavior, love and forgiveness reappear as visceral premonitions and prophesies of danger. The danger is both physical and linguistic – communication ceases to be transparent. Epistemology is reduced to the *creaturely*, to animality, to phenomenology, so that people become "dog-men." A new moral matrix must be established in order for readers to understand characters such as Bev Shaw (Lucy's friend, and a dog-woman), Petrus, (Lucy's neighbor, and the dog-man), and, last but not least, Lurie, who finds it in himself to be uniquely compassionate at the animal shelter. Lurie's love for animals is put in direct and sharp contrast with his rape of Melanie. Within this context, what can his affection and care towards dogs even mean?

Petrus, who calls himself the "dog-man," is Lucy's neighbor and assistant (Coetzee 1999, 64). Yet he is soon to be her co-proprietor, buying a land tract and building a new home for his pregnant wife out back. Lurie, meanwhile, begins his transformation on his daughter's rural farm. Can these farmers teach Lurie to trust in neighborly love and friendship? It is ironic that Lurie says, "I'm old-fashioned, I would prefer simply to be put against a wall and shot. Have done with it" (ibid, 66). Something like this happened at the inquiry committee, when Lurie refused to give a confession, insisted that a penalty be meted out to him, and was disgracefully dismissed. Later, Lucy will treat her father like a *creature*, saying that he is the one among the three monkeys who covers his eyes with his palms, refusing to see reality for what it is. Lucy will stress that, in South Africa, one has to be exposed in the public sphere and trust the possibility of neighborly love and friendship. Lurie subscribes to a neoliberal ideology: economic desire and autonomy propel development when they are overseen by the law. This will change, however, and Lurie will curb his desire in order to save his daughter.

Lucy asks that her father help Bev Shaw, who works at the animal shelter helping farm animals die with dignity. Initially Lurie dislikes Bev, because she is unattractive and he feels that the shelter must be "a losing battle." In the face of so much good, Lurie wants to do "some raping, and pillaging. Or to kick a cat" (73). The privileged Lurie exemplifies a caricature philosopher, or perhaps a Romantic poet, skeptical of everyday goodness and worldly poverty. In contrast, Bev prioritizes her engagement with animals, not any epistemological ideal. Despite Lurie's concern, he eventually begins to behave as if goodness and losing battles are the only worthy, human causes for socialization and action in the spirit of minoritarianism, or rejection of majoritarian ideologies and institutions.

Lurie often refers to himself as the "dog-man" (e.g., Coetzee 1999, 146). He makes it his job to dispose of the dead dogs' bodies. He rolls the corpses into bags, carries them, and loads them into the incinerator. Other men, who are paid for this work, bend and break the organs of the dogs' corpses in order to fit them into the incinerator. Lurie, on the other hand, decides to facilitate the corpse's entry into the fire with less breaking, "for his idea of the world, a world in which men do not use shovels to beat corpses into a more convenient shape for processing" (Coetzee 1999, 146). The dignity of the dead dogs' bodies registers for Lurie as responsibility. As a responsible member of the community, Lurie is in a disturbing and complicated moral state because he is changed: he undertakes moral dissensus, he undergoes and suffers emotions, he does not rationally apply morals to his actions without regard to affective reactions.

This change underscores that the present dog-man is a changed man, different from the man Lurie was when he raped Melanie Isaacs. The rapist could not have cared less about the dogs or the dog-man. Yet the world is not yet morally revolutionized, primarily because Lurie is not the same man anymore. He is a "good man" who remains a "servant of Eros" (Coetzee 1999, 52). How does love or Eros change through the difference that permeates Lurie's life? Lurie stops to lead a life based on the binary opposition between reasoned morals and sensual emotions, but subjects love and desire to configurations of action. Lurie ceases to impose an automatic, narcissistic meaning on love. He ceases to believe in the right to satisfy desire by violating the wants of the Other. Conversely, the love that Lurie extends as dog-man is personal – though in an impersonal situation, where the dogs are dead and to burn their corpses is a form of social or municipal necessity. Lurie's love brings moral change to the community, the kind of moral change that the community benefits from but cannot exploit. He extends noneconomic love in plurality.

Ubuntu signifies that we – human and nonhuman animals, along with the rest of nature – belong in a bundle of life. Lurie is close to goodness when he bestows dignity on nonhuman animals and on nature. If the meaning of Descartes' dictum *I think therefore I am* is that human life is a function of thinking, then when human beings do not think they rattle around like a pea in an empty shell. Lurie does not believe that living without thinking is what true morality is about. Rather, he affirms the idea that thinking, in order to disavow our corporeality, passions, and emotions, makes us evil. He is denying the Western epistemology that postulates a binary opposition between sensuality and thinking, conscious and unconscious imagination, emotion and judgment.

*Disgrace* is obligated to repeat past ideas in conjunction with an emerging difference. As emotions are projected onto the realm of the creaturely body, prosopopoeia becomes a litmus test for how far the text moves away from the dominant ideals of Western epistemology. "Prosopopoeia" means repetition, both when the text alludes to another text and when the text gives a face to a dead being through imagery. The changes that Lurie undergoes are so radical that it's unclear whether he is remotely himself by the end of the novel. What sustains Lurie's identity? Is he stark mad? Lurie's convictions change after three Black Africans, not from the neighborhood, force their way into Lucy's house and rape her while they incapacitate Lurie, who can neither help nor save his daughter. Two of the robbers rape Lucy, and all three of them beat up and burn Lurie's scalp. They then rob the house and steal Lurie's car. They viciously shoot and murder the guard dogs in their kennels. On the surface, *Disgrace* seems an extremely racist book revolving around a white man's experience. Yet the novel weaves Black and white experience in a complex cloth of relationships, so that a reader is left asking what will it take for white men to change. Why do Black Africans pillage and rape in the aftermath of receiving moral and political acknowledgement by the Truth and Reconciliation Committee, when they have achieved representation in the social and political realms?

Lucy's rape scene is an inverted image of Lurie's rape of Melanie Isaacs. In both the patriarchal logic remains intact, so that men are superior to women both when they harm and protect them. But the racial disenfranchisement is equally divided, so that both white and Black women suffer exclusion and assault. Unlike Melanie, Lucy does not want to inform the authorities; "it is my business, mine alone," she tells her father (Coetzee 1999, 112). Lucy feels that the law cannot order personal relations between neighbors. She is socially and politically privileged enough to be able to cope with the new reality of South Africa. When it is revealed that Petrus, Lucy's neighbor, knew the rapists, Lurie insists that Lucy make this information public. She refuses, adamant that these new facts should not alter her attitude toward Petrus. Lucy remains silent, bound by neighborly love (Coetzee 1999, 112). Ultimately, Lurie redefines the emotions that guide his life as "Lucy's secret, his disgrace" (ibid, 109). He commits to understanding the particulars of "disgrace" and "shame," at the same time as he ceases to understand how language can guide him (ibid, 115).

In confrontation language and meaning disintegrate: "More and more, he is convinced that English is an unfit medium for the truth of South Africa. Stretches of English code whole sentences long have thickened, lost their articulations, their articulateness, their articulatedness." In the end, Lurie understands that the language silencing him and his daughter is the very same language that has reduced Black South Africans to silence: "Pressed into the mold of English, Petrus's story would come out arthritic, bygone" (ibid, 117).

It is only when his entire world has been shaken by the violent assault that Lurie begins to examine the world around him from the viewpoint of Black people, the victims of colonialism. In South Africa, English is the language of Apartheid. It cannot properly designate the difference between good and evil, neighborly love and neighborly hatred, sexuality, desire, violence, or race. Lurie is unable to detach Lucy's rape from the politics of the nation. He views the rape scene as political revenge. So does Lucy, but Lurie scolds his daughter's resignation and silence: "You want to make up for the wrongs of the past, but this is not the way to do it" (ibid, 133). Lucy will not relent. She keeps reminding her father to "[w]ake up, David. This is the country. This is Africa" (ibid, 124).

Lurie accepts his daughter's chastising because he agrees with her: in South Africa, emotions have been corrupted. Lucy's rape is unique, and yet "it happens every day, every hour, every minute, he tells himself, in every quarter of the country" (ibid, 98). When Lurie tries to make sense of love and friendship in this evil reality, he resorts to etymology: "Modern English, *friend* from Old English *freond*, from *freon*, to love" (ibid, 102).

English is the colonizer's language. Still, the repetition that Lurie clings to, in order to find safety, dates so far back that it reaches the source of his pain and confusion. Lurie translates the English language, restores the ability of English to be embarrassed by its own automatism, makes English know when it is caught off guard, allows difference to emerge in the context of colonialism. Neighbors need not abuse each other. Friendship and love need not be in opposition. Old English instructs Lurie that emotions can continuously evolve, can create a matrix on which love, a private emotion, is needed, and can exist in the public sphere, where friendship normally presides. Can Old English teach English speakers to assign new meaning to neighborly love? Did the meetings of the Committee expose the corruption of language by English-speaking torturers and killers?

This is not just a philosophical reflection, but a practical one, because Petrus is Lurie's neighbor, the one whom Lurie tries and fails to trust and respect. He suspects that the history of colonial abuse of Black Africans teaches Petrus not to be interested in emotions. But, like the next-door successful Boer, Petrus yearns for economic stability, at the expense of his neighbor Lucy. Current American scholars[6] speculate that when Black Americans perform *like* lovers, involving af-

---

[6] In this context the most interesting texts are fiction and essays by James Baldwin, including *Another Country* (1962) and "The Fire Next Time" (1998). Butorac (2018) seeks to explain how Baldwin imagines love to be a performative speech-act that is useful in politics. In a similar vein, John D. Barbour examines *The Autobiography of Malcolm X* in order to show that, when Malcolm

fect in political speech and action, they introduce an unexpected form of commitment and responsibility to the racial dialogue in American democracy.

Is Petrus acting *like* a lover when he agrees to protect Lucy, or is he a shrewd businessman, who does what it takes to buy more land in a new South Africa? What do Petrus' actions mean? Despite his deep wrestling with friendship, Lurie remains weary of Petrus. He suspects that it is not in Petrus's interests to display the kind of neighborly love that Lucy stands for, but to follow Western, neoliberal values, which tell him to try and seize as much as he can of Lucy's land. Lurie therefore considers what it might take to allow three Black men to savage his and Lucy's lives: "The real truth, he suspects, is something far more – *anthropological*, something it would take months to get to the bottom of, months of patient, unhurried conversation with dozens of people, and the offices of an interpreter" (Coetzee 1999, 118).

Lurie reterritorializes race. He correctly recognizes that Black South Africans cannot succumb to the discourse of forgiveness, which suits the needs of whites. The political speech and action of Blacks problematizes moral emotion, when they insist on their right to demand reparations, express resentment, and exact revenge. Lurie reaches the limits of his emotional considerations when he seeks to find an "anthropological" rather than a social and political "truth" that could explain the trauma he and Lucy suffered (ibid.).

The language that Lurie uses parallels the workings of the Committee, which investigates the "anthropology" of evil using many "interpreters." Its work is caught up in questions of de- and re-territorialization, because race is not a clear quality to differentiate perpetrator from victim. Racial questions bleed into the order of emotions. Blacks perpetrated evil against their brothers, while whites brought criminal charges against their own to protect the rights of Blacks.

When Lurie identifies the fear and suspicion entrenched in the public sphere, he becomes a recluse. He fears that freedom and love are disappearing from his private sphere: "Who would have thought it would come to an end so soon and so suddenly: the roving, the loving!" (ibid, 120). The longing to be free soon reap-

---

X begins to address the question of "public virtues," his politics evolve and he moves away from *ressentiment*, endorsing "courtesy, kindness, and above all, respect, the word he uses again and again to describe what is missing in America's racist society" (1992, 137). These emotions or "public virtues" correlate with Arendt's (1958) discussion on how love transforms to friendship and respect in the political sphere (Arendt 1958, 243). Barbour quotes Malcolm X's demand that whites respect the humanity of Black people; that they ground the relationship with Black people on the question of *who* is Black, not just *what* does the Black, the Other, want: "Human rights! Respect as *human beings!* That's what America's black masses want. That's the true problem." (cited in Barbour 1992, 138).

pears in unconscious form. Lurie's dreams transform his fear into images of trauma. In these nightmares he is wallowing in blood, escaping from "the man with the face like a hawk, like a Benin mask, like Thoth" (ibid, 121). Fear and trauma are translated, so that Lurie's unconscious emotions are revealed. The dream acknowledges difference. The masks and the gods expose different forms of love and knowledge, including unknown forms of communal worshiping and magic.

This unconscious work of translation brings new meaning to conscious freedom, to desire, and to neighborly love in South Africa. Lurie is a proper name, as is English, yet in both the proper name becomes subject to the unexpected forces of the social and the political. It is imposed on and altered by the exigencies and intensities of deterritorialization, so that Lurie cannot rationally explain the boundaries of his relationships with Lucy and Petrus. Lurie's dreams force him to imagine new conditions that make Ubuntu accessible to him. More importantly, Lurie's dreams signify that he will undergo extreme changes before he is forced to give up his Western epistemology, accepting that emotions belong in a sense of embodied freedom.

In one key scene, Lurie attends Petrus' party to celebrate the newly acquired land deed. Petrus slaughters a sheep. When Lurie reflects on this slaughter, he notes that only one part of the sheep escapes from destruction; "no one will eat" the gall bladder." "Descartes should have thought of that. The soul, suspended in the dark, bitter gall, hiding" (ibid, 124). At this moment in the story Lurie and Lucy's souls are also hiding, nursing their disgrace and shame. Yet this is also the state which allows difference to emerge, not in the light of reason, but in the darkness of nightmares, murmurs, and physical endurance that takes shape in the slaughtered animal, the slaughtered safety of a proper name.

*Disgrace* suggests that Western epistemology will be valuable if it survives deconstruction. Lurie is a visionary social and political agent: "By the time the big words come back reconstructed, purified, fit to be trusted once more, he [Lurie] will be long dead" (ibid, 129). But Lucy might still be alive. According to Petrus, Lucy will see a change for the better in South Africa, because she is different from her father. She is "forward-looking," says Petrus, " a forward-looking lady, not backward-looking" (ibid, 136). Lurie, on the other hand, is disillusioned, convinced that, in the aftermath of the most terrible historical crimes, it isn't easy to find closure. Lurie is a paradox: if contradiction had overpowered him, Lurie would have been reduced to sameness, not pervaded by the passivity of love.

## Love and shame in the public sphere

Shame is all encompassing. It emerges when one has betrayed one's better judgement, not just one's victim, when society utterly fails. One is ashamed when one is convinced that one should have known the right path, should have behaved differently, should have chosen better. Martha Nussbaum examines questions of shame, disgust, and morality through psychoanalytic and legal frameworks. She argues that omnipotence is the ground for shame, rather than guilt. And adult feelings of omnipotence, she points out, develop from an infantile belief in omnipotence.

Lurie feels shame because he refused to acknowledge that he was not omnipotent. In front of the inquiry committee he declares his limited guilt. He refuses to acknowledge that he is not omnipotent. He feels that morality is lost to him. Lurie cannot reveal the ways in which he failed Melanie Isaacs, her father, his own daughter, his ex-wife. Instead, he becomes consumed by the failure of his own ideals. Rather than facing his shame in public, Lurie chooses to go to Lucy's farm, a hiding place where he can wallow in his shame. The committee has humiliated him, Melanie's father and boyfriend have humiliated him, and Melanie's denunciation humiliated for him. In Nussbaum's terms:

> It [shame] often tells us the truth: certain goals are valuable and we have failed to live up to them. And it often expresses a desire to be a type of being that one can be: a good human being doing fine things. In that sense, shame should not be thought of as a nonmoral emotion, connected only with social approval or disapproval. Here I agree with Bernard Williams: it often has a moral content (Nussbaum 2004, 207).

On this count Nussbaum agrees with Bernard Williams, who argues that shame is equal to a witnessed loss of power. One's loss of power is always witnessed either by an internalized critic or by a real bystander, the one who exposes the wrong action. How can this loss of power propel one into action, into the social and the political?

Shame demands the recognition of another person's moral value. Eventually, Lurie visits Melanie's family and has dinner with her parents and younger sister. He repents. He asks for forgiveness. But shame is the driving force behind these acts. They leave him exposed, performing his regret. Mr. Isaacs voices condemnation: "How are the mighty fallen!" Yet Lurie feels shame, not might: "Does *mighty* describe him? He thinks of himself as obscure and growing obscurer. A figure from the margins of history" (Coetzee 1999, 167). The "obscurity" that envelops Lurie is a moral state. When the women in the house hear that Lurie is their guest, they think of him as "the man whose name is darkness" (ibid, 168). As part of his expiation, Lurie goes into the women's private room: "With careful ceremony he gets to his knees and touches his forehead to the floor. Is that enough?

he thinks. Will that do? If not, what more?" (ibid, 173). This ambiguous gesture is accompanied by "a current of desire." Either Lurie remembers his desire for Melanie or he desires her pretty sister. Disgrace and desire are interwoven. To be full of life is to allow shame and love to propel one into undergoing change.[7]

In the Western epistemological tradition, if we are given the time to mature and accumulate experience, we will reach the right conclusion through reason alone, discovering the demands that the moral law makes of us, of our actions, of our existence. But what if we are not purely rational? What if there is something Other, like emotions, lurking within us?

If we commit to the inflection of law when it suits our selfish needs, we construct a morality that depends on heteronomy, not autonomy. Shame is heteronomous and not autonomous. It emerges from one's connection to, and dependence on, others. Shame is phenomenological. It is uncomfortable. One wants to hide, to avoid public space. In *On Shame*, Michael Morgan claims shame is a more appropriate moral reaction to the Holocaust than guilt: "Something in us, really in us or only apparently in us, or something we have done or seem to have done, elicits in us a sense of distress about how we seem to us to be perceived by others, real or imagined" (Morgan 2008, 40). Shame can arise from a particular infraction, or a specific failure. Guilt stops with the specific action. Shame never stops. We feel ashamed of everything that we stand for: "we feel guilty about what we have done; we feel ashamed about who we are" (ibid, 46). Morgan concludes that shame "is a feeling we have about how we see ourselves *in terms of how others see us*" (ibid, 47).

Apartheid in South Africa was an organized national betrayal. The question then becomes: how does one correct a flaw in which others share? South Africa

---

7 Adriaan van Heerden argues that Coetzee meticulously uncovers the disparity between shame and disgrace in order to show that Lurie is in an existential state of disgrace. It is important for van Heerden to affirm that Lurie remains loyal to the law. He further suggests that Lurie does not cease to belong to the cult of unrestrained masculinity, and concludes that Lurie did not undergo radical change. In his celibacy, he is not acting on his desire, but neither is he reckoning with the impact of his behavior. Van Heerden claims that Lurie supports the rights of desire and the necessity of a strong law in post-apartheid South Africa. I disagree with both of these conclusions. As I mention above, Lurie is exposed in the public sphere and does not remain the isolated, indicted, guilty, sovereign individual that he was at the beginning of the novel. This change makes him a better person, a person who can relate to love and shame, in addition to acknowledging the necessity of determining guilt in the eyes of the law. Lurie is more intimately attached to his desire because he is able to feel joy. Lurie's visit to the Isaac's family and his love for Lucy takes on a new shape, a shape connected to respect. In fact, it is love for his yet unborn grandchild that forces Lurie to undergo this, anticipating the baby's arrival with joy. See Van Heerden, 2010, 50–55).

instituted the Truth and Reconciliation Committee in order to restart cross-racial relationships. Ubuntu cannot control the change that single individuals undergo, but it can facilitate people's recognition of love and shame in themselves. Morgan suggests that "we can change the circumstances that gave rise to it [shame], or it can lead us to change ourselves in some fundamental way . . . As a result we can individually change ourselves into persons who care and invest ourselves in contributing to the prevention of atrocity and genocide" (ibid, 54). Shame, like love, can be the harbinger of change.

When Bev Shaw asks Lurie if he regretted his actions in Cape Town, Lurie refuses to be exposed and replies that what happened there brought him to where he is. "I'm not unhappy here," he says (Coetzee 1999, 149). Boldly he tells Bev that "in the heat of the act there are no doubts. As I'm sure you must know yourself." Bev "blushes" with shame (ibid, 148). Lurie is referring to the brief fling he had with Bev. Bev is married. She and her husband Bill Lurie's friends. The affair stopped because Bev and Lurie lost interest in each other.

In Lurie's last visit to Cape Town, when he's thinking of selling his house, he is overwhelmed by a sweep of moral emotions. His house is destroyed, despoiled by, he knows, Black looters, much like the Black looters who emptied Lucy's house earlier. Lurie accepts that his love and shame are not alleviated when the once victimized Black South Africans perpetrate crimes against white property. He exists within the bounds of his love and shame, despite the fact that Blacks also act on the basis of unwarranted desire when they thieve or vandalize. These opportunities to wrestle with what equality means sustain Lurie, until he returns to Lucy and receives the most harrowing news yet. He learns that Lucy is pregnant as a result of the rape. He "heaves and heaves and finally cries" (ibid, 199).

Western epistemology is reduced to silence in the face of these extreme moral situations. Petrus offers to marry Lucy, to protect her from the dangers of robbery and rape. But, as they all know, in so doing he would also gain ownership of her land. Lurie resents this. "This is not how we do things," he retorts, but then remembers that, by now, the personal pronoun "we" is deterritorrialized: *"We*: he is on the point of saying, *We Westerners*" (ibid, 202). Lucy accepts the marriage proposal.

This does not prevent Lurie from beating up Pollux, one of the three men who facilitated Lucy's rape and whom he recognized at Petrus's party. Lurie feels that his blows are justified, and yet, "at the same time, he is ashamed of himself. He condemns himself absolutely" (ibid, 208). Lurie feels shame for the world that he belongs to, a world in which neither Blacks nor Boers are capable of substituting neo-liberal interests with emotions that lead to moral relationships.

Lucy decides to keep her child, and tells her father he "should try to be a good person too." "A good person," Lurie muses. "Not a bad resolution to make, in dark times" (ibid, 215–216).[8] This sounds simple, against the backdrop of the apparatus of Western epistemology that limits the social and political reach of goodness. *Disgrace* dissolves the moral limits by flooding them with emotions. Western epistemology is so thorough that it purges al the nouns, verbs, and emotions that remain relevant to love, shame, and desire; these are entirely "forgotten," (ibid, 217).

At the end of the novel, Lurie agrees to euthanize his favorite dog. The dog's soul has to leave its body. Lurie must pack him in a bag and burn him: "He will do all that for him when his time comes. It will be little enough, less than little: nothing." (ibid, 220). And yet, even this "nothing" becomes a moment of moral choice. Lurie declines to postpone the action, despite his narcissistic desire to keep his friend around a little longer. The novel closes with Lurie's words: "Yes, I am giving him up" (ibid, 220).

Here the narrative emphasizes "killing," "giving," and "love." Rather than remain self-indulgent, Lurie paces his actions according to the rhythm of his dog's *joy*. Lurie is not guided by epistemological abstractions, but by the practices that emerge from love and concern. Ultimately, he is transformed, he is made better, by shame and love.

## Global themes: Love, forgiveness, nonviolent resistance

The Argentine literary critic Walter Mignolo (2013) notes that First World thinkers adopt the literature and philosophy of the Other, through the prism of "area studies," in order to more accurately recognize the gendered, racial, and immigrant Other within their own nations. Although Black people are indigenous to South Africa and deserve to be treated as equal citizens, they are marginalized and decimated.

Both Mignolo and Coetzee are interested in the West's blindness toward the disenfranchised, toward those who are Other. Mignolo uses the term *humanitas* to refer to the Eurocentric reaction to the Other.[9] Europeans employ *humanitas* to

---

**8** When Nelson Mandela was a prisoner on Robben Island, he often used the phrase "dark days," which parallels Coetzee's and Arendt's use of "dark times." Mandela construes his politics around the value of *moral force*. Anthony Bogues, who met with Mandela in 1994, explains that for the inmate, violence brings about defeat, but *moral force* accumulates and helps build a new system of communication.

**9** Mignolo offers a definition of border thinking and its relation to a revolt against the concept of *humanitas*: "Border thinking is, in other words, the thinking of us, the *anthropoid*, who do not aspire to become *humanitas*, because it was the enunciation of the *humanitas* that made us *anthropoi*. We delink from the *humanitas*, we become epistemically disobedient, and think and

diminish the colonized, continually re-situating what it means to be human. The humanist definition imposed on the colonized Other is polluted by epistemological superiority. Europeans *enunciate*; that is, they make epistemological claims about the *enunciated*. These are the populations whose cultures are defined as "area studies." The subaltern does not *enunciate*. Her/his language is not accepted as a text that produces knowledge. To the colonizer, the subaltern remains a threatening enigma. Mignolo puts it thus:

> Connectivity and epistemic convergence seem to be ways to delink from the legacy of area studies, to turn the tables and focus on the enunciation rather than on the enunciated. If the enunciation remains within the boundaries of Western scholarship, and Asia, Africa, and the Mediterranean provide the cultural resources to be processed by Western social sciences and the humanities (independently of the fact that processing information is carried on in New York, Singapore, or Johannesburg), then the possibilities of delinking from area studies remain limited (Mignolo 2013, 270).

Mignolo predicts that decoloniality will follow the European invasion only if the colonized seize the opportunity to "create the conditions for the emergence of a new type of existence and thinking by the population being invaded: dwelling in the borders and, therefore, thinking in the borders appears" (Mignolo 2016, 185). To rethink, and thereby re-inhabit racism, gender, and immigration is to delink ones' self from three pillars of Eurocentric knowledge: what Derrida calls "phalogocentrism," what Michel Foucault calls "biopolitics," and what Adam Smith and Karl Marx call "division of labor" and "the proletariat," respectively. People, not states, create decoloniality. If it is people who claim their rights, as racial, gendered, or migrant populations, then these people can break free from an epistemology that universalizes and thereby annihilates their everyday experience of what Mignolo calls "a border," a unique space and time in which emotions are of paramount importance.

I want to return to *Disgrace* for a brief moment. European colonialism and Apartheid in South Africa are the backdrop of David Lurie's trauma. Lurie's infractions of the law signify thinking in Western universal terms, not in "the border." Mignolo stresses that border thinking belong to us, "the *anthropoid*, who do not aspire to become *humanitas*," and the reason is that those interested in humanitas turned those who engage border thinking to an anthropoid (Mignolo 2013, 137). Within the reality of a racially-charged politic, Lurie is forced to confront difference while carrying the weight of embodied emotions, of love and shame. He undertakes a singular existence in "the border" when his action is in-

---

do decolonially, dwelling and thinking in the borders of local histories confronting global designs" (Mignolo 2013, 137).

stigated by embodied emotion. This triggers his transformation, makes him an anthropoid which belongs in a larger assemblage of embodied differences, which prosper as they live within and refashion the border. Lurie's identity is in the state of becoming different, even as his actions delineate, and activate deterritorialization within concrete borders. He no longer enunciates abstractions in a universalizing gesture.

Lurie moves from having power and sovereignty to being disenfranchised. Yet the move is fuzzy, for, within the culture in which this transformation occurs, Lurie finally becomes equal to Lucy and Petrus. Mignolo wants to address the needs of the anthropoi, those people who suffer marginalization, but what does this mean within the world of *Disgrace*? I suggest that love and the emotions that are related to it attach themselves to the anthropoi because love, forgiveness, and resentment are forged by the people whom Eurocentrism systematically erases. Resentment, in turn, sustains marginalized communities, and allows them to live in the borderlands, influencing social and political realms within and outside of the clan, the pack, the community.

In the work of Wole Soyinka and Judith Butler, resentment and love are understood as embodied phenomena. Western culture teaches that the death of certain bodies does not merit grief. Bodies become grievable or nongrievable based on their value to the state. This means that those who are powerful and privileged have their deaths memorialized and grieved, while the deaths of all the rest are anonymous, forgotten, nongrievable. Soyinka and Butler argue that love, within disenfranchised communities, can lead to active resentment and resistance to the State.

## Judith Butler: Nonviolent resistance and moral substitutability of "I" and "You"

In *The Force of Nonviolence*, Butler understands the anthropoi, the oppressed, as radically dependent on others. Butler explains how dependence creates the phantasy of substitution in checking the sovereignty of the subject. She follows Melanie Klein in asserting that love is an emotion that ushers the notion of substitutability into the infant's life. The infant is dependent on her/his mother, and confronts the maternal environment with both love and hatred. When the infant is hostile, s/he feels that s/he can destroy the maternal environment in order to salvage her/his sovereignty. This animates the principle of substitution. A phantasy is formed in the infant and makes her/him feel: if I can be hostile toward my environment (mother), then I am in danger, because the environment (mother) can retaliate, direct hostility at me. This paranoid phantasy becomes integral to every adult's ability to analyze her/his social position.

This same structure of interdependence and substitution exists in national and international contexts. A sovereign state (I) is powerful when it has allies (you) and depends on treaties that limit its sovereignty. Therefore the ally threatens the sovereignty of the presumably sovereign state. The "you" could threaten the interests of the "I," for the ally contemplates how to remain allied to, and yet resents, the state that threatens its sovereignty. What begins as love and infantile paranoid phantasies within the familial context becomes political power struggles in adult relationships.

Butler does not ignore this. She adds several reasons why the paranoid position, although inevitable, does not have to be terminal. First, the infant learns that, within family relationships, the "I" and "you" are not separate, the environment (mother) is internal to the infant, the "you" is organized inside the "I," and a phantasy assures the developing infant that, for the environment (mother), it is also true that the infant ("I") is integral to the environment (mother) "you." This structure of mutual interdependence enhances love and gratitude to the one who is outside the "I." And yet this same subject is inside, integral to the "I." Paranoia is modulated by love, while a loss of sovereignty produces gratitude for the birth of relationality and reciprocity.

In the national and international contexts, it is more difficult to dismantle the violence projected onto the "outsider (you)," the one who does not belong to the patriarchal or Eurocentric "nation (we)." The racial, gendered, and migrant bodies do not belong to *us*, the white, male, citizen. A phantasy is projected onto *you*, namely, *you* belong to those who want to abuse or annihilate *us*. How do *we*, the ones who presume to be sovereign, white male citizens of prosperous nations, willful descendants of a Eurocentric epistemology, acknowledge *our* violent, radicalized fantasies? How does one take stock of the violence that *we* want to inflict on these racialized, gendered, and migrant bodies in order to keep *our* social and political institutions intact? In *Disgrace*, David Lurie starts out as this privileged white man fully committed to Eurocentric epistemology because it gives him, not just power, but the justification to abuse power. By the end of the novel, Lurie embodies how difference is found in alternate systems of action, those that facilitate our access to knowledge and connections with the Other.

Butler argues that nations offer protection in agreement with patriarchal logic. According to this logic, it is the man (I) who protects the life of the woman (you), the rich (we) who protect the lives of the poor (you), and the citizens (we) who protect the lives of the migrants (you). She suggests that we have to develop a systematic critique of violence in order to protect those whose lives are nongrievable (nonsovereign). It is easier, she argues, to annihilate a life that has always been understood as nongrievable and is interested in the following question: "how do unconscious forms of substitution come to inform and vitalize what we might call 'moral sentiments?'" (Butler 2020, 87).

Equal recognition "produces the condition of becoming, of living, of futurity, where the content of that life, that living, can be neither prescribed nor predicted, and where self-determination emerges as a potential" (ibid, 94). And this condition points the way towards love on a social, national, global level. This love is not pure, because the prosperous disciples of Eurocentrism, whom *we* are in the beginning, undergo change in the encounter with the different, the *you*, and thereby *we* come to internalize and rely on *you* in the same fashion that *you* undergo transformation when *you* internalize and rely on *us*.

Diversity is not just anthropological or economic. It is a psychosomatic state of transformation and transmogrification. Nongrievable lives are often described with the language of *they*, not *us*. They are seen as *outside* society and state, not *inside* the social and economic order. Why? Because the outsider poses a threat to those who belong to the system. Under these conditions, what motivates us, those in power, to save lives? Butler replies: "A life can register as a life only within a scheme that presents it as such" (ibid, 112).

Mignolo anticipates Butler's question, as does Hannah Arendt. Mignolo and Arendt are concerned with the lives of the slaves, the colonized, the gendered, the religious Other, the refugee. When Butler explains how law enforcement can be manipulated, she has Black Americans in mind:

> The violence that the policeman is about to do, the violence he then commits, has already moved toward him in a figure, a racialized ghost, condensing and inverting his own aggression, wielding his own aggression against himself, acting in advance of his own plans to act, and legitimating and elaborating, as if in a dream, his later argument of self-defense (Butler 2020, 118).

Butler's description captures the logic that underpins the Truth and Reconciliation Committee. In the investigation into the "Guguletu 7 Incident," the Committee demanded that the perpetrators explain why they shot unarmed Black men who had already surrendered, or were lying dead in the dirt. Unfortunately, as Lurie intuits in *Disgrace*, "the real truth" would take "months to get to the bottom of, months of patient, unhurried conversation with dozens of people, and the offices of an interpreter" (Coetzee 1999, 118).

The "offices of an interpreter" make it possible to realize that a Black life is valuable "within a scheme that presents it as such," as Butler puts it (Butler 2020, 112). The Committee enabled, demanded, a new epistemological and legal scheme when it showed that, for *us*, the Apartheid regime required interpretation, a change of heart and of structure. Whites, seen as bodies in possession of grievable lives, became subject to interrogation, punishment, and interpretation, while Black bodies, whose lives are nongrievable, were granted the power to give or withhold forgiveness, accept or reject existing practices of memorialization, and resent or wield political authority.

The Committee made it clear that the positive presence of nonviolence is integral to translation, inevitable for conversation and negotiation. The nonviolent force of good translation changes the original and thereby gives the original its afterlife. Coetzee's translation of emotions helps to forge understanding in situations that are mired in conflict. In the meetings of the Committee, this technique of nonviolent translation was extra-juridical, and it focused on conflict resolution. Mignolo wants to translate Eurocentrism by allowing the subaltern to enunciate, while Butler wants to translate the patriarchal scheme by shining light on the value of the lost lives of the nongrievable. How do we show that lost lives are grievable?

Butler asks whether violence is "an interdependency of, or part of the polarity of love and hate that characterizes human relations, part of what threatens human communities or lets them cohere?" (Butler 2020, 147). She replies that interdependency does not have to undergo translation to substitutability. As Tutu asserts:

> A person with Ubuntu is open and available to others, affirming of others, does not feel threatened that others are able and good, for he or she has a proper self-assurance that comes from knowing that he or she belongs in a greater whole and is diminished when others are humiliated or diminished, when others are tortured or oppressed, or treated as if they were less than who they are (Tutu 1999, 29).

Substitution is one aspect of non-sovereignty, but this does not mean that Black people's lives are less singular than are white people's. Both are caught up in social connections that are as necessary as they are ambivalent. Butler concludes that "the obligation not to destroy each other emerges from, and reflects, the vexed social form of our lives, and it leads us to reconsider whether self-preservation is not linked to preserving the lives of others. The self of self-preservation is defined, in part, by that link, that necessary and difficult social bond" (Butler 2020, 148). Emotions allow us to experience the self as tied up with other selves. It is the work of emotions that catalyzes processes by which all lives can be seen as equally grievable.

## Memory as restitution in the wake of difference, translation of identity

In his book *The Burden of Memory, the Muse of Forgiveness,* Wole Soyinka (the first African laureate of the Nobel Prize in Literature) demonstrates how reparations are paramount in the field of history and in the lives of individual victims.

Like Améry, Soyinka's assertions circumambulate around the moral value and necessity of resentment. Soyinka reveals his resentment when arguing that South Africa must secure a forgiveness that does not reach closure, nor does it induce amnesia. Resentment is a critique that continues to expose and tell the truth of corruption, murder, and everyday enslavement in Africa. Soyinka effectively argues that in South Africa, the Truth and Reconciliation Committee only created a short-term knowledge of the truth, by telling the stories of localized atrocities, while avoiding an inclusive, historical narrative of enslavement and violence.

The story of slavery is eliminated from historical memory by both whites and Blacks. What facilitates this abuse is "a yet unexpiated past" (Soyinka 1999, 19).

Soyinka's claims mirror those made by Jankélévitch and Butler. Questions about the past matter. If the past is evil beyond legal expiation, then memory is morally necessary. But Soyinka argues that the Committee encouraged the foreclosure of memory. Indeed, he feels that this was the goal of the Committee: "cathartic bliss, the healing that comes with closure" (ibid, 20).

What does Soyinka mean when he insists that the past of Africa must be continually redressed, that historical reparations and national reconciliation must remain pressing? I believe he is thinking about a form of negative possession. What does the world owe Africa? Soyinka's call for reparations is a call from the present. Justice must punish African violence, not just white perpetrators. It must also expose the racial violence that still inflicts enslavement and murder on whole African populations.

Soyinka stresses that the question "what is Africa to me?" inspired poetry and rhetoric, but, more importantly, "it informed, in one way or another, the socio-political existence of many" (ibid, 145). Africa deserves the restitution of diverse anterior and interior cultural concepts, values, and institutions that were destroyed. As long as European, American, and African leaders refuse to make reparations for slavery, reconciliation is but a "chimera" (ibid, 64). Difference can emerge from translation, but repetition emerges from amnesia:

> Now, it is possible that there is something about the magnitude of some wrongs that transcends the feeling of vengeance, even of redress in any form. A kind of crimino-critical mass after which wrongs and sufferings are transmuted into a totally different stage of sensibility from which can only derive a sense of peace, a sense of truth that overawes all else and chastens the human moral dimension. It is not a surrender to evil, not a condoning of wrongs; perhaps it is akin to a balm that comes after a cataclysm of Nature, even when clearly of man's making. It overrides grief and despair, diffuses rage, infuses one with a sense of purgation, the aftermath of true tragic apprehension (ibid, 68).

These emotions can appear when ethics are immoral and self-aggrandizing. Without emotion memory is incapacitated. Recognition "overrides grief and despair, diffuses rage, infuses one with a sense of purgation, the aftermath of true tragic apprehension (ibid, 68). The truth is insufficient. Recognition is the urgent moral emotion. The lives of slaves, of the victims of genocidal violence, are denied lives, lives that the colonizer, the slave trader, and the contemporary neoliberal, all deny.

At the very end of *Disgrace*, Lurie is thinking about living close to his daughter in a divided, racially charged, rural society. In the aftermath of Lucy's rape, Lurie observes, "Everything is tender, everything is burned. Burned, burnt" (Coetzee 1999, 97). Coetzee does not idealize love in times of crisis, when all meaning evaporates. Like Soyinka, he shows that humanity remains where love is constantly translated, preserved as meaningful and necessary, when the victim and the perpetrator document and broadcast negative possessions.

## Conclusion

*Disgrace* redistributes "guilt" and "shame" in post-apartheid South Africa, and ties together "truth" and the local genius of negative possessions. After Lucy's rape and Lurie's burning, Lucy finally speaks to her father. Lurie's response takes into consideration the fact that the Black perpetrator is propelled by the history of victimization – "it was history speaking through them" (ibid, 156). *Disgrace* recognizes the historical structure in a society that has always demanded and produced closure: subjection and subjugation are the opposite of becoming different, be it personal or social. It does not conclude with a utopia of forgiveness but rather with a paradox of resentment. The novel closes with words that forego sovereignty and economic triumphalism and instead introduces the value of "giving up." I understand this to mean that, in the aftermath of great catastrophe, an acknowledgement of injustice effects the restitution of memory. This in turn promotes passivity – the kind of passivity that is related to passion. A passive passion does not infringe on the rights of the Other in order to satisfy the need of the "I." A passive passion is enhanced when the needs of the "I" take the time, practice patience. An "I" who succumbs to a passivity explores ways to express her/his passion in assemblages, in ways that make differences proliferate. The passive "I"s, with their passion and patience, have Ubuntu in them.

# Interchapter 4
# Memory and nonviolence – on Raoul Peck's *I Am Not Your Negro*

The documentary film *I Am Not Your Negro* is based on an unfinished James Baldwin manuscript from 1979. Baldwin's thoughts and words are accompanied by relevant historical and contemporary footage, which show him and his ideas in action. The voice-over narration is provided by Samuel L. Jackson, a Black actor whose many film personas, perhaps more than anyone's, embody the fact that Blackness has come to occupy in American entertainment a very different place from the stereotypical one that was assigned to it. The film follows Baldwin on a journey to the South, to Georgia and Alabama, and from there to Harlem; it is a journey of remembrance and rediscovery.

The footage covers several familiar moments in the history of the Civil Rights Movement – the Montgomery bus Boycott, Malcolm X's "Uncle Toms" speech and his subsequent murder, as well as the assassinations of Medgar Evers and Martin Luther King, Jr. Baldwin calls himself "a witness," not least because he stood near the casket of each of these three great men. As a witness, he publicized their actions—through essays and reports and lectures and interviews—on university campuses and on television, where he was tasked to explain the Black experience in America, to America, including the anger, resentment, and yearning for change.

In his role as witness, Baldwin refused to write a book that speaks of the Black struggle in the white, the majoritarian language. He chose instead to tell the story of America through an examination of the lives of its most important Black leaders and the movements they inspired. Through the deterritorialization of white epistemology, when America was depicted not as the end result of segregation but as a nation of many peoples and many historical narratives, Baldwin uncovered the true significance of Medgar, Malcolm, and Martin. Through their experiences, Baldwin afforded Black Americans the opportunity to understand themselves, both as the product of a horrific history of enslavement and as a counterbalance to majoritarian America, and to view themselves as a force of cultural, economic, and political renewal.

In his public addresses, Baldwin relentlessly attacked the dominant white epistemology, which understood the Black experience in the most limited and limiting ways. He poked holes into white epistemology and forced it to face its inconsistencies, its ignorance, and its fears. White America's epistemology was

**Note:** See page numbers of citations on the bibliography.

https://doi.org/10.1515/9783111317694-009

(is) dishonest, because it justified the use of brute force to maintain segregation, discrimination, and an immoral discrepancy of power. The status quo against which he spoke relied on institutions that prevented Black people from bettering their lives, keeping them down, powerless and disenfranchised, while at the same time perpetuating white America's insecurity and paranoia. Baldwin didn't directly speak of the tropes of forgiveness and resentment, but he was interested in a possible restoration of the American qualities of sincerity, simplicity, and innocence. This is why he embraced nonviolent resistance.

Innocence precedes the possibility to forgive the offender as well as the possibility to acknowledge guilt and shame. The innocence that supports forgiveness has nothing to do with immaturity. On the contrary, it belongs to a sincere witness, one who knows the wounds of the past and the injustices of the present, but who is open to the new languages of Black leaders: the language of suffering, the language of nonviolent resistance, and the language of revolution, a revolution in the form of being involved in the everyday life of the community. Nonviolent resistance is tied to resentment and remembering, but this doesn't mean that the pain of the past must remain in the present. The act of Remembrance involves seeking out transformation, and when the leaders turn to direct action it propels structural change, the innocence of the witness and the nonviolent resistance of the activist join hands, in the service of instituting diverse transformations in local and national politics.

## Detour: On globalism and nonviolent resistance

Mahatma Gandhi and Martin Luther King Jr. did not demand that forgiveness and resentment remain pure when they entered into politics. On the contrary, they valued the sincerity of forgiveness precisely when, paradoxically, forgiveness was tied up with a kernel of resentment. The resentment that gnaws at us when we sincerely forgive is a valuable form of visceral remembering, but it does not diminish true forgiveness. Gandhi and King taught that forgiveness is learned through nonviolent resistance, and that the victim can resist only when he feels neighborly love toward the transgressor. This political ethos is on par with J. M. Coetzee's in *Disgrace*, particularly at the enigmatic end of the novel. Lurie's decision to euthanize the maimed dog that he loves is a form of mercy, which involves curbing desire in the service of truth. Lurie extends the same kind of love to Petrus, his daughter's co-proprietor of the land. This reconfiguration of desire, truth, and mercy or love has political implications. But the political parameters that cause Lurie to feel the dog's pain and right to die peacefully, and that make him affirm Petrus's suffering and his right to gain from a new distribution of land ownership in South Africa, do not sever these practical actions from the realm of morality. In the same vein as Gandhi and King, Coetzee too recognizes that to feel neighborly love toward the one who is different curbs one's desire and leads one's resentment to be expressed in a morally valuable way.

Nonviolent resistance emerges in the context of diversity. Gandhi's autobiography and King's papers show the two leaders engaging in repetition in the service of discovering domestic, social and political possibilities for the emergence of difference. The oppression of African-Americans and Indians are examples of mass atrocities towards which forgiveness and resentment are both appropriate ethical and psychological reactions because I accepted and am trying to prove the philosophical argument that a mortal crime must seek forgiveness, the unforgiveable atrocity has to be forgiven. Gandhi and King articulated political translations to emotions like forgiveness and resentment, at the same time that they translated British and American definitions of oppression when they chose to include Black people and Indians. Gandhi and King demanded the application of universal principles of archived historical knowledge, present repetition of the exclusion of Blacks and Indians, and future differences in creating new assemblages that accept the direct action of Black people and Indians and their equal involvement in shaping the social and political realms.

Gandhi, a London-trained lawyer, used Western legal and religious concepts to support the struggle against imperialism. He argued for a distinctly Asian form of nonviolent resistance. King, in turn, imported Gandhi's ideas and transformed nonviolent resistance into a method appropriate to African-American culture. King crafted a narrative of the Black experience that covered slavery and sanctioned segregation up to the plight of Black Americans in the 1960s. Both Gandhi and King, then, created narratives that spoke from within an oppressed culture. They were not ashamed of their own culture's myths and traditions, but knew how to use Western aesthetic and political symbols in transgressive ways, in ways that stressed difference. In so doing, they gave voice to the ideals of freedom among the poor in India, and the descendants of slaves in the Deep South. The narratives and protests that these two men created and mobilized into action contributed to shaping mental and political open fields, not defined or known in advance. They made it possible to pit racial and cultural specificity against Western epistemology and legal universalism, and encouraged others (meaning, other peoples, other cultures) to familiarize themselves with difference whether it emerges from different histories or from different socioeconomic positions. For it is in the quest to find equality without reducing differences to sameness and blindness to the diversity that the calls for freedom and justice are born.

In the 1960s, German politicians and writers, such as Chancellor Willy Brandt and the novelist Heinrich Böll, became interested in forgiveness and resentment.

At about the same time, Jewish thinkers in the diaspora articulated the paradox of forgiveness and resentment; Hannah Arendt focused on the paradox of forgiveness while Jean Améry and Vladimir Jankélévitch focused on the paradox of resentment. The thinkers on this subject – European, Indian, American – all deployed aesthetics and politics that brought to the fore traumatic wounds, wounds which in the political atmosphere of reconciliation between peoples and nations demanded emotional responses such as forgiveness, repentance, resentment, guilt, and shame. These thinkers stressed a sense of place, and in doing so gave concrete reality to the narratives of victimization and the demands for justice.

Gandhi began to use concepts like *Ahimsa* (love), *Satyagraha* (passive resistance), *Moksha* (servitude), and *Bramacharya* (abstinence) in the early nineteen hundreds, while working as a barrister in Natal, South Africa. His autobiography is rife with descriptions of the discrimination he suffered because he was a brown man. Yet, his writing brims with empathy and the search for compromise: "I saw in later life that this spirit [of compromise] was an essential part of *Satyagraha* [passive resistance]" (Gandhi 1927, 123). Passive resistance itself is a form of compromise, an affirmation that the resister acknowledges an inextricable connection, a bond of relationality, with the defenders of unjust laws.

Gandhi's philosophy displays features that are neither European nor Western but rather completely Indian or simply his. He demands that the same moral judgments be exercised in ordinary, personal life as in leadership. In his autobiography, *The Story of My Experiments with Truth*, Gandhi explains that a leader can induce people to relinquish desire only if he curbs his own excessive desire. In his own life, Gandhi chose restraint and denied his personal desires, even in the face of death. He learned to practice *bramacharya*, abstinence from sexual activity, and quit cooking altogether, instead eating small quantities of fresh fruits and nuts, interspersed with periods of fasting. He preached care for the nonhuman animal and for the environment, at the same time as he studied the needs of the human body.

Gandhi stands in radical opposition to the European tradition represented by Nietzsche, who argues that the master is not reactive but rather acts from an unconscious immediacy. Gandhi is conscious enough to completely repress his desires. How does self-rule, the control of the self, exert political force on others? By being active instead of reactive. Gandhi restructures the power relation of desire and action, conscious and unconscious actions, and successfully undertakes to control instincts that he believes lead to immoral action. He dismisses the Nietzschean dictum that defines the slave as passive and the master as active: "What is 'passive?' – To be hindered from moving forward: thus an act of resistance and reaction. What is 'active?' – reaching out for power" (Nietzsche 1967, 657).

Gandhi brings together the themes of action and servitude, or power and passive resistance. The British empire enters a state of anxiety when the colonized have a voice. It is not just that Gandhi acted like a master when he allowed "soul-force" in the form of restraining personal desire (Gandhi 1997, 90) to guide his actions. He is not deluded that he is sovereign, and his philosophy of abstinence, love, servitude, and passive resistance is proof that the Indian and the imperialist are interconnected in their humanity as well as in the political realm because the ruler and the ruled are dependent on each other in fashioning a sustainable sociopolitical organization of structural equality between singularities that generate collaboration and dependencies. He also preaches that a political leader must offer a personal example and implement the sacrifices that he demands from his followers. Gandhi's ability to offer a personal model of "soul-force" made him a world leader, despite the fact that in the Western world nothing in politics is more inappropriate than to probe a leader's abstinence from sexual relationships, and nothing is as insignificant as a leader's dietary habits, or a leader's devotion to symbols like weaving one's clothes on a loom.

In a 1945 letter to Jawaharlal Nehru, Gandhi contends that "without truth and nonviolence there can be nothing but destruction for humanity [. . .]. Man should rest content with what are his real needs and become self-sufficient [. . .]. After all the world is made up of individuals just as it is the drops that constitute the ocean" (Gandhi 1997, 150). This socialist vision of self-rule is by extension a vision of healthy national and world governance. The self-sufficient citizen is truthful because s/he is not sovereign, but is equally connected to the other members of the community, as India should be equal and connected to other countries. Gandhi envisions a world organized as an assemblage of self-sufficient governments, all tied together into a larger body politic of peoples, the way raindrops form an ocean.

Decades after Gandhi, Desmond Tutu offered a similar vision when he envisioned South Africa as a state grounded in Ubuntu: "a person with *Ubuntu* [. . .] has a proper self-assurance that comes from knowing that he or she belongs in a greater whole and is diminished when others are humiliated or diminished, when others are tortured or oppressed, or treated as if they were less than who they are" (Tutu 1999, 29). Ubuntu ushered into global politics a moral structure that transgressed, and surpassed, the Western democratic vision, because it recalled Gandhi's demand that the state be truthful and generate equality.

The connection between nonviolent resistance, leadership, and ethics is paramount in King's autobiography, sermons, and essays. King recognizes that passive resistance enhances a sense of dignity in the victim. The use of nonviolent resistance during the fight for civil rights enabled Black Americans to hate the illegal deeds of white people – who claimed to be acting within the bounds of the law –

while offering love, forgiveness, and mercy to white people as human beings: "Here we rise to the position of loving the person who does the evil deed while hating the deed that the person does." (King 1997, 459).

Judith Butler, following in the footsteps of Walter Benjamin, shows that much of white or state violence was and still is legalized, and comes to the conclusion that nonviolence is the only force that can change the social and political schemes that allow white people to treat Black lives as if these lives were ungrievable. Changing the scheme relies on re-defining the value of love, because, in this new context, the self and the Other are split by the *who* and the *what*. This view echoes and transgresses Arendt's definition of love in *The Human Condition*: "For love, although it is one of the rarest occurrences in human lives, indeed possesses an unequaled power of self-revelation and an unequaled clarity of vision for the disclosure of *who*, precisely because it is unconcerned to the point of total unworldliness with *what* the loved person may be, with his qualities and shortcomings no less than with his achievements, failings, and transgressions" (Arendt 1958, 242). They simultaneously become substitutable, or equal to one another, and indispensable to the welfare of home, society, and politics.[1] Each member of society is a singular human being and therefore is capable of endless action and transformation within assemblage that form and reform the existing structure of society and politics.

While it is possible to explain the infraction of law by the police as a mechanism to spread fear, Butler suggests that nonviolence is a force that can change social and political schemes in a specific way that allows love to be not "unworldly," but concerned with *what* the self and the Other can achieve as equals in their humanity, their *who*. Similarly, King co-opts and translates St. Augustine's definition of *agape*, the love of God for the human being, into the secular, political context where forgiveness, nonviolent resistance, and reconciliation are necessary to restore justice to the daily lives of people in the aftermath of mass atrocity.

*I Am Not Your Negro* opens with images from Montgomery, but does not specifically mention that the bus boycott is a good example of a new assemblage. The sustained action of Black people from all walks of life together and in concert is a

---

[1] In a similar study that applies Benjamin's "Critique of Violence" to the infractions of the law committed by the police, the American anthropologist Michael Taussig cites Benjamin and argues that "'[it] really marks the point at which the state [. . .] can no longer guarantee through the legal system the empirical ends it desires at any price to attain.' This terrifying assertion means that the people we pay to maintain the law are free of it so as to be able to get on with their job" (Taussig 2006, 176). The police enforce the law but is not subject to it. To protect state power, the police break the law.

new assemblage. The protracted protest shows how Gandhi's ideas were present in a Southern American city known as "the Cradle of the Confederacy." When Rosa Parks refused to give up her seat on the bus to a white man, she demonstrated dignity and a commitment to justice. Parks did not resent this specific man, but reacted to the state violence committed against her in a way that caused segregation to be brought to trial, and ultimately declared illegal. Parks's show of civic responsibility caused members of her community to feel empathy. They chose to emulate her refusal to endure state violence.

The face of the Civil Rights Movement was communal and popular. It was not only the familiar face of Rosa Parks or that of Martin Luther King. Members of the community and unionized workers decided to stay off buses on Monday, December 5$^{th}$, 1955, the day Parks stood before a judge with her Black attorney, Fred Gray, who also represented Claudette Colvin, a fifteen-year-old girl who had refused to give her seat on the bus to a white woman. Unity in the face of segregation happened on its own, yet a new political assemblage emerged from this event. The Montgomery Improvement Association taught the community how to remain nonviolent in the face of state violence.[2] Grassroots resistance strengthened communal bonds of love and loyalty. The community organized a fleet of private cars and minibuses to shuttle people to and from work, but the law, interested in protecting state interests, stood in their way. The legal means to combat the movement were many, including bogus fines for the bus drivers, refusals to renew vehicle registrations, and even incarceration of drivers on the grounds of false traffic violations. For a full year, thousands of Black people in Montgomery practiced love and loyalty, to each other and to the cause, and in so doing turned into a tightly-knit group.

When a federal court in Alabama concluded that segregation was unconstitutional, King was optimistic that the state's appeal process in the Supreme Court would fail. He was right. Still, in his work King cautions that a boycott is not an end in itself: "it [boycott] is merely a means to awaken a sense of shame within the oppressor and challenge his false sense of superiority. But the end is reconciliation; the end is redemption; the end is the creation of the beloved community" (King 1997, 458).

Gandhi and King both see forgiveness and nonviolent resistance, or *Ahimsa* (love) and *Satyagraha* (passive resistance), as paths to compromise and reconciliation, not as conditional emotions. While Derrida and Améry disconnect emotion

---

[2] There were organizing efforts on a grassroots level prior to Parks's act, planned in conjunction with the NAACP. See Samir Sonti at: https://www.salon.com/2013/03/15/the_progressive_legacy_of_rosa_parks_partner/ Accessed July 17, 2022.

from politics, Gandhi and King perceive emotion as critical to politics. If the victim gains any political advantage the forgiveness is not a gift, say Derrida and Améry. The forgiveness that Gandhi and King envision is not a gift because it aims to bring about compromise, reconciliation, and transformation of both the victim and the offender. Political equality is useless if politics does not shake up the existing structure of prejudice.

Racist schemes can be changed only if translation of Western epistemology and paternalism allows white people to view the lives of Black people as part and parcel of the social bond. These different lives are equal, valuable, and active. For Derrida, forgiveness signifies radical openness without any literary or historical closure. This is the gesture of ethics beyond ethics. Butler morally indicts a society that tolerates and produces ungrievable lives, yet she analyzes the possibilities for the creation of a new society, one in which all lives are equally grievable. In this society, lives remain open and can endlessly remain potentials for action. They are not compelled by fate.

Améry's resentment demands that the perpetrator document all crimes committed against the victims: in literature, history, education, and the law. The perpetrator must accept these crimes as a negative possession of the nation, the culture, and each one of the individual offenders. The concept of negative possession means that the offender is open to a psychological transformation and fully accepts guilt. Negative possession also means that the offender undergoes moral transformation, and accepts guilt as an ethical precept that forces him to know, speak of, and record in art and history the crimes that he committed. He should seek to hear and understand the resentment of the victims, and acknowledge that moral responsibility for atrocity cannot expire or reach closure. Negative possession can also assist in the creation of new frameworks that transform the unequal distribution of power. It must be rethought and reevaluated by every future generation that wants to belong to the culture and its historical and moral heritage. King finds the discussion of emotions useful in the context of nonviolent resistance when he resorts to "shame," the same moral emotion in which Coetzee is interested. King suggests that "shame," not just guilt, is the proper emotion that must plague the "oppressor" (King 1997, 458).

## Is memory's language wrong?

> What are the kinds of stories to be told by those and about those who live in such an intimate relationship with death? Romances? Tragedies? [. . .] How does one revisit the scene of subjection without replicating the grammar of violence? Saidiya Hartman, "Venus in Two Acts"

> In effect, it is not modern Jewish historiography that has shaped modern Jewish conceptions of the past. Literature and ideology have been far more decisive. That this should be so seems to me sufficiently interesting to make one pause and reflect. Yosef Haim Yerushalmi, *Zakhor*

Early in *I Am Not Your Negro*, Baldwin states that he wants to tell the stories of Medgar, Malcolm, and Martin because to bring these three lives together reveals their relevance to one another. To interweave them together reveals all the more about each of the men and about the country that betrayed them. He hypothesizes that historicization will make sense not just of the past but also of contemporaneity. And yet, as Yerushalmi suggests in the epigraph above, the contemporaneous challenges historical memory, it does not rely on historical memory. Literature, film, and ideology are in a better position to explain and influence contemporaneity than is systematic historical documentation, which seeks a grand narrative, a cohesive explanation of *all* the "facts."

Baldwin is aware that the stories of active singularities, singular leaders are a better tool to effect societal change than are grand narratives. Right from the beginning, Baldwin tells the story of singularity. The topic is the formation of a new assemblage of people. Baldwin's obligation is to write. But what instigates the writing of this testimony is murder. Baldwin seeks to name the emotional, intellectual, and social transformations that these specific groups brought to the nation.

This is illustrated in the film with the famous photo of a young Black girl in Little Rock, Arkansas, who in 1957 attended an integrated school for the first time.

**Figure 10:** *I Am Not Your Negro*, a Black girl is choosing to go to a desegregated school, DVD screen shot.

She is alone, surrounded by a large crowd of white people, who jeer at her and block her way. In his writing, Baldwin wants to avoid the repetition of the violence of slavery, repeated in segregation, in jeering at a schoolgirl practicing her right to study in a desegregated school as if she were not as much a human being with legal rights as are those who offend her. Baldwin's text has to open the image to new possibilities because the image captures suffocating blind white power that seeks to impose limitations on a young student.

Before that first day of school in 1957, the Black journalist and activist Lorraine Hansberry met with Attorney General Robert Kennedy to try and devise a way to diffuse the fear and fury, to try and make this day when Black students went to desegregated schools a day of national moral reckoning. She asked him to suggest to his brother, President John F. Kennedy, that he escort this little girl on her first walk to school. Robert Kennedy was annoyed. He didn't understand why this would matter. But both Baldwin and Hansberry understood that it would be a meaningful moral gesture. If anyone spat on the girl in the presence of the President they would be spitting on the entire nation. The language of violence would have failed if President Kennedy had walked to school with the girl.

Saidiya Hartman suggests it might be that, in retrospect, the very request – made by a Black journalist to the Attorney General or the President – triggered exaggerated hope and mobilized into action the language of romance, a language that attaches itself to hope, as if for a brief moment the majoritarian language of hierarchical power would bow down, show empathy towards those whom the country systematically disenfranchised. This vignette shows how the language of violence was dealt a blow because the Black representative addressed the humanity of the Attorney General, *who* he is as a human being who can affect the administration's political decisions, *what* are his actions. It did not prevail, even if the girl was the target of violence and hatred. Deterritorialization of the national, hierarchical structure occurs when Lorrain Hansberry and James Baldwin affirm that Black children go to desegregated schools in the face of jeering. Activists don't expect white people to welcome the children to school. Children have the soul-force it takes to face hardship because they're thinking about a future in which they become equal in a changed structure of power. Activists and Black families alike see that desegregated education gives knowledge in the hands of the children, the kind of knowledge that enhances the potential that these children will bring about the transformation of the existing communities of knowledge and make America a place where Black people are equal in their contribution to the nation and in the rewards that they reap as designers of new assemblages of knowledge and power.

The epigraph by Saidiya Hartman belongs to a text which follows the case of a slave-ship captain suspected of raping and killing two young female slaves. Hartman uncovers all the available facts about the murder and the trial (the captain was acquitted). But her true focus is her own distress at realizing that the historical record deprives slaves of a voice, in the same way that the institution of slavery deprived them of freedom or the ability to defend their own lives. The archive perpetuates institutional deafness and dumbness. The law does not rectify the wrongs of slavery. On the contrary, the system is institutionally deaf when faced with the rights of the slaves. It returns verdicts that ignore the violence perpetrated against the slaves. A verdict that does not ignore the violence inflicted on the murdered girls would record their words, treat the slaves as reliable witnesses, and yet the very concept of slavery means that these are not human beings with a language, a voice, a means of communicating.

At the same time, when a contemporary reader examines the records, in an attempt to understand the lives of those tortured, raped, murdered, the result is silence. The pain of the slaves, their hopes, and their friendships are lost – as if they were less than human, unable to hurt or love, unable to tell the stories of their lives, devise ways out of subjection. Hartman asks how contemporary scholarship can counter this epistemology, which offers silence about the victims while dishing out detailed life stories of the slave traders. Hartman's text rises from the silence of the archive, the caesura, the murmurs that remain from the destroyed lives of the slaves. This silence is honest and valuable. It enables transference between the reader and the text, the pain that the reader can feel emerges from the inarticulateness of the text, the fact that no words can describe the suffering that silence elaborates.

Transference already opens up the potential for new assemblages of knowledge and action. Through transference, the reader can acknowledge that slaves occupied a socio-economic position in which life was already destroyed. Black Americans to this day hurt, love, raise families, study, and have careers, but they cannot change the white supremacist scheme of unequal distribution of power, and so they are within their rights to upset the structure, to create literature and film, and to formulate ideologies that challenge the structural inequalities that imprison them. To understand the past, to say things out loud, launches the deterritorialization or the destruction of a majoritarian distribution of power inscribed in the territories of language, and of action, in the patriarchal family, community, and in the nation.

*I Am Not Your Negro* shows that it is a work of love to articulate the facts and expose the pain, to protect the silence of the disenfranchised when silence leaves open the interstice through which transference can permeate both discrete, singular and transcommunal interactions. King understood, as did the older Malcolm X, that love has nothing to do with romance or desire. Love makes Black people strong when they choose it and rather than act-out on hatred they practice love and forgiveness, not just of resentment and resistance. At the same time, this love that brought about Black action makes white people acknowledge that they themselves are not just monsters: they can be loved and they are human even though the socio-economic structure of power that they perpetuate is monstrous. Black leaders and thinkers aim to change the structure of power. The aim is to open spaces in which reciprocal respect prevails, so that America can rid itself of brutality and exclusion.

In 1957, Baldwin decided to return home from his self-imposed exile in Paris. He was driven to do so by the image of the young Black girl going to school alone, harassed by an angry white mob. He didn't return because he missed the majoritarian symbols of American culture – Times Square or baseball or Lady Liberty. He missed Harlem: "I missed the style. That style possessed by no other people in the world. I miss the way the dark face closes. The way dark eyes watch, and the way when a dark face opens light seems to go everywhere. I missed in short, my connections. I missed the life which had produced me and nourished me. Now though I was a stranger I was home."

This love, which literature can ignite, is deterritorializing because it destroys known epistemological systems of belief and diffuses the rhetorical force of political structures that generate an unequal distribution of power. It gives Black people great force, the force to love Black life and heritage despite the fact that white society impels them to feel self-hatred, as if Black people were guilty of having no means to change their socio-political situation for the better, to protect their lives against the constant threat of destruction.[3] The average Black child of Baldwin's time grew up seeing musicals and films featuring white heroes like John Wayne and beautiful white women like Doris Day, but only saw Black actors on screen who played caricatures of Black people, never heroes, rarely even real people. Baldwin remembers one genuine Black face on film, which became etched in his mind: Clinton Rosemond plays a janitor in the 1937 film *They Won't Forget*. Although it is a small part, the horror on the janitor's face is real. The body of a young girl is found on the premises for which the janitor is responsible and he is accused of raping and killing her. The horrified face, the janitor's sobbing, are as real as are the faces and sobs of real live Black people. The character reminded Baldwin of his father.

Baldwin is a writer, a witness, not an activist. Unlike Evers, he was not charged by his Black brothers to restore justice to the people. Evers was asked to find the murderers of a Black man. Baldwin merely escorted him on his journey.

---

3 In a letter to his nephew, Baldwin reminds the young man that he is part of a great family, of a beautiful tradition, even if he feels that to need love is a weakness and a shame: "You can only be destroyed by believing that you really are what the white world calls a *nigger* [. . .] The really terrible thing, old buddy, is that *you* must accept *them*. And I mean that very seriously. You must accept them and accept them with love. For these innocent people have no other hope. They are, in effect, still trapped in a history which they do not understand; and until they understand it, they cannot be released from it" (Baldwin 1998, 293–94).

Baldwin clarifies that as a writer he was relatively safe and did not carry direct political responsibility: he was not a Muslim, like Malcolm X, nor did he belong to the NAACP. Baldwin did not believe that all white people were devils, nor did he want young Blacks to believe it. He sought to deterritorialize the white language of power, to echo the Black language of the activists, and to bring the subcultural force of, say, the face and voice of Ray Charles into American culture, so that Black children could grow up loving their own beauty and talent.

While he was in elementary school, Baldwin had a white teacher who took him under her wing. The teacher gave him books and talked to him about them, took him to see films that no family would take a seven-year-old to see. In the film Baldwin reveals his debt to her. She came into his life at such an early age that, he muses, she is probably the reason why Baldwin was never able to hate white people. Memories of that teacher belong to the prehistory of Baldwin's life, in the same way that the archive that imposed the silence of the slaves is part of the prehistory of contemporary Black life.

**Figure 11:** *I An Not Your Negro*, James Baldwin, DVD screen shot.

## Memory and difference

> To be in the wake is also to recognize the ways that we are constituted through and by continued vulnerability to overwhelming force though not *only* known to ourselves and to each other *by* that force. Christina Sharpe, "The Wake," 2016

It is we ourselves, however, who are always standing at the center of these rare images. Nor is this very mysterious, since such moments of sudden illumination are at the same time moments when we separated from ourselves, and while our waking, habitual, everyday self is involved actively or passively in what is happening, our deeper self rests in another place and is touched by the shock [. . .] It is to this immolation of our deepest self in shock that our memory owes its most indelible images. Walter Benjamin, "Berlin Chronicle" [1932] 633)

Medgar Evers was murdered in his parked car. His wife and children saw him die. Malcolm X was murdered while Baldwin was enjoying a good meal in a London restaurant. And Martin Luther King, Jr. was murdered in a hotel room. Baldwin was in Hollywood at the time, turning the autobiography of Malcolm X into a screenplay.

**Figure 12:** *I Am Not Your Negro*, Malcolm X, Martin Luther King, Jr., Medgar Evers, DVD screen shot.

The shock of these murders is manifest in Baldwin's text in two ways. Baldwin returns to his childhood, to memories steeped in the precarity of Black lives. At the same time, he also reaches for the contemporaneity, new mental images that the murders provoke.

The images of the precarity of Black lives about which Baldwin writes in a new language should diffuse repetitions of violence in the present state of diversity, propel into existence different potentials in the lives and actions of Black leaders, speakers, and thinkers, and integrate new social and political causes, suggesting new goals to be pursued. Yet, the sense of a self in "immolation", to use Benjamin's language, means that Black people—who inherit subjection to violence in the form of a feeling of nonbeing or of inexistence from their parents' generations whom the whites suppress and oppress—can belong to becomings or to responding to, and instigating transformations only through exploring new relations to, and contacts among Black and with white people in, their actions of the everyday.

How does one insert a distance between the shock of the present and the dangers of the past? The film stresses that Black lives are still in danger. Baldwin created distance when he declared himself to be a witness, one who gives testimony, and not a political activist. That said, he slightly misjudged his own situation: The FBI had a file on him.

Baldwin believed that those who cannot rest do not survive the battle. Medgar, Malcolm, and Martin aimed to detach Black people from the repetition of violence, from the stereotypes imposed on them by white people. They aimed to help Black communities pull themselves out of the traps of racism and violence. The rope that they through and the others could hold on to was the new language of love and non-violent resistance.

*I Am Not Your Negro* commemorates the death of Tamir Rice in 2014 and those of Darius Simmons and Trayvon Martin in 2012. Their faces flicker on the screen and sink the viewers back into shock, a shock that gives power and truth to Baldwin's words, that Black people are "blood of the country, flesh of the nation, bone of the bones of white people." White Americans fear love for they are evaluated within a structure of power distribution on the basis of what they are, not on the basis of *who* they are. They fear that this love will bring about the loss of their privileged lives. They dread the Black people who embody the kind of family and community immersed in the love that they lack, and hate them for it. White persons fear the Black entity they created, which lives only in their heads.

For Baldwin, the United States is a very complex democracy choosing to be narrow-minded. The film contains footage of many politicians saying "I am sorry." Repentance and regret repeat themselves over and over again, from different mouths in different places, on different dates, alluding to different offenses against the victims of racism and sexism. Those who apologize say that they take "fully responsibility" for the wrongs they perpetrated, but, as the existing structure of power distribution does not change, Baldwin concludes that America remains immature; it does not grow up.

At the backdrop of this American refusal to mature is humanism, which is Western Civilization's great lie. Western democracies have no moral authority. Americans live in a world of unending prosperity, while ignorant of what that prosperity costs. Baldwin is convinced that to change America one does not need to think about numbers but about people. Those white Americans who claim to care about change are lying. They care about their safety and their profits. Baldwin writes that prophets and angels weep when they look on America. It is not the home of the free, though sometimes it is the home of the brave.

Baldwin's concluding remarks employ King's interweaving of love and nonviolent resistance. King trained his demonstrators to love the white people who would assault them with clubs and send dogs at them. They were only allowed to suffer violence, never to reciprocate. The white offender is forgiven despite the violence. In the same vein, Baldwin wants to disabuse his readers of the hold, the power that white words have over us all. Baldwin suggests that white and power are not synonyms because when we say white power we use a metaphor for Chase Manhattan Bank, we describe the existing structure of exclusion: we show that we know that whites created an unjust structure of power distribution, a structure that generates innumerable social and economic failures; we do not prove that the world is white when we think of white power. Black people see whites but white people don't see Blacks and become monstrous. On film, Baldwin suggests that the future of the Black people in America is as bright or as gloomy as the prospects of America itself.

# Coda
# Forgiveness, justice, and historical responsibility

Walter Benjamin begins "The Meaning of Time in the Moral Universe" by showing that retribution and justice are different from forgiveness. He puts to task a divine form of forgiveness that lays waste to the world in the process of forgiving, but only so as to show that human forgiveness keeps the world intact. For forgiveness takes place in time, in daily living, in the infinite postponement of judgment. Benjamin denies that a statute of limitations can take the place of forgiveness. It rather signifies the law's refusal of retribution until, he says, the time of the Last Judgment, which is endlessly postponed: "This significance is revealed not in the world of law, where retribution rules, but only in the moral universe, where forgiveness comes out to meet it. In order to struggle against retribution, forgiveness finds its powerful ally in time" (Benjamin 1996 [1921], 286).

This is important to students of forgiveness, who wrestle with whether or not statutes of limitations are applicable to crimes against humanity. Arendt agrees that forgiveness comes into the world like a miracle, because it unexpectedly breaks the vicious cycle of retribution. She clearly sees forgiveness as closer to love and respect than to justice (Arendt 1958, 242). When Arendt rejects forgiveness for crimes against humanity, she is relying on a legalistic outlook: "It is therefore quite significant, a structural element in the realm of human affairs, that men are unable to forgive what they cannot punish and that they cannot punish what has turned out to be unforgivable" (Arendt 1958, 241).

For Derrida, the application of a statute of limitations to crimes against humanity does not amount to expiating these crimes, but to ceasing to seek retribution, and leaving the matter in the hands of the Last Judgment:

> One can maintain the imprescriptibility of a crime, give no limit to the duration of an indictment or a possible pursual before the law, while still forgiving the guilty. Inversely, one can acquit or suspend judgment and nevertheless refuse to forgive. It remains that the singularity of the concept of imprescriptibility (by opposition to 'prescription' . . .) stems perhaps from what it also introduces, like forgiveness or the unforgiveable, a sort of eternity or transcendence, the apocalyptic horizon of a final judgement: in the law, beyond the law, in history beyond history (Derrida 2001, 33).

This ties to Benjamin's insistence that the significance of forgiveness "is revealed not in the world of law, where retribution rules, but only in the moral universe, where forgiveness comes out to meet it. In order to struggle against retribution, forgiveness finds its powerful ally in time" (ibid.). I understand this to mean that forgiveness comes face to face with retribution in order to struggle against it.

In this book I have contested Derrida's conclusion that crimes against humanity institute the aporia of forgiveness because, if "forgiveness forgives only the unforgiveable," then "forgiveness must announce itself as impossibility itself. It can only be possible in doing the impossible" (Derrida 2001 32–33). My main argument is that resentment is necessary to forgiveness, in the same way that forgiveness is necessary to the resentful survivor: because they allow for the possibility of negative possession. The second reason that I part from Derrida's notion of forgiveness is related to Benjamin's notion of the relevance of forgiveness to time. The past changes when it is illuminated by the present, and the meaning of retribution exists only in flux, in a blur of emotions that in the face of difference keep insisting on sameness. Time is a strong ally of forgiveness. This is why Améry, referring to the moral abyss between victim and perpetrator, says that "someday *time* will close it, that is certain" (Améry 1980 ix). I see forgiveness as the bridging of the moral breach between victim and perpetrator. But bridging of the abyss does not come about automatically, because of forgetfulness or usefulness, but because new assemblages form between communities, because people find new reasons to trust each other.

\*

Daniel Levy and Natan Sznaider worry that forgiveness, if it is historically material, allows the perpetrator to avoid responsibility. In order to eliminate this possibility, they argue that forgiveness must be inextricable from reconciliation: "At the level of states and ethnic collectivities, money is exchanged for forgiveness. Legal and political consequential forgiveness are distinct from feelings of forgiveness. And at the level of individuals, the act is of closure. Money symbolizes the irrevocable admission that a crime has been committed" (Levy and Sznaider 2006, 93).

Levy and Sznaider deploy the kind of political language for which Benjamin has no use. When they say that compensation is the kind of forgiveness that states dispense, they are not using a metaphor but a metonymy. They allude to the reparations agreement between Germany and Israel, and suggest that survivors are not obliged to forgive their fellow Germans just because two states came to monetary and diplomatic accord.

For Benjamin, forgiveness and reconciliation are inassimilable. Time helps to "complete the process of forgiveness, though never of reconciliation" (Benjamin 1996 [1921], 287). Forgiveness ushers in a history of acknowledgement, but this "postponement" to the time of the Last Judgement has nothing in common with financial agreements between states. "Postponement" signifies openness and constant transformation.

Benjamin's examination of divine law in "The Critique of Violence" is, as I have discussed, likewise related to forgiveness. Divine law engages legitimate violence when it obliterates the sinner along with every trace of the crime committed against God. God does not wrest a bloody sacrifice, does not magnify His own power. Eli Friedlander argues that "the divine manifestation of sovereign power [. . .] dissolves law for the sake of life itself" (Friedlander 2012, 132). This echoes Benjamin's contention that divine law inflicts "a retribution that 'expiates' the guilt of mere life – and doubtless also purifies the guilty, not of guilt, however, but of law" (Benjamin 1978, 297).

Divine law destroys and forgives simultaneously when it eliminates the existing structure of law.[1] Benjamin says of the commandment "Thou shalt not kill," that "it exists not as a criterion of judgment, but as a guideline for the actions of persons or states who have to wrestle with it in solitude and, in exceptional cases, to take on themselves the responsibility of ignoring it" (Benjamin 1978, 298). In the same spirit, Butler argues that divine law leads to freedom in relation to the law: "One must, as it were, wrestle with oneself in relation to it. But the wrestling with oneself may well yield a result, a decision, an act that refuses or revises the commandment, and, in this sense, the decision is the effect of an interpretation at once constrained and free" (Butler 2006, 213). Benjamin's image of divine wrath is different from retribution in the Last Judgment and different from forgiveness in time. He envisions forgiveness as a destructive storm that precedes the Last Judgment:

> This storm is not only the voice in which the evildoer's cry of terror is drowned; it is also the hand that obliterates the traces of his misdeeds, even if it must lay waist to the world in the process. As the purifying hurricane speeds ahead of the thunder and lightning, God's fury roars through history in the storm of forgiveness, in order to sweep away everything that would be consumed forever in the lightning bolts of divine wrath (Benjamin 1996 [1921], 287).

That the two exist simultaneously, the annihilation of existing law and the sinner's cry of terror, signifies that the wrath of God is also the space where persons and communities can "wrestle" with forgiveness. It is in the storm of the present that past guilt and shame turn to a future of new assemblages and connections between singularities that are not locked up in identities but are in flux, being reshaped by differences.

\*

---

[1] Illegitimate violence is characteristic of both mythic and state law. In the hands of these systems, the individual becomes a plaything of fate when both myth and the state inflict on her/him bloody reprisals of infractions of the law. The sufferer of punishment in the myth is a tragic hero, because he is sacrificed to the gods and becomes a moral example that humanity can emulate. The sufferer of punishment in the state becomes an example of the fact that the law's violence is self-serving, not obligated to the use of just means and the advancement of just ends.

In *The Time That Remains*, Agamben suggests that forgiveness becomes meaningful when one remains loyal to one's resentments. Resentment as a precondition of forgiveness gives meaning to history. Agamben is inspired by Améry, who never let go of his resentment toward the Gestapo man who tortured him. In the form of a daydream, Améry shares the following memory:

> SS-man Wajs from Antwerp, a repeated murderer and an especially adroit torturer, paid with his life. What more can my foul thirst for revenge demand? But if I have searched my mind properly, it is not a matter of revenge, nor one of atonement. The experience of persecution was, at the very bottom, that of an extreme *loneliness*. At stake for me is the release from the abandonment that has persisted from that time until today (Améry 1980, 70).

According to Agamben, Améry's commitment to resentment is a commitment to remembering, which he terms, with Benjamin in mind, a "messianic" modality or exigency. In Benjamin, according to Agamben, the history of society is engraved in a forgotten history that is documented nowhere. But this chaos of forgotten knowledge is useful. The forgotten works in us with the same force that consciousness works in us, only in a different way. The forgotten remains in us and makes us react to it as forgotten. It is unforgettable. The unforgettable is transmittable because we bear it in our core. We must remain loyal to that which has always been forgotten but must remain unforgettable. This exigency is our historical responsibility (Agamben 2005, 40).

Historical responsibility inheres in Benjamin's storm of forgiveness, because it equals to a brainstorm that involves recollection and acknowledgement from a messianic modality. The storm is purifying not of law/crime, but of the fact that history encourages us to forget the unforgettable. That is the violence that emerges during historical "states of exception," which is Agamben's term for occasions in which a tyrant eliminates the law in order to protect the structure of the state. Violence is inescapable during states of exception – as it was during World War II, during the reign of Apartheid in South Africa and of racial segregation in the American South. The unforgettable belongs in human time, according to Benjamin and Butler, even if God forgives and forgets.

I am interested in the fact that resentment and forgiveness are associated with Power(lessness), by which I mean that the forgiving/resentful survivor is not sovereign and yet has Power, the power to make choices about whom to remain connected with, and what shape this connection is to have. Non-sovereignty enables the survivor to forgive the evildoer from the position of a storm, not the statist or legalistic position of formal reconciliation. The Power(lessness) of forgiveness and remorse enables recalling the unforgiveable, the unforgettable. Derrida endorses this attitude toward forgiveness: "What I dream of, what I try to think as the 'purity' of a forgiveness worthy of its name, would be a forgiveness without power: *unconditional but without sovereignty*" (Derrida 2001, 59).

Agamben refers to an *event* that binds past and present, so that the past appears in the present as the flash of an image. The past is recognized in the present while the present recognizes its context in the past, so that they both acquire new meanings (Agamben 2005, 142). Améry's daydream is illuminating because, Améry argues, "At stake for me is the release from the abandonment that has persisted from that time until today" (Améry 1980, 70). The dialectical image can remedy the illness that time inflicts when it salvages historical crimes from abandonment.

In "A Berlin Chronicle," Benjamin attaches language to both memory and specific places:

> Language has unmistakably made plain that memory is not an instrument for exploring the past but its theater. It is the medium of past experience, just as the earth is the medium in which dead cities lie buried. He who seeks to approach his own buried past must conduct himself like a man digging. This determines the tone and bearing of genuine reminiscences . . . the images, severed from all earlier associations, that stand—like precious fragments or torsos in a collector's gallery—in the sober rooms of our later insights (Benjamin [1932], 611).

Benjamin gives meaning to central concepts such as "sudden illumination" and "image" when they affect memory and hence our relation to the present:

> It is we ourselves, however, who are always standing at the center of these rare images. Nor is this very mysterious, since such moments of sudden illumination are at the same time moments when we separated from ourselves, and while our waking, habitual, everyday self is involved actively or passively in what is happening, our deeper self rests in another place and is touched by the shock . . . It is to this immolation of our deepest self in shock that our memory owes its most indelible images (Benjamin [1932], 633).

In *Walter Benjamin's Grave*, Michael Taussig turns into a sudden illumination the fact that Benjamin does not have a proper grave. But Taussig would like to show that in Port Bou it is Benjamin's "Shadowy existence" that presides. Benjamin's spirit creates the "*genius loci*" (Benjamin [1932] 612–613) of Port Bou, and thus it disables abandonment and reaches out to forgiveness (Taussig 2006, 612). Benjamin committed suicide, yet he was the victim of a war that generated mass graves. Taussig admires Dani Karavan's monument to Benjamin (completed in 1994). The underground shaft ends in a large glass window where a quote from Benjamin is engraved: "It is more arduous to honor the memory of the nameless than that of the renowned. Historical construction is devoted to the memory of the nameless" (cited in Taussig 2006, 16). The monument stands in the midst of the *fosa comun*, a mass grave. If you were buried there you ended up nameless. Bodies that want to be redeemed are severed from history.

Benjamin believed that in "order for the past to be touched by the present, there must be no continuity between them." The image of the past is superimposed on the present suddenly, and thus "jump-starts" redemption. The past is dislodged from its entrenchment and installed on a new track (Taussig 2006, 17–19). This is the exact opposite of a monument. Améry's daydream embodies such an overwhelming moment of realization. The meaning that emerges from the superimposition of the past on the present originates in Power(lessness), not in sovereignty, "trembling with the pathos of forgiveness and reconciliation" (Améry 1980 65).

# Bibliography

*Aftermath*. Dir. Wladyslaw Pasikowski. Apple Film Productions, Menemsha Films, 2012.
Agamben, Giorgio. *The Time that Remains*. trans. Patricia Dailey. Stanford, California: Stanford University Press, 2005.
Amery, Carl. *Capitulation: An Analysis of Contemporary Catholicism*. trans. Edward Quinn London: Sheed and Ward, 1967.
Améry, Jean. *At the Mind's Limit Contemplations by a Survivor on Auschwitz and Its Realities*. trans. Sidney Rosenfeld and Stella P. Rosenfeld. Bloomington: Indiana University Press, [1966] 1980.
Améry, Jean. "On the Necessity and Impossibility of Being a Jew." *At the Mind's Limits*. trans. Sidney Rosenfeld and Stella P. Rosenfeld. Bloomington: Indiana University Press, 1980. 82–101.
Améry, Jean. "Resentments." *At the Mind's Limits Contemplations by a Survivor on Auschwitz and Its Realities*. trans. Sidney Rosenfeld and Stella P. Rosenfeld. Bloomington: Indiana University Press, [1966] 1980. 62–81.
Améry, Jean. "Torture." *At the Mind's Limits Contemplations by A Survivor on Auschwitz and Its Realities*. trans. Sidney Rosenfeld and Stella P. Rosenfeld. Bloomington and Indianapolis, Indiana University Press, 1980. 21–40.
Appelfeld, Aharon. *The Story of A Life*. trans. Aloma Halter, New York: Schocken Books, 2004. 69, 50, 76, 105.
Arendt, Hannah. *The Origins of Totalitarianism*. New York: Harcourt, Brace and Company, 1951.
Arendt, Hannah. *Rahel Varnhagen: The Life of a Jewess*. Jerusalem: Leo Baeck Institute, 1957.
Arendt, Hannah. *The Human Condition*. Chicago: University of Chicago Press, 1958.
Arendt, Hannah. "The Meaning of Love in Politics: A Letter by Hannah Arendt to James Baldwin." 1962. https://www.hannaharendt.net/index.php/han/article/view/95/156%20accessed%20July%2026 (May 13, 2023).
Arendt, Hannah. *Eichmann in Jerusalem: A Report on the Banality of Evil*. New York: Penguin Books, 1963.
Arendt, Hanna. *On Revolution*, New York: Penguin, 1965.
Arendt, Hannah. *Men in Dark Times*. San Diego: Harcourt Brace and Company, 1968.
Arendt, Hannah. *Crisis of the Republic*. New York: Harcourt Brace Jovanovich, Inc., 1969.
Arendt, Hannah and Jaspers, Karl. *Hannah Arendt Karl Jaspers Correspondence 1926–1969*. Trans. Robert and Rita Kimber. San Diego, New York, London: Harcourt Brace and Company, 1992.
Arendt, Hannah. *Love and Saint Augustine*. Chicago: University of Chicago Press, [1929] 1996.
Arendt, Hannah. *Essays in Understanding 1930–1954 Formation, Exile, and Totalitarianism*. ed. Jerome Kohn. New York: Schocken Books, [1950] 1994.
Arendt, Hannah. "The Aftermath of Nazi Rule: Report from Germany." *Essays in Understanding 1930–1954, Formation, Exile and Totalitarianism*. ed. Jerome Kohn. New York: Schocken Books, [1950] 1994. 248–269.
Arendt, Hannah. "Collective Responsibility." *Responsibility and Judgment*. ed. Jerome Kohn. New York: Schocken Books, 2003. 147–158.
Arendt, Hannah. "Personal Responsibility Under Dictatorship." *Responsibility and Judgment*. ed. Jerome Kohn. New York: Schocken Books, 2003. 17–48.
Arendt, Hannah. *The Promise of Politics*. ed. Jerome Kohn. New York: Schocken Books, 2005.
Augstein, Rudolph. "Heinrich Bölls Ansichten eines Clowns" *Die Zeit*, 14 Juni, 1963. https://www.zeit.de/1963/24/heinrich-boells-ansichten-eines-clowns/seite-4 (June 3, 2020).

Aavitsland, Vilde Lid. "The Failure of Judgment: Disgust in Arendt's Theory of Political Judgment." In *The Journal of Speculative Philosophy*, Volume 33, Number 3, 2019, 537–550.

Badiou, Alain. *Saint Paul: The Foundation of Universalism*. trans. Ray Brassier. Stanford: Stanford University Press, 2003.

Baker, Emily-Rose. "Memorializing the (Un)Dead Jewish Other in Poland: Spectrality, Embodiment, and Polish Holocaust Horror in Wladyslaw Pasikowski's *Aftermath* (2012)." *Geneology*, 2019. 3, 65, 5/14.

Baldwin, James. *Another Country*. New York: Penguin Books, 1962.

Baldwin, James. "The Fire Next Time." *Collected Essays*. ed. Tony Morrison. New York: The Library of America, [1985] 1998, 291–296.

Baldwin, James. "My Dungeon Shook: Letter to My Nephew." *Baldwin Collected Essays*. ed. Tony Morrison. New York: The Library of America, [1962] 1998. 291–295.

Barbour D, John. "*Ressentiment*, Public Virtues, and Malcolm X." *The Conscience of the Autobiographer, Ethical and Religious Dimensions of Autobiography*. London: Macmillan, 1992. 120–142.

Bataille, George. *Erotism, Death and Sensuality*. trans. Mary Dalwood. San Francisco: City Lights Books, 1962.

Bataille, Georges. *Inner Experience*. trans. Leslie Anne Boldt. Albany: State University of New York Press, 1988.

Bégin, Richard. « [. . .] d'un temps qui a déjà servi » L'imaginaire des ruine de Bruno Schulz à Wojciech Has. *Protée*, (2007), 35: 2, 27–36.

Benjamin, Walter. "Critique of Violence." *Reflections*. trans. Edmund Jephcott. New York: Schocken Books, 1978. 277–300.

Benjamin, Walter. "The Meaning of Time in the Moral Universe." [1921] trans. Rodney Livingstone. *Walter Benjamin Selected Writings Volume 1 1913–1926*. eds. Marcus Bullock and Michael W. Jennings. Cambridge, Massachusetts: Harvard University Press, 1996. 286–287.

Benjamin, Walter. "The Task of the Translator." *Walter Benjamin Selected Writings, Volume 1, 1913–1926*. eds., Marcus Bullock and Michael W. Jennings. Cambridge: Harvard University Press, 1996. 253–263.

Benjamin, Walter. "A Berlin Chronicle. [1932]" *Selected Writings* Vol 2. 1927–1934. Trans. Edmund Jephcott. Cambridge, Massachusetts: Belknap Press, 1999. 595–635.

Benjamin, Walter. "Berlin Chronicle." In *Selected Writings* Volume 2, Part Two, 1931– 1934. trans. Rodney Livingstone et al. Editor, Michael W, Jennings et al. Cambridge, Massachusetts, Harvard University Press, 1999, 595–637.

Bion, W. R. "The Psychoanalytical Study of Thinking; A Theory of Thinking." *International Journal of Psychoanalysis*, vol. 43, 1962, 306–310. http://www.pep-web.org.ezp.lib.cam.ac.uk/document.php?id=ijp.043.0306a (July 3,2020).

Birmingham, Peg. *Hannah Arendt and Human Rights: The Predicament of Common Responsibility*. Bloomington: Indiana University Press, 2006.

Blanchot, Maurice. *L'espace littéraire*. Paris: Gallimard, 1955.

Blustein, Jeffrey M. *Forgiveness and Remembrance Remembering Wrongdoing in Personal and Public Life*. Oxford: Oxford University Press, 2014.

Bluestein, Jeffrey. "Forgiveness, Commemoration, and Restorative Justice." *Forgiveness and Remembrance: Remembering Wrongdoing in Personal and Public Life*. New York: Oxford University Press, 2014. 143–177.

Bogues, Anthony. "Nelson Mandela: Decolonization, Apartheid, and the Politics of Moral Force." *Boundary* 41, no. 2 (2014): 34–36.

Böll, Heinrich. *Billiards at Half-Past Nine*. trans. Patrick Bowles. New York: Melville House, 1959.

Böll, Heinrich. *The Clown*. trans. Leila Vennewitz. New York: Melville House, 1963.
Böll, Heinrich. "Epilogue." *Capitulation: An Analysis of Contemporary Catholicism*. trans. Edward Quinn. London: Sheed and Ward, 1967. 225 –231.
Böll, Heinrich. "Freedom is Fading Every Day, The Last Major Interview with Margarete Limberg." *Heinrich Böll On his Death, Selected Obituaries and the Last Interview*. Bonn: Inter Nationes, 1985. 22–31.
Böll, Heinrich. "An Approach to the Rationality of Poetry, *Nobel Address Delivered on 2 May 1972 in Stockholm*." *Heinrich Böll On his Death, Selected obituaries and the last interview*. Bonn: Inter Nationes, 1985. 32–46.
Böll, Heinrich. *Lettre à un jeune Catholique*. trans. Josette Calas and Fanette Lepetit. Paris: Éditions Mille et une nuits, 1996. 5–39.
Böll, Heinrich. *Werke, Kölner Ausgabe*. Herausgegeben von Árpád Bernáth, Hans Joachim Bernhard, Robert C. Conard et. al.; Band 10 (1956–1959). Herausgegeben von Viktor Böll. Köln: Kiepenheuer & Witsch, 2005, S. 452.
Bowen-Moore, Patricia. *Hannah Arendt's Philosophy of Natality*. London: Macmillan, 1989.
Boyle, Patrick, S. J. "Elusive Neighborliness: Hannah Arendt's Interpretation of Saint Augustine." *Amour Mundi: Explorations in the Faith and Thought of Hannah Arendt*. Eds. S. J. James and W. Bernauer, 81–113. Boston: Martin Nijhoff Publishers, 1987.
Brinkema, Eugenie. *The Forms of the Affects*. Durham: Duke University Press, 2014. 105
Brudholm, Thomas. *Resentment's Virtue: Jean Améry and the Refusal to Forgive*. Philadelphia: Temple University Press, 2008.
Brudhom, Thomas and Rosoux, Valérie. "The Unforgiving: Reflections the Resistance to Forgiveness After Atrocity." *Law and Contemporary Problems*, vol. 72, no. 33, (2009): 33–49.
Bulgakov, Mikhail. *Master and Margarita*, trans. Mira Ginsburg. New York: Grove Press, [1967] 1995.
Butler, Judith. "Critique, Coercion, and Sacred Life in Benjamin's "Critique of Violence."" *Political Theologies Public Religions in a Post-Secular World*. eds. Hent De Vries and Lawrence E. Sullivan. New York: Fordham UP, 2006. 201–219.
Butorac, Sean Kim. "Hanna Arendt, James Baldwin, and the Politics of Love." In *Political Research Quarterly*, 2018, 1–12.
Butler, Judith. *The Force of Nonviolence, an Ethico-Political Bind*. London and New York: Verso, 2020.
Celan, Paul, *Collected Prose*. trans. Rosemarie Waldrop. Lancashire: PN Review, Carcanet, 1986.
Char, René. *Hypnos*. trans. Mark Hutchinson, London: Seagul Books, 2014. Fragment 106; 30.
Coetzee, J. M. *Disgrace*. New York: Penguin Books, 1999.
Deleuze, Gilles and Guattari, Felix. *Kafka, Toward a Minor Literature*. trans. Dana Polan. Minneapolis: University of Minnesota Press, 1986.
Deleuze, Gilles, and Guattari, Felix. "Becoming-Intense, Becoming-Animal, Becoming Imperceptible." *A Thousand Plateaus: Capitalism and Schizophrenia*. trans. Brian Massumi, Minneapolis: University of Minnesota Press, 1987.
Deleuze, Gilles. *Cinema 2*. trans. Hugh Tomlinson and Robert Galeta. Minneapolis: University of Minnesota Press, 1989.
Deleuze, Gilles. *Difference and Repetition*. trans. Patton Paul. New York: Columbia University Press, 1994.
De Man, Paul. *The Rhetoric of Romanticism*. New York: Columbia University Press, 1984.
De Man, Pau. "Excuses (*Confessions*)." *Allegories of Reading, Figural Language in Rousseau, Nietzsche, Rilke, and Proust*. New Haven: Yale University Press, 1997. 278–301.
Derrida, Jacques. "Cogito and the History of Madness." *Writing and Difference*. trans. Allan Bass. Chicago: University of Chicago Press, 1978. 31–63.

Derrida, Jacques. *Specters of Marx.* trans. Peggy Kamuf. London: Routledge, 1993.
Derrida, Jacques. *The Gift of Death*, trans. David Wills. Chicago: University of Chicago Press, 1995.
Derrida, Jacques im Gespräch mit Michel Wieviorka, "Verzeihen ohne Macht: unbedingt und jenseits der Souveränität, *Jahrhundert der Vergebung.* " *Lettere Internationale* volume 48 (2000): 10–18.
Derrida, Jacques. *On Cosmopolitanism and Forgiveness.* trans. Marl Dooley and Michael Hughes. London: Routledge, 2001.
Derrida, Jacques, "On Forgiveness," *On Cosmopolitanism and Forgiveness*, trans. Mark Dooley and Michael Hughes. London: Routledge, 2001. 1–24.
Derrida, Jacques. "On Forgiveness." in *Cosmopolitanism and Forgiveness.* trans. Mark Dooley and Michael Hughes. London: Routledge, 2001. 25–60.
Evans, C. Stephen."Faith and Reason in Kierkegaard's Concluding Unscientific Postscript." *Kierkegaard's Unscientific Postscript A Critical Guide*, ed. Rick Anthony Furtak. Cambridge: Cambridge University Press, 2010. 2014 –218.
Feinsilver, June, "Testimony no. 2463." Interview from *Fortunoff Video Archives of the Holocaust*, Yale University. Video.
Felstiner, John. *Paul Celan: Poet, Survivor, Jew.* New Haven: Yale University Press, 1995. xvi; 64; 141–146.
Freud, Sigmund. *The Interpretation of Dreams*, trans. James Strachey. New York: Basic Books, [1900] 1995.
Freud, Sigmund. "Leonardo Da Vinci A Memory of His Childhood." *Sigmund Freud: Art and Literature.* Trans. James Strachey. New York: Penguin Book, [1910] 1985. 151–231.
Freud, Sigmund. "Repeating, Remembering, and Working Through." *The Standard Edition of the Complete Psychological Works of Freud*, trans. James Strachey. Vol. XII. Psychoanalytic Electronic Publishing: 1914. 145–156.
Freud, Sigmund. "The Moses of Michelangelo," *The Standard Edition of the Complete Psychological Works of Freud*, trans. James Strachey. Vol. XIII. Psychoanalytic Electronic Publishing: 1914. 209–238.
Freud, Sigmund. (1917) "Mourning and Melancholia," *The Standard Edition of the Complete Psychological Works of Sigmund Freud*. trans. James Strachey. Volume XIV, 1957.
Freud, Sigmund. "Remembering, Repeating and Working-Through." *The Standard Edition of the Complete Psychological Works of Sigmund Freud Vo XII.* trans. James Strachey, 147–156. London: Hogarth Press, 1958.
Freud, Sigmund. *Civilization and Its Discontents*, trans. James Strachey. New York: W. W. Norton and Company, [1930] 1961.
Freud, Sigmund. *Moses and Monotheism*, trans. James Strachey. Vol. XXIII. Psychoanalytic Electronic Publishing: 1964 [1939], 1–138.
Freud, Sigmund. "Mourning and Melancholia." *On Metapsychology, The Penguin Freud Library Vol 2.* trans. James Strachey. London: Penguin Books, 1984. 245–267.
Friedlander, Eli. *Walter Benjamin A Philosophical Portrait.* Cambridge Massachusetts: Harvard University Press, 2012.
Gandhi, M. K. *An Autobiography or The Story of My Experiments with Truth.* Ahmedbad: Navajivan Publishing House, 1927.
Gandhi, M. K. *Hind Swaraj and Other Writings.* New York: Cambridge University Press, 1997.
Gardner, Jonathan. "Beneath the Rubble, the Crystal Palace! The surprising persistence of a temporary mega event," *World Archeology*, vol. 50, no. 1, (2018): 185–199.
Garloff, Ktja. "Conclusion: Toward the Present and the Future, *Gershom Scholem, Hannah Arendt, Barbara Honigmann.*" *Mixed Feelings*: *Tropes of Love in German Jewish Culture*. Ithaca: Cornell University Press, 2016. 171–187.

Garloff, Katja. "Introduction." in *Mixed Feelings: Tropes of Love in German Jewish Culture*, 1–18. Ithaca: Cornell University Press, 2016.

Gasyna, George. "Tandeta (Trash): Bruno Schulz and the Micropolitics of Everyday Life." *Slavic Review* vol. 74, no. 4 (2015): 760–784.

General Assembly of the United Nations. Universal Declaration of Human Rights. Paris: 10 December, 1948. https://www.ohchr.org/EN/UDHR/Documents/UDHR_Translations/eng.pdf (July 30, 2020).

Govier, Trudy. *Forgiveness and Revenge*. London: Routledge, 2002.

Griswold, L. Charles. *Forgiveness*. Cambridge: Cambridge University Press, 2007.

Gross, Jan T. *Neighbors the Destruction of the Jewish Community in Jedwabne, Poland*. Princeton and Oxford: Princeton University Press, 2001. 48; 3.

Grossman, David. "The Age of Genius, the Legend of Bruno Schulz." Trans. Stuart Schoffman. *New Yorker*, June 8, 2009. https://www.newyorker.com/magazine/2009/06/08/the-age-of-genius (August 26, 2021).

Grunebaum, Heidi. "Talking to Ourselves 'Among the Innocent Dead': On Reconciliation, Forgiveness, and Mourning." *PMLA* 117. 2 (2002): 306–310.

Hartman, Saidiya. "Venus in Two Acts." *Small Axe*, 28 (2008): 1–14.

Hieronymi, Pamela. "Articulating an Uncompromising Forgiveness." *Philosophy and Phenomenological Research 62*, no. 3, (May 2001): 529–555.

Hobbes, Thomas. *Leviathan*. Great Britain: Oxford, [1651] 1909.

*Holy Bible, the*. Translated out of the original tongue. London: Oxford University Press.

Hollier, Denis. *Against Architecture*. Trans. Betsy Wing. Cambridge, Massachusetts: MIT Press, 1992.

Hughes, Paul M. "What is Involved in Forgiving?" *Philosophia 25*, no.1 (1997): 33–49.

*I Am Not Your Negro*. Dir. Raoul Peck. Narr. Samuel L. Jackson. Velvet Film. Artemis Productions, 2016.

Jacobs, Carol. "What Does It Mean to Count? W. G. Sebald's The Emigrants" *MLN* vol. 119, no. 5 (2004): 905–929.

Jankélévitch, Vladimir. "Should We Pardon Them?" *Critical Inquiry 22*, no. 3 (Spring 1996): 552–572.

Jankélévitch, Vladimir. *Le Pardon*. Paris: Aubier-Montaigne, 1967.

Jankélévitch, Vladimir. *Pardonner*. Paris: Le Pavillon Reger Maria Éditeur, 1971.

Jankélévitch, Vladimir. *Forgiveness*. trans. Andrew Kelley. Chicago: The University of Chicago Press, 2005.

Jaspers, Karl. *The Question of German Guilt [Die Schuldfrage]*. trans. E. B. Ashton. New York: Fordham University Press, 2000.

Kampowski, Stephen. *Arendt, Augustine, and the New Beginning: The Action Theory and Moral Thought of Hannah Arendt in the Light of her Dissertation on St. Augustine*. Cambridge: Eerdmans, 2008.

King, Martin Luther. "Facing the Challenge of a New Age," *The Papers of Martin Luther King Jr. Vol. III, Birth of a News Age*. ed. Clayborn Carson. Berkley: University of California Press, 1997. 451–463.

Klein, Melanie. "Notes on Some Schizoid Mechanisms (1946)." *Envy and Gratitude and Other Works 1946–1963*. New York: Free Press, 1975. 1–25.

Kluger, Ruth. "Forgiving and Remembering." *PMLA* 117. 2 (2002): 311–313.

Kristeva, Julia. "Forgiveness an Interview." trans. Alison Rice, in *PMLA* 117.2 (2002): 279–295.

Lacan, Jacques. "The Direction of the Treatment and It's Power." *Écrit*. trans. Alan Sheridan. New York: W. W. Norton and Company, 1971.

LaCapra, Dominique. *Writing History Writing Trauma*. Baltimore: Johns Hopkins University Press, 2014.

Laplanche, Jean, and Pontalis, Jean- Bertrand. *The Language of Psychoanalysis*. trans. Donald Nicholson-Smith. New York: W. W. Norton and Company, 1973.

Lear, Jonathan. "Radical Evaluation." *Love and Its Place in Nature*. New York: Farrar, Straus and Giroux, 1990. 183–222.

Levi, Primo, *The Drowned and the Saved.* trans.Raymond Rosenthal. New York: Vintage International, 1988.
Levinas, Emmanuel. *Éthique et infini: dialogue avec Philippe Nemo*. Fayard, 1982, 81, 97.
Lévinas, Emmanuel. *Le temps et l'autre*. Paris: Presses Universitaire de France, 1983.
Levinas, Emmanuel. "The Temptation of Temptation." *Nine Talmudic Lectures*. trans. Annette Aromowicz. Bloomington: Indiana University Press, 1990. 37; 38; 39.
Levinas, Emmanuel. *Ethics and Infinity*. Wiley, 1984. Vol 34. No. 2: 192; 194; 195; 196; 201; 202. https://www.jstor.org/stable/24458756?seq=1#metadata_info_tab_contents (January 18, 2022).
Levy Daniel and Sznaider Natan. "Forgive and Not Forget: Reconciliation Between Forgiveness and Resentment." *Taking wrongs Seriously: Apologies and Reconciliation*. eds. Elazar Barkan and Alexander Karn. Stanford, California: Stanford University Press, 2006. 83–98.
Loewald, Hans. "Transformations of Passion and Their Vicissitudes." *Sublimation*. New Haven: Yale University Press, 1988. 9–14.
*Long Night's Journey Into Day*. Dir. Hoffmann, Deborah and Reid, Frances. Iris Films, 2000.
Malabou, Catherine. "Repetition, Revenge, Plasticity." *e-flux*.com, October 27–28, 2017. https://www.e-flux.com/architecture/superhumanity/179166/repetition-revenge-plasticity/ (July 20, 2022).
Margalit, Avishai. *The Ethics of Memory*. Cambridge, Massachusetts: Harvard University Press, 2002.
Margalit, Avishai. "Forgiving and Forgetting." *The Ethics of Memory*. Cambridge, Massachusetts: Harvard University Press, 2002. 183–209.
Marx, Karl. "The Eighteenth Brumaire of Louis Bonaparte." *Selected Writings*, ed. Laurence H. Simon, 187–208. Indianapolis: Hackett Publishing Company, Inc., 1994.
McCullough, E. Michael. "Forgiveness: Who Does It and How Do They Do It?" *Current Directions in Sociological Science*, vol. 10, no. 6 (December 2001): 194–197.
Mignolo, Walter. D. "Point of Nonreturn: The Emergence of the Disavowed." *Comparative Studies of South Asia, Africa and the Middle East* 33, no. 3 (2013): 268–271.
Mignolo, Walter D. "Geopolitics of sensing and knowing: On (de)coloniality, border thinking, and epistemic disobedience." *Confero* 1, no. 1 ( 2013): 129–150.
Mignolo, Walter D. "The Making and Closing of Eurocentric International Law: The Opening of a Multipolar World Order." *Comparative Studies of South Asia, Africa and the Middle East* 36, no. 1 (2016): 182–195.
Morgan, Michael L. *On Shame*. New York and London: Routledge, 2008.
Neiman, Susan. *Evil in Modern Thought: An Alternative History of Philosophy*. Princeton and Oxford: Princeton University Press, 2002.
Nietzsche, Friedrich, *The Will To Power*. trans. Walter Kaufmann and R. J. Hollingdale. New York: Vintage Books, 1967.
*Night and Fog*. Dir. Alain Resnais. Argos Films, 1956.
Nussbaum, C. Martha. *Hiding from Humanity: Disgust, Shame, and the Law*. Princeton: Princeton University Press, 2004.
O'Keeffe, Brian. "Deleuze on Habit." *The Comparatist* 40:2016, 71–93.
Pelbart, Peter Pal. "Images of Time in Deleuze; Naked Life, Dumb Life, A Life; How to Live Alone." *Deleuze Studies* 8.1, (2014): 111–140.
Philips, Adam and Barbara Taylor. *On Kindness*. London: Hamish Hamilton, 2009.
Pihlström, Sami. "Why there should be no argument *from* evil: remarks on recognition, antitheodicy, and impossible forgiveness." *International Journal of Philosophy and Theology*, vol. 78, no. 4–5 (2017): 523–536.
*Phoenix*. Dir. Christian Petzold. IFC Films, 2014.

Quart, Leonard. "Breaking National Taboos, An Interview with Wladyalaw Pasikowski and Darius Jablonski." *Cineast*, 2013. 22–25; 25.

Reich-Ranicki, Marcel. "Writer, Jester, Preacher." *Heinrich Böll on His Death Selected Obituaries and the Last Interview*. Bonn: Inter Nations Bonn, 1985. 10–13.

Roth, Joseph. "Solomon's Temple in Berlin." *What I Saw: Reports from Berlin, 1920–1933*. trans. Michael Hofmann. New York, London: W. W. Norton & Company, 2003, 41–44.

Rothberg, Michael. *Multidirectional Memory Remembering the Holocaust in the Age of Decolonization*. Palo Alto: Stanford University Press, 2009. 1–29.

*Sanatorium Pod Klepsydra*. [*The Hourglass Sanatorium*], Dir. Wojciech Has. Zespol Filmowi "Silesia", 1973.

Sanders, Mark. *Ambiguities of Witnessing, Law and Literature in the Time of a Truth Commission*. Stanford: Stanford University Press, 2007.

Scholem, Gershom. "Jews and Germans." *On Jews and Judaism in Crisis, Selected Essays*. Edited by Werner J. Dannhauser. New York: Schocken Books, [1966] 1976. 71–92.

Scholem, Gershom. "Against the Myth of the German-Jewish Dialogue." *On Jews and Judaism in Crisis, Selected Essays*. Edited by Werner J. Dannhauser. New York: Schocken Books, [1962] 1976. 61–64.

Scholem, Gershom. *A Life in Letters: 1914–1982*. trans. Anthony David Skinner. Harvard University Press 2002.

Scholem, Gershom, *A Life in Letters: 1914–1982*, trans. and ed. Anthony David Skinner Cambridge, Massachusetts: Harvard University Press, 2002. 394–398.

Schulz, Bruno. *The Streets of Crocodiles and Other Stories*. trans. Celina Wieniewska. New York: Penguin, 1963.

Schulz, Bruno. "The Republic of Dreams." *Letters and Drawings of Bruno Schulz*." ed. Jerzy Ficowski. trans. Walter Arndt. New York: Harper and Row, 1988. 217–223.

Schulz, Bruno. *The Collected Works of Bruno Schulz*. Ed. Jerzy Ficowski. London: Picador, 1998.

Schulz, Bruno. "The Sanatorium under the Hourglass." *Bruno Schulz Collected Stories*. trans. Madeline G. Levine. Evanston, Illinois: Northwestern University Press, 2019. 83–237.

Scott, Jill. "Poetics and Performative Forgiveness in the South African Truth and Reconciliation Commission." *A Poetic of Forgiveness, Cultural Responses to Loss and Wrongdoing*. New York: Palgrave Macmillan, 2010. 141–165.

Sebald, G. W. "Max Ferber." *The Emigrants*. trans. Michael Hulse. New York: New Directions, 1996. 149–237.

Sebald, W. G. "Max Ferber." *The Emigrants*. trans. Michael Hulse. New York: New Directions Book, 1996, 157.

Sebald, G. W. "Against the Irreversible." *On the Natural History of Destruction*. trans. Anthea Bell. New York: The Modern Library, 2003, 143–167.

Sebald, W. G. *On the Natural History of Destruction*. trans. Anthea Bell. New York; random House, 2003. 26–30; 34; 35.

Sebald, G. W. *Die Ausgewanderten: Vier lange Erzählungen* (Frankfurt: Fischer, 2013).

Sieg, Christian. *Die, engagierte Literatur´und die Religion*. Berlin and Boston: Walter de Gruyter GmbH, 2017.

Shakespeare, William. "A Midsummer Night's Dream." *The Riverside Shakespeare*. Boston; New York: Houghton Mifflin, 2009.

Sharpe, Christina. *In the Wake: On Blackness and Being*. Durham: Duke University Press, 2016. 1–24.

Sholokhova, Lyudmila. "NYPL Researcher Spotlight: Idit Alphandary." https://www.nypl.org/blog/2022/05/05/researcher-spotlight-idit-alphandary. May 5, 2022. (August 1, 2022).

Sonti, Samir. "Rosa Parks' Activism Wasn't Limited to a Montgomery Bus." *Salon*, March 15. 2013.

Soyinka, Wole. *The Burden of Memory, the Muse of Forgiveness*. New York: Oxford University Press, 1998.
Staat, Wim. "Christian Petzold's melodramas: from unknown woman to reciprocal unknownness *Phoenix, Wolfsburg,* and *Barbara.*" *Studies in European Cinema*, 2016. Vol 13. No. 3. 185–199.
Stern, Daniel N. *The First Relationship, Infant and Mother*. Cambridge, Massachusetts: Harvard University Press, 2002.
Taussig, Michael, *Walter Benjamin's Grave*. Chicago: The University of Chicago Press, 2006.
Taussig, Michael. "NYPD Blues." *Walter Benjamin's Grave*. Chicago: The University of Chicago Press, 2006, 175–187.
*They Won't Forget*. Dir. Mervin LeRoy. Warner Brothers,1937.
Tömmel, Tatjana Noemi. "Vita Passiva: Love in Arendt's Denktagebuch." *Artifacts of Thinking: Reading Hannah Arendt's Denktagebuch*. eds. Roger Berkowitz and Ian Storey. New York: Fordham University Press, 2017. 106–123.
Tutu, Desmond Mpilo. *No Future Without Forgiveness*. New York: Doubleday, 1999.
Vetlesen, Arne Johan. "A Case for Resentment: Jean Améry versus Primo Levi." *Journal of Human Rights* 5 (2006): 27–44.
Weigel, Sigrid. "Secularization and Sacralization, Normalization and Rupture: Kristeva and Arendt on Forgiveness." *PMLA 117*, no. 2 (March 2002): 320–323.
Williams, Bernard. *Shame and Necessity*. Berkeley: University of California Press, 1993.
Winnicott, D. W. "Ego Distortion in Terms of True and False Self." *The Maturational Processes and the Facilitating Environment*. London: The Hogarth Press and the Institute of Psycho-Analysis, 1965. 140–152.
Witzthum, David. "David Ben-Gurion and Konrad Adenauer: Building A Bridge Across the Abyss." *Israel Journal of Foreign Affairs*, vol. 13 no. 2 (2019): 223–237.
Worthington, Kim. "Suturing the Wound: Derrida's "On Forgiveness" and Schlink's *The Reader*." *Comparative Literature*, vol. 63, no. 2 (2011): 203–224.
Yerushalmi Haim, Yosef. *Zakhor*. Seattle and London: University of Washington Press, 1982, 96.
Young-Bruehl, Elizabeth. "The Origins of Totalitarianism and the Twenty-first Century." *Why Arendt Matters*. New Haven: Yale University Press, 2006.
Žižek, Slavoj, Eric L. Santner, and Kenneth Reinhard. *The Neighbor: Three Inquiries in Political Theology*. Chicago and London: University of Chicago Press, 2005.
Zolkos, Magdalena. "Jean Améry's Concept of Resentment at the Crossroads of Ethics and Politics." *The European Legacy, Toward New Paradigms*, vol. 12. no.1 (2007): 23–38.

# Index

active 1, 41, 65 n. 2, 67 n. 5, 82, 87, 88, 94, 115, 131–132, 159, 160 n. 2, 178, 187, 191–192
acting out 75, 111 n. 4
archive 22, 134, 194, 196
Agamben, Giorgio 25, 31, 203–204
affects 2, 7, 14, 42, 43, 70, 71, 105, 134–135, 139, 145, 161 n. 2, 209
anti-Semitism 5, 10, 22, 32, 61, 80, 94, 134, 144
Appelfeld, Aharon 95, 142–143

bare life 6, 8 n. 3, 15, 80, 83
Bataille, George 28 n. 8, 35 n. 14, 58, 208
Ben-Gurion, David 24, 76 see also Witzthum, David
Benjamin, Walter 18, 26, 144, 166 n. 5, 189, 189 n. 1, 197, 200–205, 208, 210, 214
Bion, Willfred 63 n. 1, 208
Brinkema, Eugenie 209 see also *tableaux vivant*
Brudholm, Thomas 4, 24 n. 4, 28, 110 n. 2, 209
Bulgakov, Mikhail 26 n. 7, 209

Celan, Paul 9, 25, 93–94, 101–105, 150, 210
Char, René 133, 209
compensations 37, 131

Deleuze, Gilles 1, 16, 28 n. 8, 40–43, 47–48, 51, 209, 212
De Man, Paul 13, 156 n. 1, 209
destruction 5, 27, 32, 38, 57, 58, 69, 78, 81, 94, 95, 101, 172, 188, 194–195
deterritorialization 3, 55, 172, 178, 184, 193, 194
dream 14, 30, 31–36, 47, 60, 148, 172, 180, 203, 213

Eichmann 63, 76, 78, 80, 85, 94, 117

Feinsilver, June 117 n. 12, 210
Felstiner, John 96, 210
Freud, Sigmund 31 n. 12 see also naval of the dream
Friedlander, Eli 25, 29, 202, 210
Foucault, Michel 114 n. 9, 177

Gandhi, M. K. 185–188, 190, 191, 210
Garloff, Ktja 90, 118–119, 210, 211
Gasyna, George 35 n. 14, 211
Griswold, L. Charles 111 n. 3, 211
Gross, Jan T. 133, 137, 211
Grossman, David 58, 211
Grunebaum, Heidi 18, 162–163, 211
Guattari, Felix 16, 40, 41, 42, 47, 48, 209

Hartman, Saidiya 191, 193–194, 211
Hobbes, Thomas 66, 66 n. 4, 211
Hoffmann, Deborah 24 n. 4, 161 n. 2, 212 see also *Long Night's Journey Into Day*, see also Reid, Frances
Hollier, Denis 35 n. 15, 211
Human rights 65 n. 2, 79, 82–83, 92, 153, 158, 165, 165 n. 6, 208, 211, 214

ideology 5, 95, 136, 143, 167, 192

Jankélévitch, Vladimir 10–11, 18, 74 n. 9, 111 n. 3, 112 n. 5, 128, 150, 182, 187, 211
Jaspers, Karl 5, 10, 14, 15, 46, 64, 72, 92, 110–111, 207, 211

Kafka, Franz 36, 42, 209
Klein, Melanie 64 n. 1, 68, 178, 211

Lacan, Jacques 17, 30, 211
LaCapra, Dominique 4, 211
Laplanche, Jean 66 n. 3, 69, 211 see also Pontalis, Jean-Bertrand
leap of faith 3, 124
Lear, Jonathan 65 n. 2–66, 211
Levi, Primo 8, 14, 92, 95, 116, 116 n. 10, 212, 214
Levinas, Emmanuel 28 n. 8, 98–100, 212
Levy, Daniel 201, 212 see also Sznaider, Natan
line of flight 3, 57, 59, 60
Loewald, Hans 75 n. 11, 212
*Long Night's Journey Into Day* 24 n. 4, 160 n. 2, 212 see also Hoffmann, Deborah, see also Reid, Frances

madness 11, 28, 80, 108, 111–114, 209
Malabou, Catherine 164 n. 4, 165, 212
Margalit, Avishai 17, 26 n. 6, 212
Marx, Karl 113 n. 6, 177, 210, 212
memorial 57, 109, 113, 114
memorialization 4, 7, 44, 46, 57, 109, 111, 115, 133, 148, 178, 181
Mervin LeRoy 214 see also *They Won't Forget*
messiah 53–54
messianic 31 n. 11, 203 see also Agamben, Giorgio
Mignolo, Walter 176–181, 214
minoritarian 41–42, 48–50, 54, 58–59, 151, 168
Morgan, Michael L. 174, 175, 212
*Mourning and Melancholia* 9, 11 n. 4, 210

naval of the dream 31 n. 12 see also Freud, Sigmund
Neiman, Susan 81, 212
Nietzsche, Friedrich 23, 131, 132, 187, 209, 212
*Night and Fog* 103, 104, 212 see also Resnais, Alain

Oedipal 43, 50, 138, 143

paradox 3, 9–12, 14, 17, 18–19, 62, 64, 77, 82, 90, 93, 94, 95, 96, 98, 100, 102, 104, 105, 112, 117 n. 10, 124 n. 13, 125 n. 13, 134, 135, 139, 140, 159, 172, 183, 187
pariah 88–91, 94
Parks, Rosa 190, 190 n. 2, 213
passive and passivity 8, 22 n. 2, 23, 70, 94, 137, 172, 183, 187–188, 190, 195
patriarchal 40, 47, 51, 143, 154, 169, 179, 181, 194
Philips, Adam 68, 212 see also Taylor, Barbara
Pihlström, Sami 16, 212
Pontalis, Jean-Bertrand 66 n. 3, 69, 211 see also Laplanche, Jean
prosopopoeia 9, 10, 13, 15, 19, 21, 27, 33, 130, 169
psychoanalysis 28 n. 9, 61–62, 65, 65 n. 2, 67, 75–76, 91, 91 n. 20, 208, 211

Reid, Frances 212 see also *Long Night's Journey Into Day*, see also Hoffmann, Deborah

Reinhard Kenneth 82 n. 14, 214 see also Žižek, Slavoj; see also Santner, Eric L., see also Space
Roth, Joseph 31, 213
Rothberg, Michael 1, 4 n. 2, 213

Sanders, Mark 163, 213
Scholem, Gershom 29 n. 10, 65 n. 2, 115, 118–119, 210, 213
Scott, Jill 162–164 n. 3, 213
Shakespeare, William 69 n. 7, 213
silence 7, 15, 21, 25, 36, 37, 93, 107, 114 n. 9, 137, 142, 160 n. 2, 165, 170, 175, 194, 196
singularity 4, 30, 45, 48, 77, 118, 192, 200
Soyinka, Wole 178, 181–183, 213
space 7, 24, 30, 31, 59, 61, 81, 82, 82 n. 14, 85, 115, 119, 134, 174, 177, 202 see also Reinhard, Kenneth
speech and speech act 5, 6, 7, 14, 18 n. 1, 25, 71, 77, 80, 83 n. 16, 85, 87, 93–94, 114 n. 9, 116, 119, 121, 136–137, 139, 143, 154, 162, 164, 165, 170–171, 184
sublimation 61, 65, 66, 66 notes. 2, 3, 69–71, 74, 79, 84–86, 90–92, 101, 149, 212
Sznaider, Natan 201, 212 see also Levy, Daniel

*tableaux vivant* 205 see also Brinkema, Eugenie 209
Taussig, Michael 189 n. 1, 204–205, 214
Taylor Barbara 68, 212 see also Philips, Adam
*They Won't Forget* 195, 214 see also Mervin LeRoy
thinking 4 n. 2, 6, 8, 18, 25, 28, 29 n. 10, 40, 43, 62–64, 67, 71, 78, 80–82, 114 n. 9, 159, 165, 168, 175–177, 182, 183, 193, 208, 212, 214
Tömmel, Tatjana Noemi 6, 214
torture 23, 36, 37, 106, 115, 117, 135, 136, 152, 170, 207
trauma 1, 2, 4, 7, 11, 19, 45, 103, 148, 157, 171–172, 177, 211 see also LaCapra, Dominique
Tutu, Desmond Mpilo 1, 2, 152, 158, 162, 163, 181, 188, 214

ubuntu 1, 16, 152, 153, 162, 163, 168, 172, 175, 181, 183, 188 see also Tutut, Desmond Mpilo

Vetlesen, Arne Johan 116 n. 10, 132, 214
violence 4, 8, 63, 67, 68, 83, 99, 104–105, 111,
    134, 145, 148, 154, 159, 170, 176 n. 8, 179,
    180, 181, 182, 183, 189, 189 n. 1, 190, 191,
    193, 194, 197, 198, 199, 202 n. 1, 203, 208,
    209

Williams, Bernard 173, 214
Winnicott, D. W. 64 n. 1, 214
Witzthum, David 24 see also Ben-Gurion,
    David

Yerushalmi Haim 192, 214
Young-Bruehl, Elizabeth 81 n. 13, 214

Žižek, Slavoj 82 n. 14, 214 see also Eric
    L. Santner, see also Kenneth Reinhard
Zolkos, Magdalena 25 n. 5, 116 n. 11,
    117 n. 11, 214

www.ingramcontent.com/pod-product-compliance
Lightning Source LLC
Chambersburg PA
CBHW020230170426
43201CB00007B/375